# LOUISE SAUVAGE
## — MY STORY —

**LOUISE SAUVAGE WITH IAN HEADS**
FOREWORD BY DAWN FRASER

HarperSports
An imprint of HarperCollins*Publishers*

Article published in the *Sydney Morning Herald* on 22 August 1998 reproduced by kind permission of Mike Carlton.
Extracts from article published in the *Daily Telegraph* on 14 August 2000 reproduced by kind permission of Miranda Devine.
Article published in the *Sydney Morning Herald* on 29 September 2000 reproduced by kind permission of Caroline Overington. Caroline is a journalist with the *Age* and the *Sydney Morning Herald*.

*All the images contained herein have been provided for publication from the private collections of Louise, Rita and Maurice Sauvage, unless specified otherwise. Every effort has been made by the authors to contact the copyright holders of the aforementioned images, however in some cases credit is missing, illegible or insufficient. Any information regarding the ownership of copyright of these images is welcomed by the publishers.*

**Harper*Sports***
An imprint of HarperCollins*Publishers*, Australia

First published in 2002
Reprinted in 2002
by HarperCollins*Publishers* Pty Limited
ABN 36 009 913 517
A member of the HarperCollins*Publishers* (Australia) Pty Limited Group
www.harpercollins.com.au

Copyright © Louise Sauvage and Ian Heads 2002

The right of Louise Sauvage and Ian Heads to be identified as the moral rights authors of this work has been asserted by them in accordance with the *Copyright Amendment (Moral Rights) Act 2000* (Cth).

This book is copyright.
Apart from any fair dealing for the purposes of private study, research, criticism or review, as permitted under the Copyright Act, no part may be reproduced by any process without written permission.
Inquiries should be addressed to the publishers.

**HarperCollins*Publishers***
25 Ryde Road, Pymble, Sydney, NSW 2073, Australia
31 View Road, Glenfield, Auckland 10, New Zealand
77–85 Fulham Palace Road, London, W6 8JB, United Kingdom
Hazelton Lanes, 55 Avenue Road, Suite 2900, Toronto, Ontario M5R 3L2
*and* 1995 Markham Road, Scarborough, Ontario M1B 5M8, Canada
10 East 53rd Street, New York NY 10022, USA

National Library of Australia Cataloguing-in-Publication data:

Sauvage, Louise.
    Louise Sauvage: my story.
    Includes index.
    ISBN 978 0 7322 7263 0.
    1. Sauvage, Louise. 2. Physically handicapped athletes –
    Australia – Biography. 3. Wheelchair track and field –
    Australia – Biography. 4. Women track and field athletes –
    Australia Biography. I. Heads, Ian. II. Title.
796.0456092

Front cover photograph by Jacqui Henshaw
Back cover photograph by David Lange
Photograph on spine courtesy of AAP
Cover and internal design by Luke Causby, HarperCollins Design Studio
Typeset by HarperCollins in Sabon 10.5/16

*For my family and my friends,*
*who always supported and encouraged me –*
*whatever path I chose to take.*

# APPRECIATION

This book has been a long time in the making and, just like my career in sport, has had its ups and downs. It would not have been possible without so many people. First and foremost, my thanks are with my family – my mum Rita, my dad Maurice and sister Ann – for being there for me and for always believing in me and for giving me every possible opportunity throughout my life.

And my thanks are with so many other people too:

- My cousin Jacqueline, who makes me feel just so special.

- Lee, for being in my life.

- All the medical staff who looked after me in the early days.

- My coaches over the years – Frank Ponta, Jenni Banks, Andrew Dawes and Gary Foley – who guided and supported me. They knew I would be at training, no matter what.

- All the sports associations I have belonged to: Western Australian Wheelchair Sports, Western Australian Disabled

Sports Association, Victorian Wheelchair Sports, New South Wales Wheelchair Sports and the Australian Paralympic Committee.

- My sponsors, past and present. Without you I couldn't have been as succesful as I have been. You shared the vision and believed in me.

- My bestest friends who stuck by me and understood why I was in bed by nine o'clock! – Karen Long, Shona Casey, Tracey Harnett and Chris and Rozi Shaw.

- Karen McBrien ... there's so much to say – part of my life since 1997, my manager up until 2000, bringing control and order to my sometimes out-of-control life. Thank you, Karen – for being there and for being my friend.

- Ian Heads, for all the hours and hours we spent together on this book. Thank you for your patience and dedication.

- All the many race officials and competitors who made all my competitions possible. Without you there is no race.

- And to all the people who have supported me throughout – especially the fans who scream and shout and cheer me on. You make a difference.

– Louise Sauvage

# CONTENTS

| | |
|---|---|
| *Foreword* by Dawn Fraser | ix |
| *Introduction* by Ian Heads | xiii |
| CHAPTER 1 – THE WIND BENEATH MY WHEELS | 1 |
| CHAPTER 2 – DON'T CRY FOR ME | 3 |
| CHAPTER 3 – SPORTS GIRL | 19 |
| CHAPTER 4 – THE WORST YEARS OF MY LIFE | 27 |
| CHAPTER 5 – WORLD CHAMP … AND STARRY-EYED! | 37 |
| CHAPTER 6 – THEY SAID I'D NEVER MAKE IT! | 46 |
| CHAPTER 7 – BARCELONA – OLÉ! | 51 |
| CHAPTER 8 – NEXT STOP: THE WORLD | 60 |
| CHAPTER 9 – 'MELT INTO OBSCURITY, MR TUNSTALL' | 71 |
| CHAPTER 10 – ATLANTA GOLD | 82 |
| CHAPTER 11 – ATLANTA BLUES | 87 |
| CHAPTER 12 – THE LONG ROAD HOME | 97 |
| CHAPTER 13 – THE GREAT RACE | 110 |
| CHAPTER 14 – WIN SOME … LOSE SOME | 124 |
| CHAPTER 15 – THE GATHERING STORM | 136 |
| CHAPTER 16 – COUNTDOWN! | 152 |
| CHAPTER 17 – LET THE GAMES BEGIN | 176 |
| CHAPTER 18 – ONE DOWN … A LONG WAY TO GO | 197 |
| CHAPTER 19 – DOING IT MY WAY | 233 |
| CHAPTER 20 – BACK TO THE FUTURE | 246 |
| *Appendix 1 – Awards & Recognition 1990 to 2001* | 266 |
| *Appendix 2 – Performance Record 1990 to 2001* | 269 |
| *Index* | 289 |

# FOREWORD

BY DAWN FRASER

My links with Louise Sauvage, the world's greatest wheelchair racer, go back a fair way. Louise has a memory of my presenting her with a prize winner's medal at the National Games in Sydney some years ago, when she was an unknown teenager – and so do I. I admired her that first day, and I have admired her ever since. The medal I presented to Louise back then was in my sport, swimming. But her sporting life was to change, and wheelchair racing became her chosen sport – a sport she was to grace, and dominate, in the years ahead. It became increasingly obvious to me as time went by that she was a very special package, mixing high-level ability, grit, intelligence and unbending competitive spirit.

Over the years Louise and I have got to know each other well – and gradually become firm friends. Increasingly, as she came into prominence as a true 'great' of her sport, our paths would cross at sporting functions and dinners. For me, that was always a source of considerable enjoyment. I have thought quite often that in Louise I could glimpse more than a little of my own make-up. Like me she came from a working-class family in a working-class suburb. As with my own story, there were few favours. She battled her own way up... cut the cloth her way. And through sheer willpower and dedication, matched by natural ability... she became a champion.

Louise did it far tougher than I ever did – tougher, I'm sure, than most people who will read this book. The early chapters, listing the struggle she had with her health (twenty-one operations before she was ten!) hit with a powerful impact – making you realise the height of the hurdle she had to negotiate. Yet, as Louise says, she never regarded herself as disadvantaged, despite the lot that life dealt her. She was just herself: Louise Sauvage, wheelchair racer. And she just got on with it.

I remember so well a wonderful night in Monte Carlo, Monaco, in Sydney Olympic year, 2000, when she was named World Sportsperson of the Year with a Disability at the prestigious Laureus Awards. This was quite a night. I had a lively exchange of words with Boy George, one of the celebrities on display, we couldn't get a feed despite all the glitz and glamour – yet it was all still terrific... and such a thrill that she won. She was in glittering company: Tiger Woods and Marion Jones were other winners on the night. But how well she handled it, how much she deserved the honour bestowed on her – and how proud my daughter Dawn Lorraine and I were of 'Louie'.

Louise, of course, has won just about everything there is to win. I was looking on at Stadium Australia in September 2000 the night she came surging home to win the 800 metres demonstration race at the Sydney Olympics, before a roaring crowd of more than 100,000 people. What a reception the fans gave her! It proved to me something that I had already known: that for someone who is so modest about her achievements Louise is loved very deeply by Australians at all levels of society.

I am honoured to be her friend. And I feel privileged that she asked me to make this small contribution to the book that tells her story – tracing her history, as it does, all the way from the day in Perth on which she arrived in this world, bringing with her a congenital spinal condition that would shape the direction of her whole life.

The story told here is nothing short of inspiring. I would urge anyone feeling a bit sorry for themselves to read this book, and marvel. Never at any stage – even when things are very tough (and they do get extremely tough now and then) – does Louise give any hint of falling back into some sort of cocoon of self-pity, even though fate has made her life tougher than it might have been. Always, somehow, she is able to stay strong. Right from the start it seems she set out on a quest in her life to find something at which she could excel, in which she could make her mark. And she did that in the sport of wheelchair racing in a way that was nothing short of brilliant – as the trophies that fill her home in Sydney and the family home in Perth testify.

Louise Sauvage is one of the great Australian athletes of modern times. Because of what she has achieved, the Aussie flag has flown high and proud at so many places around the world. Now her story is being told . . . and what a story it is. Good on you, Lou – we are all so proud of you.

# INTRODUCTION

BY IAN HEADS

This book was a year and a half in the making, beginning with moments of interview grabbed in the high-tension period before Sydney's Olympic and Paralympic Games in the spring of 2000 – and re-engaging as the world's finest wheelchair racer Louise Sauvage carved out a near-invincible run of success throughout a more relaxed 2001. It was the time of her life – the time that put the seal on Louise's greatness as an athlete, although by then of course she had long been high among the elite in world sport. The triumphs of Sydney's two Games (gold before a crowd of 110,000 in the 800 metres demonstration race at the Olympics, two golds and a silver at the Paralympics) were monumental feats – achieved as she battled illness and injury. The full story – never before told – of just *how* tough it became for her unfolds in these pages, and especially so in Louise's personal diary of the six weeks of the Games, document that dips now and then into heart-wrenching despair.

In the end Louise Sauvage's story, with its marvellous punchline of Sydney's Games, is an inspiration in any telling. The cards dealt her at birth all those years ago in suburban Perth would have blunted many a life. Born with a congenital spinal condition called myelodysplasia, which meant she had virtually no use of her legs, Louise was to undergo twenty-one correctional operations in the first ten years of her life and then three more in her early teenage years, which would take her away for a long period from the sports activities she had already grown to love. In formative years she responded to the urgings that she should try to walk, on legs that were not of much help in that pursuit – and she stumped doggedly around on her callipers and splints. Eventually, Louise chose the freedom, mobility and independence that only a wheelchair could give her. And with that decision an unlikely career in global sport was begun . . .

Through it all Louise sought no word of sympathy. She does not see herself as different or disadvantaged: 'I'm just me – just the way I am', she says in this book. And 'the way she is' is just this: a wonderfully brave, focused and determined and extraordinarily talented Aussie athlete. Almost single-handedly she has raised the profile of sport for athletes with a disability to unprecedented levels in Australia. Her achievements as a wheelchair racer on the world stage and her determination to make sure her fellow athletes, and people with a disability generally, get a fair go make her a seminal figure in Australian sport – one who is probably unmatched. The huge crowds that poured in to watch the Sydney Paralympics – after the handfuls who attended Atlanta four years earlier – were testimony to the risen status of sport for athletes with a disability here. Most were at the Paralympics to see Louise Sauvage – and there were reports of how the stands emptied to an extent once she had raced.

The stories of Louise's athletic triumphs, on track and road, are told in full in the pages of this book: Olympic gold, Paralympic gold, World

Championship gold, and the amazing saga of her Boston Marathon battles with America's Jean Driscoll, a tale surely as rich and colourful as anything modern international sport has produced. There are controversies too – such as the behind-the-scenes story of the 800 metres race at the Paralympics in which she went down to Canada's Chantal Petitclerc. The glittering prizes that have come her way, in the decade since she took the Paralympic sports world by storm with her achievements at the 1992 Barcelona Games, fill the Sauvage family home in Perth and her own house in Sydney's northwest. But to Louise, though she is proud of them, they are no more than the tip of the iceberg. For her, better by far is the raw appeal of the sweet, hectic moment of victory in a tight finish – for she is a racer, first and foremost – or the modest acceptance that just maybe another of her achievements has helped the cause of sport for athletes with a disability.

For me, as Louise's helping hand in this telling of her story, primary images of her emerge.

I picture her at an airport, with her two chairs and all her baggage. Alone. She is awaiting another plane, to fly to another faraway race. Maybe in America, maybe Europe. This is what she does. There are no members of the media in attendance, no attention. Unfussed, she just gets on the plane and goes. And races. And almost always wins. And, as she reveals, flying is no great pleasure for people with a disability. When Australia's rugby league team, the Kangaroos, were dithering about whether they should take the 'risk' and fly to England a month after the terrorist attacks on New York in September 2001, Louise Sauvage travelled to Sydney's Kingsford-Smith Airport, flew to the US west coast, then took two more internal flights to meet her commitments at a 10-kilometre road race in middle America. She won, collected her prize money – and quietly flew home.

The second image is of a wet and cold and windy Sydney morning. In the city's beautiful Centennial Park or out on the trails that surround the Olympic rowing venue at Penrith, Louise Sauvage is training, hunched against the weather, wondering now and then whether it really *is* all worthwhile . . . but doing it just the same. Like all true champions, she has always been prepared to pay the price. Training goes on, whatever happens, whatever the weather. It is one of her big secrets.

It is from the messages *behind* the success that the true inspiration of the Louise Sauvage story emerges. From her beginnings in Joondanna, Perth, a loving family gave her every possible chance to become what she became. Mum and dad, Rita and Maurice, supported her budding sporting career every inch of the way, and determined from the start to provide her with a life of normal opportunity and bright promise. Her parents, plus sister Ann and Louise's network of friends and, in recent years, coaches, make up a vibrant 'Team Sauvage', providing the support and sustained positive vibes that underpin her career. Her unstinting hard work and ability to ride through pain, backing the ability she already has, are the other factors. Those things, plus her successes as probably the best wheelchair racer in the world, explain why she is so much in demand now as a public speaker. The messages she offers are as important to the corporate world as they are to primary school children.

Yet, for all of that success and adulation, she remains a truly modest champion. At times, in fact, her gentle disinclination and discomfort in talking in depth about her successes made the book's progress slow going. But with friends, coaches and others generously filling the information gaps here and there – and via the steady, long conversations at her home, with her beloved pup Penny the ever-present third member of the group – the story has gradually emerged.

And what a story it is. Alix Louise Sauvage is a national Australian treasure – an achiever almost beyond belief in the world sporting arena, and an inspiration for all Aussies, especially those who play their sport or live their lives under the shadow of physical disability. As the message aboard the Sydney Harbour Supercat 3 named in her honour in October 2001 states: 'You'll never know what you can achieve or do until you try'.

It is the creed by which a great Australian sportswoman has lived her life.

CHAPTER 1

# THE WIND BENEATH MY WHEELS

Never in my years as a wheelchair racer had I experienced anything like the tremendous blast of noise and energy that swept me home to an Olympic gold medal that Sydney evening – Thursday 28 September 2000. Probably I never will again. After more races than I can begin to remember over many years, this was a once-in-a-lifetime event.

I learned that night that a crowd of 110,000 in a great stadium can muster an amazing *physicality* when it is willing someone to win. Making my challenge with 150 metres to go, out in Lane Three on the brick-red Stadium Australia track, I felt as if I were almost picked up and carried along by the roar of the crowd, the *breath* of the crowd. Almost literally, they propelled me to the line . . . to the gold.

Only later was I told of how people had risen to their feet almost as one, clambered up on seats, to add their determination to my own in the 800 metres final. I will never forget the feeling that night, the 'rush' that supported my charge in the home straight. It is not easy to put into words . . .

To win there in front of a home crowd (I have been a Sydney girl these past five years!) was both a wonderful thrill and a magnificent relief. The build-up to the Games, as you will come to appreciate, had not been easy. To come out and win the 800, before a huge crowd draped in green and gold and waving flags, was one of the great moments of my life. Later, I will also tell you tales of the second leg of 2000's amazing sporting double: the Paralympic Games. For four intense years, my life had circled these twin targets. Never were they out of my view. One goal, clung to tightly through good days and, particularly, bad, was to win gold at both.

But my overall goals were wider than that. Especially I wanted to do whatever I could via the Olympics and Paralympics to teach the public about wheelchair sport and to change people's perceptions about athletes with a disability. My hope was that any personal success I gained at either Games, or both, would add to the vastly wider positives that I expected a successful Sydney Paralympics to bring. I hoped it would be a further step along the path towards the complete acceptance and understanding of sport for athletes with a disability – and the complete acceptance and understanding of the athletes themselves.

I had raced, swum, thrown discuses, shot puts and javelins and played basketball in sport for athletes with a disability since I was a little girl. Now, in Sydney, came the most important competition of my life to date.

It had been a long haul – eleven back-to-back years of representing Australia at international wheelchair racing. All of it was hard to believe, considering how simply it had all started many years before – when a Perth mother had trundled her daughter along to a neighbourhood swimming pool a couple of days a week. Just for some exercise and therapy.

I'll tell you the story . . .

CHAPTER 2

# DON'T CRY FOR ME

I never thought of myself as being different, or disadvantaged. I'm just me – the way I am. The circumstances of my life put me in a wheelchair – but it has been my own efforts that have taken me around the world, and to the successes I have had.

Even as a kid I never really thought about my disability, because I didn't know anything else. Of course, I accepted that in one way I was not quite the same as the other kids – that I couldn't get around as well as they could. But as far as I was concerned (and *am* concerned!) that just happened to be the way it was – and, well, I had to simply get on with my life.

I can remember people asking my mum with worried faces when I was little, 'What's wrong with her?'. At those times I would look up at my mother and say, 'What do they mean what's wrong with me? There's *nothing* wrong with me!'. And that's exactly the way it was, the way I felt back then – and the way I feel now. Other people's perceptions aren't something I think about . . . I just get on with it.

I do not believe my life has been any more difficult than those of many people who confront challenges every day. Each one of us faces obstacles in one way or another. I believe I've had a very good life and I know I've done everything I've ever wanted to do – without a second thought.

Many people say to me, 'Oh, you must have overcome so many barriers in your life'. But I don't see it that way at all. In fact I don't see myself as having overcome *anything*. What I have to deal with is what I have had to deal with all my life; it's not as if I have gone from being an able-bodied person to being in a wheelchair, and had my life suddenly turned upside down. If there is any message in the story I tell in this book, it's about being determined and believing in yourself. With me it's always been a case of saying, 'If everyone else can do it . . . then so can I!'.

\* \* \*

Let me tell you something about the Sauvage family into which I was born back in 1973. My mum Rita (née Rigden) is an English lass, from the town of Oadby in Leicestershire, and my dad Maurice is a Seychellois – from the French- and Creole-speaking island of the Seychelles, in the Indian Ocean off Africa's northeast coast. From such beginnings they met at a dinner dance, in an unlikely place, far away from both their homelands: Perth. Arriving in Australia in 1967 as a 'ten-pound Pom' (on a £10 assisted sea passage), Mum had lived and worked in Sydney for a time, gone back to England and hated it – and headed back to Perth, to stay with relatives. It was there that she met Maurice Sauvage, something of a traveller himself at the time. (Incidentally, the family name – Sauvage – means 'wild' in French.)

They were married in 1968 and in the years that followed had two daughters, Ann (1969) and me four years later. I was christened

Alix Louise Sauvage – the Alix after my nanna. It's the French or Creole version of Alice. But in line with a family tradition not to use first given names – a tradition that comes from my father's side of the family – I have always been known as Louise.

I'm twenty-eight as I write these words – born 18 September 1973 at King Edward Memorial Hospital, Perth, on what must have been an especially difficult day in the lives of my mum and dad. I arrived at the starting line of life with one leg trapped under and around my body and the other up over one shoulder.

Obviously there were serious problems with my hips and legs, and what followed must have been terrible for my mum. 'Oh my God ... what's wrong?' she asked the doctors. She has told me about how people grilled her – virtually accused her of having been on some medication or drug that had caused the problem. What should have been the happiest of days turned into a terribly difficult one. The fact was that my mum had done absolutely nothing wrong. There was, and is, no explanation for the condition I was born with. It just happened.

The condition is called myelodysplasia, a congenital spinal condition (i.e., one existing from birth) that restricts the function of the lower half of the body, which meant that I had (and have) only very limited control over my legs. As I said, they don't know how or why it happens. Put simply, the base of my spinal cord was not properly formed when I was born. It left me with curvature of the spine, which progressed up to 90 per cent but was then corrected (to 49 per cent) by operations I was to have in my teenage years.

> *Rita Sauvage: She had one leg underneath her and one over the top, right up to her shoulder. That's how she was born. We had no hint of a problem, and I had had the tests and everything, although I remember she didn't kick like Ann had. She was born at King Edward Memorial Hospital, by caesarean. She was four and a half hours old when they gently pulled her leg down. It snapped like a piece of cheese. They told me not to look, but I looked.*

> *She was in plaster, in a little crib with her legs strung up in the air, for the first two weeks of her life. When the plasters came off her legs were bowed, but they eventually managed to get them straight. Then she had an operation on a foot when she was about eight weeks.*

When I was old enough to understand, I learned I had had my first operation four hours after I was born.

> *Dr F. B. (Don) Webb A.M., orthopaedic surgeon: I was asked to see Louise at the King Edward Memorial Hospital when she was four hours old. She had dislocated hips, she had contractures of her knees and she had very severe club feet. And she had a broken left femur . . . when they had been examining her . . . her bones were fragile and someone had managed to break [it] . . .*
>
> *In my hands over the next eight or nine years she had twenty-two different operations, mainly on her knees and feet, although also on her hips . . . and then she had a spinal fusion.*

In my early years the Princess Margaret Hospital in Subiaco, Perth, was my home away from home. It got to the point where I almost lived there, to the point where I knew it better than my home, or (later) my school. I didn't have a lot of choice. Medical decisions were made constantly, in the interest of trying to make my life easier and better. It meant many operations and long stays in hospital. Mum and Dad used to take me home on weekends in the family's canary-yellow Kingswood wagon, with me lying on a mattress in the back.

Over the years my sister Ann has kept a sort of scorecard of the total number of operations I have had on my hips and legs and back. I think the tally now is up around twenty-three or twenty-five. My mum tells me she's lost count. My hips are the part of me that has been operated on the most. I've had one side 'done' five times, and the other three.

> *Rita Sauvage: Of all the operations, the worst was on her hips, which wouldn't stay in their sockets; it took more than five hours. The doctor said afterwards that he would never do such an operation again. She was in a full cast and we could barely lift her.*
>
> *When she was three she had an operation in which they had to snip the spinal cord away from the spinal wall. She got very sick, had a raging temperature, and on one particular night we thought we might lose her. I sat there with her until ten o'clock, then went home to a sleepless night.*
>
> *When I went back in the morning she was putting paper on this blooming balloon to make a pig. She was OK. But she told me, 'I never want to come back to hospital, Mum'. Of course she did, many times.*

Out the back of our suburban home in Joondanna are six or seven steps down to the yard. I still can't get down them. Mum tells how when I was really little, I was in plaster – 'Edinburgh splints', with my legs splayed by a metal rod – for almost three years on and off, and she couldn't cuddle me. And I used to clonk down the stairs in my plasters. There was no stopping me, apparently.

> *Rita Sauvage: Every week without fail we had to go to the hospital on Monday morning and get her plasters renewed. She had worn them out. But the additional problem was she used to sometimes clomp down the steps without her plasters on too, and put bruises all over her legs. The doctors used to think I was belting her up!*
>
> *The worst time came when she broke a leg one day – just after she had got rid of her plasters after being in them for two years. Her bones were soft. That was terrible. It had been so nice to be able to hold her again; when she was little I couldn't hold her because of the*

> plasters. Then she was back in blooming plasters again. Poor kid. We used to go to the hospital three times a week for physio.

Stomping down the back steps is certainly one strong early memory I have of our house, and my life. My father made me a little V-shaped trolley of wood with foam on top and rubber wheels, on which I could scoot around, lying face down. I had a little red car too, which I called, for reasons that escape me after all these years, Doo-Da. I would whiz up the side of the house in it and eat the strawberries (which I called 'gips') that my dad had planted there, whether or not they were ripe.

> *Rita Sauvage: At home she would zoom around on her trolley, lying face down in her plasters, dragging herself around with her arms. You couldn't slow her down. We used to put her food on the floor. It sounds terrible ... but it was the only way. Maurice and I just did the best we could for her.*

Growing up, in many ways I was a pretty normal girl, but I didn't have any special crushes as far as I can recall. I didn't have any posters of movie stars or bands or anything like that on my walls. I liked Garfield, though! I remember being sent a lot of Garfield stuff when I was in hospital being operated on. I thought he was cool. I shared a room with my sister until about the time when she went to high school.

> *Ann Sauvage: I have many memories of Louise and me at home in those early years. I remember days during the school holidays when we would play 'dollies' hour after hour. We'd build dolls' houses out of boxes, and throughout the day Mum would have to do no more than look in on us and give us a sandwich. We had an operating theatre too and we used to do 'operations' on*

*the toy dog 'Doggie', sew on a bit more fabric here and there. We'd be there for eight hours or more . . .*

*I remember the endless games of 'Marco Polo' in the pool, so much fun, and I remember Louise with a mullet haircut. She might deny that – but I have photographic evidence! And I remember a day when she was mad with me – and chased me with a knife!*

*I remember too when I was studying to be an accountant – and I worked damned hard for that – and she'd be in her room with the music blaring. 'Turn it down!' I'd yell. She wouldn't. It can be like that with sisters.*

\* \* \*

Much as I loved home, my experiences of world travel, so much a part of what I do today, started early in life.

I was about five when the family went on holiday to the old French colony of the Seychelles, where my dad was born. All these years on he still speaks with a strong French (Creole) accent; I don't notice it, but people who ring up still sometimes have trouble understanding him. I learned French for three years at school and Dad helped a bit – but there was no French spoken around the house, which I think is a shame. I'd love to be able to speak it now.

I don't remember much about that trip, but I visited again in 1999, when my aunty over there celebrated her seventy-fifth birthday. This was a great trip and one I won't forget, especially as it's unlikely I'll go back to the Seychelles again. I met lots of rellies I'd never known before and came to realise I looked more like Dad's side of the family than Mum's, and I saw all the places where Dad grew up. And I met my father's nanny – Nanny Simone – who had looked after him when he was a little boy. We went to her house, and the conversations brought back a lot of memories for them both and taught me more about my father's upbringing. She was very old then – in her nineties – and the occasion was sort of sad and happy at the same time. It was the last time that Dad and Nanny Simone were ever going to see each other.

On the first trip to the Seychelles we also visited my nanna and my aunty Mary in Kenya, where they owned a property in Nairobi and another one in Mombasa. We went back when I was twelve and again when I was fifteen. On those occasions there were opportunities to visit game parks and see the animals up close, with monkeys climbing all over the car, trying to get at the bananas we had. We got close to a lot of different animals – my mum nearly freaked out one day when we got *too* close to a rhino, and it was ready to charge. I got to feed the giraffes at one place . . . and they are the coolest animals of all. Anyone who has ever visited my place will realise that I am keen on giraffes. They're all over my house these days. It probably all started on my first trip to Africa. I'd love to have a real one out the back . . . as long as it was a miniature one. That would be my first choice of pet if there were such a thing. I suppose I like them because they are kind of awkward, just not your regular animal – but they make the most of what they've got.

Africa is a wonderful place to visit for its scenery and wildlife – but difficult for someone like me. It is not a very accessible place for people in wheelchairs. There were a number of times on our trips when I just couldn't go out with everyone else – and that was so frustrating. I was something of a novelty to them, I suppose. I'd go into towns and people would freak out because I was in a chair. I was stared at big-time over there, wherever I went. It was as if no-one had ever seen a person in a wheelchair before. You would see all these people with different deformities sitting there on skateboards in the streets, begging for money. And here I was in a wheelchair that had probably cost more money than they would ever see in their lives. They had never seen anything remotely like it before – a human being riding around in a chair on wheels! That made me sad in one way . . . and also made me realise how fortunate I was. People over there with similar disablities to mine will probably never have the opportunities that I have had, or the quality of life that I have had.

On each of our family vacations we spent up to six weeks in Africa, and they are memories I value, that chance I had to experience a very different way of life. My aunty Mary had servants who worked in her house, at a time in Africa when there were huge differences in status between black and white. But my memory of my aunt's house is that it was like a big happy family where we, the guests, talked and laughed and got to know the people working there in a very harmonious atmosphere. I remember going over one day to the home of John, the driver, to meet his wife and children.

We got around quite a lot in Africa, saw plenty of animals, visited some of the tribes and saw how they lived. When I think about it, I consider myself very lucky that I had the chance to spend time there and observe their way of life. The family enjoys telling the story of one trip we took to Kenya when I was only little. We visited Fort Jesus, in Mombasa – a place where Vasco da Gama had stopped on his travels – and I demanded loudly to know where Jesus was. It seemed a fair enough question!

For me though, there is sadness in the memories of Africa, apart from the poverty and inequality I saw everywhere we went. My nanna and my aunty Mary have died in the years since. I'm happy I went. But I'll probably never go back.

\* \* \*

In 1976 I was Perth's 'Telethon Child'. Every year Channel Seven Perth would have a big Telethon to raise money for children with disabilities, and they'd pick a child of the year as the focal point, to represent all children with a disability in Western Australia. In '76, I was it.

By then I had had ten operations. I was only three, but they made such a fuss of me and it was such an occasion that I remember everything about it. There were photos of me in the paper and on lottery tickets and posters, and one with my toy Womble. And I got to wear my yellow party dress all the time.

At the studios on the big day I met Fat Cat, and Percy his offsider. They gave me a toy dog that walked and barked and wagged its tail. I clumped around noisily on the wooden walking device I had at the time. A newspaper feature referred to my 'unusually strong arms' from pulling myself along at speed on the floor at home – something that was to stand me in good stead throughout my future sporting years. I was just so excited. There was such a lot going on.

The Telethon footage, incidentally, is still around, and has surfaced now and then in TV shows looking at my career. There are photos in the family album of Ann and me out the front at home at Telethon time, selling pot plants lined up on a little table. We raised a fair bit of money that way . . .

The toy dog presented to me by the Telethon people was a special treat. We'd always had a real one at home, you see – from as far back as my memories take me. Sparky was the first – a bit of a Bitzer, with long hair, and the best dog ever. He was almost human. Every afternoon he'd come and sit by the front door when it was time for us to come home from school. He was a very tolerant dog; he'd quite happily let Ann and me dress him up and put him in a pram. There are numerous photos of us with the dog all dressed up. Sparky had quite a social life, too – he'd sneak out regularly at night and get up to who knows what. I loved him. Then, one day he went off . . . and we never saw him again. For weeks we went looking for him every day after school, but we never found a trace.

It was after Sparky's disappearance that Dad got us a Blue Heeler-Kelpie cross, whom Mum called Punch after a dog she had had in England. He was a real terror. He used to chew everything and was aggressive even when he was a pup. But he was very lovable and calmed down as he got older. He lived a long life; he was seventeen when we had to get him put down, just before Christmas 1995.

Then there was Judy, a Fox Terrier and Border Collie cross and a bicentennial baby. Judy was dumped as a pup and was advertised through the newsagent where Ann was working. The arrangement was that she would have to go to the pound if no-one took her. When the weekend came and no-one had accepted her, Ann brought her home. Judy never went back to the newsagent . . . and for years we had Punch and Judy at home. Judy developed cancer later in her life and was put down at thirteen, a very sad event for our whole family.

* * *

As far as my education went, my parents provided wonderful support to my own philosophy that there was nothing 'wrong' with me – that I was just me. Mum and Dad sent me to a regular primary school and high school, and never considered doing anything else. At Tuart Hill Primary I was the only child with a disability. Before I arrived they made ramps for me to make my life easier. They were terrific to me at Tuart Hill.

Mum tells the story of other mothers asking the question, 'Where does your little girl go to school?'. When Mum told them, 'Down the road at Tuart Hill', the startled response would inevitably be the same: 'Doesn't she go to a special school?'. Mum had pretty much a stock answer to that: 'No, there's nothing wrong with her head . . . why would she need to go to a special school?'. The fact was that most of the other mothers who had kids with disabilities sent them to special schools. Mum never even thought of doing that.

Making friends at Tuart Hill was never a problem. Adults probably have a preconceived idea about children who are 'different'. But kids aren't like that. They'd just come out and ask me stuff. I think that you get teased at school no matter what your difference is – whether you wear glasses or braces or you've got freckles or whatever. But after a while it all faded away and people just accepted: 'Oh, yeah . . . she's got a disability. So what?'. I had all my friends by then and, well, it just didn't matter. Getting teased about stuff is just part of life. We all go through some of that. In the end I still belonged . . . still felt part of the school. And with my best friend Tanya Giglia at my side, I conquered all. She was a real pal, although we headed our own separate ways once we went to high school.

During Year Four I swapped schools – to go to St Mary's (now called Aranmore), the Catholic school at Mt Hawthorn, where Ann had started high school. Mum decided to move me too, to keep us together, and I went to the lower school at St Mary's for a couple of terms. I didn't like it at all – my discontent being enough for Mum to eventually switch me back to Tuart Hill. It was there that I finished my early schooling. The specific reasons for my dislike of St Mary's have faded to an extent from my mind now. But from the start I knew I just wasn't going to have a good time. The number of stairs at the high school there meant it was not a long-term option for me anyway.

When I finished my primary years I went to Hollywood Senior High in Nedlands, a public school that was fully accessible and catered well for people in wheelchairs (which I was by then – I'll tell you about that soon). I could even travel to Hollywood High by bus. The bus would rock up to my house of a morning and they'd lift me on and I'd leave my chair at home. At the other end they'd lift me off, and into the chair I kept at school. To me this represented some degree of freedom – I didn't have to depend on Mum to cart me to and from school.

I was at Hollywood High for three years. The school sounds pretty glamorous, doesn't it? By name, anyway. It stands, in fact, just across the road from Perth's biggest cemetery, Caracutta – the place we used to go when we wagged school, which happened now and then.

In Year Nine I met Karen Long in English class one day, and from the start we just laughed and chatted and carried on, and were eventually told off. We were the best of mates from that point – and still are today, although I am in Sydney and she is based in the north of Western Australia, working as a teacher. As Karen says, even though we live on opposite sides of Australia now and lead completely different lives, when we do catch up it's as if we've never been apart.

> *Karen Long: I remember the day that Louise and I met. Both our English partners were away and it seemed a sensible thing for us to sit together. We had a double period of English and I don't think we stopped talking the whole time. From then on we were pretty much inseparable. Talking in class was something we were constantly scolded for.*
>
> *One day we encountered the wrath of our Social Studies teacher, Ms Klisc. After being berated many times in class for talking or not paying attention, we were separated. It didn't take us long to find a solution, though, because Louise then taught me to finger-spell in sign language. We would sit for hours after school, perfecting the letter formations until I was proficient enough to get a message across . . .*
>
> *Nothing stopped us. As kids we would let nothing get in the way of what we wanted to do. I don't think it ever entered our heads that something would be impossible for us to achieve. If we wanted to do it, we did it.*

Despite the ups and downs at times, life was a lot of fun . . . there were a lot of laughs, especially when Karen and I were up to some mischief or other.

> *Karen Long: I remember the first time Louise came to my house. We were out in the back yard and decided to play a trick on my sister Ali, who had never met Louise and didn't know she was in a wheelchair. We hid the chair, and when my sister arrived she thought nothing of the two kids sitting out the back playing cards. When Ali came to the back door to call us in for lunch, I jumped*

> up and ran inside to get Louise's chair. Meanwhile, Louise began to crawl towards the back steps.
>
> Then Ali uttered the words we had been waiting for: 'Don't be lazy – get up and walk!'. At the same moment I tapped her on the back of the legs with Louise's wheelchair. Well, she could just have died. We killed ourselves laughing, while my sister tried to find a rock big enough to hide under.

Karen and I had more than a few adventures back in those days, and we still laugh about them a lot when we get together.

> We went skateboarding a couple of times, and we used to go bike riding. Initially I would ride my bike and Louise (in her wheelchair) would hold on to the back and I would pull her along. That was OK for a while, but it wasn't enough. For Louise it wasn't really riding on a bike. So we tied a couple of cushions to the carrier on the back and took my bike to the brick fence out front, where Louise jumped on. Then we were off!
>
> One day we decided to go to our high school and pick roses. Away we went – as free as birds, without a care in the world. At the school I leant my bike and Louise up against a tree while I picked roses. All went smoothly until, heading home, I misjudged a jump up a curb. Flowers flew everywhere and the dust rose – and when it cleared all you could see was a mass of tangled body parts, roses strewn everywhere and a bike! All we could do was laugh. We laughed so hard that we cried. Then we had to figure out a way of getting Lou back on the bike without a brick wall – and that made us laugh more. Eventually we worked it out, and made our way home.

In 2000 I went back to Hollywood High for the school's last day. It was to be closed down – combined with another school in the district.

Hollywood High's most famous pupil, Kim Beazley, was there, and he and I spoke at the goodbye gathering – about the way the school had been in the years when we had been there. I also met teachers who had taught me, and the occasion brought back many memories. The day was effectively a goodbye . . . and that was sad.

\* \* \*

It was in primary school that I first used a wheelchair. The accepted wisdom back then seemed to be that if a child had *any* use at all of his or her legs, then walking was the best option. There was a continuing push for kids like me to walk, and keep walking.

It was as if there were two worlds, one for the people with disabilities and one for the able-bodied . . . and if you happened to be in the world of people with disabilities then you had to do whatever you could to get into the other world. That determination to make me walk caused me a lot of pain and a lot of grief. I clomped around in callipers – leg irons – and a body brace on and off throughout my primary school years. I don't think Mum was ever happy with it – sending her daughter off to school wearing all of that. I was as stiff as a board and dreadfully uncomfortable. It was just horrible.

> *Rita Sauvage: She didn't want the leg irons; I hated putting them on. The poor child had no life. She was like this the whole day – back stiff and straight, legs straight . . . she couldn't get around. When she first started to walk, she walked all flipping day. But the excitement only lasted about two days. It was terrible for her in the leg irons. She used to wear out her boots, crawling around the house.*

As you get older there are more things you want to do, places you want to go – and if you can only do it agonisingly at snail's pace, it takes forever. Around the age of eight it became apparent that walking with callipers and crutches wasn't going to work for me. It was awkward and slow. I couldn't carry my books, couldn't keep up with my friends.

I think a lot of children in my situation back then would probably have just accepted the things adults said, and still do today. They tell themselves, 'I can't do that, because the doctor told me I can't' . . . So they never really try. I'm not sure exactly what if was with me – but being told I couldn't do something usually meant that I was going to go right out and do it! So at eight I started using a wheelchair; by the time I went to high school I was in a chair full-time.

The chair gave me my freedom. And so it became part of my life. Today I sometimes wish I could walk around my house a bit, but it's not possible because of the wasting of my legs, and the fact that I can't fully straighten them. For me the chair (which was always going to happen anyway) provided the mobility I didn't have – and was much easier and quicker and more fun.

> *Don Webb: With most of these kids, we used to get them going on walkers. Most of them, the girls in particular, used to opt for a wheelchair when they were about thirteen or fourteen. At that stage they wouldn't persist with crutches and callipers. Louise made it very plain that she wanted to go into a wheelchair when she was eight years of age. She found she could get around much faster in a wheelchair, do more things in a wheelchair than she could on crutches and callipers.*
>
> *She was always a very determined kid . . . and a delight. She's a great girl. I have tremendous affection for her. One of the beauties with Louise as far as I am concerned is that, throughout, she remained the same unspoiled girl, even bearing in mind her fierce determination, even in those early days, to chart her own future and her tremendous will to succeed in her ambitions – so well demonstrated by her prowess in the sporting field, and indeed her life.*

CHAPTER 3

# SPORTS GIRL

Sporting recreation started early for me – when I was about three. It was around then that Mum first took me swimming at the Spastic Centre at Mt Lawley and then to the Tuart Hill Swimming Club, the local club not far from our home. At the start it wasn't about training or learning the strokes or anything like that. It was just about water confidence and exercise and getting active in the water. It was part of my rehab program, to build upper body strength, which I was going to have to rely on for the rest of my life.

> *Rita Sauvage: First of all I took her to the pool at the Spastic Centre at Mt Lawley. There we'd play 'Humpty Dumpty had a great fall' – dunking her in the water. She loved that. But Tuart Hill was really where she first started more seriously in swimming. The original idea of her taking*

> *up swimming was so that the two girls could do things together. At home, the girls were always in the above-ground pool we had ... they used to swim like fish.*

I think some of our swimming ability must have come from our parents. Both of them were into sport at school – Mum played netball and a bit of badminton and squash, and Dad played soccer. But neither of them ever played any high-level competitive sport. Mum swims now and enjoys it; she only learned freestyle in more recent years.

Ann was really good, something of a star at school – and I don't think there's any doubt that she could have gone further, to state level or beyond, if she had really wanted to. My mother would say, 'It's terrible ... Ann's got all these trophies and Louise is never going to be this successful'. It's funny how the tide turned. Ann, who is an accountant in her working life, still swims and had quite a long time of active involvement in the surf lifesaving movement (she was captain of Scarborough Club) – but by choice never took her sport any further than that. Both Mum and Ann still get great enjoyment out of their swimming – and swim regularly in the Aussie Masters.

> *Ann Sauvage: Mum was always worried for Louise, because I had won all the trophies. I remember how when she won her first spoon at Tuart Hill Swimming Club, Louise had this grin from ear to ear. Of course we had to have a bottle of bubbly.*

> *Rita Sauvage: Progressively both girls had a lot of success in their sport. When they were little we used to have a bottle of bubbly whenever either one of them won a race. Ann was winning them all the time – then Louise started, and we thought, 'God, we'll have to stop this!'.*

Swimming was clearly my first sporting love – and it provided my first experience of full-on training. My sister and I used to train with the squads at Inglewood Pool, three times a week to start with – we'd go down there after school.

My first-ever coach was Frank Ponta, a great guy who gave so much time and energy – not just to me but also to the countless other junior athletes he coached – and still does today, as enthusiastically and caringly as ever. In my view Frank is an amazing person, a coach who moves with the times to ensure that his charges are given the best of opportunities. His patience was amazing as he worked to gradually bring out the best in young athletes. He was a major influence in making me believe in myself – and in pushing me in his careful way to see how far and how fast I could go. Frank coached kids with disabilities to become something. There is no doubt he has touched many lives.

I'm sure the fact that Frank was also in a wheelchair meant that his words of advice to us kids carried more weight. We all related to him, and listened to him. Frank worked with kids with a whole lot of different disabilities, and figured us all out. He was the one who saw our potential much more clearly than we did. He seemed to believe in me from the start – and always pushed me further and harder because he knew I could do more. His believing in me made me want to be better. He had a way that would kind of spur you on and make you angry . . . so that you would try and go faster.

> *Frank Ponta: Sometimes Rita and other parents thought I was too tough on the kids. 'You push them too hard,' they'd say. 'Bloody rubbish,' I'd respond. 'If we don't do it this way we're never going to get anything out of them and they're never going to learn and improve.' Yes, I've pushed kids through the barriers that exist. Mainly I just give them the facts: 'You've got to work hard . . . you've got to train four or five days a week'.*

It was Frank who taught me the true meaning of sportsmanship. I was a cheeky kid – and used to tell everyone that I was going to beat them.

*Rita Sauvage: She was competing at Bateman Park one morning and Frank Ponta came to us. 'You had better have a word with your daughter,' he said. Louise was telling all the other kids she would beat them (which she did) – and they were crying. We had to tell her to stop.*

*Frank Ponta: Back when Louise was eight or nine there was this girl she competed against, Anne-Marie Soloti, who went on to become a very good field eventer and pentathlete. She and Anne-Marie raced over 200 metres in the pool. Louise was given a head start in the race, and beat Anne-Marie – and afterwards Anne-Marie broke down and cried. And Louise went up to her and said, 'Ha ha ... I beat you'. I got stuck into her. 'Don't you ever do that again,' I said. 'Be a sportsperson.' Even then she had that tough competitive spirit.*

*With Louise when we first started ... oh, she was hard going, very strong-willed. She had a mind of her own. She always had some killer instinct – even back in 1983 when Rita first got in touch with the Association and brought her down. No matter what she took on she was going to make good out of it. She had so much strength. She was always prepared to do the work, although if she didn't want to do something, she would buck. Oh yeah, she could be stubborn. But I didn't curtail that; I like a bit of spirit in people.*

There is a stubbornness deep down in me, always has been. Some people might say that 'pig-headed' is a phrase that comes to mind! As you've already seen, from very early in my life if someone wanted to tell me there was something I couldn't do, well, I'd go and do it just to prove them wrong. My parents reckon my motto for life was set early: 'Don't say I can't do it'. They reckoned they couldn't say no to me because I'd just go ahead and do whatever it was anyway. I think when you have a disability, people are always putting limitations on you, telling you, even in a nice way, what you *can't* do. My attitude to that has always been: 'You can't tell me that. I'll show you'. I probably always had that kind of personality anyway – and having limitations imposed on me by others only brought it out more strongly.

* * *

I was pretty young when I started to get 'serious' about sports, about eight when I was first introduced to sports for athletes with a disability – and I progressively got involved in them all: swimming, basketball, track and field – discus, shot put, javelin. In the field events discus was my favourite, and the discipline I was best at.

It was mad when I think about it now. I was into everything. At the weekends there'd be different track and field sports and basketball. Through the week it all revolved around swimming. And my parents never faltered – especially my mum, who used to cart me around endlessly, to training and competitions. I can never remember a time when she said 'I can't take you' or 'We're not going'. I am forever grateful for that.

I was the only kid with a disability who belonged to the swimming club. Mum did most of the trekking around with me, and my dad did what he could to make my life easier at home. My dad is a softie. And he is not a man for lots of words. I never really knew how proud he was of me until I learned years later of how he used to take newspaper clippings of some of my early wins to work, to show his workmates. He did that for a long time without my knowing.

> *Frank Ponta: Rita and Maurice were always very good, very supportive. Maurice used to work away on patching up the wheelchair, keeping it in good shape, when she was a little girl.*

My parents have been such an integral part of what I have done in my life – right from those early beginnings. I think that anyone who has had success in sport would say the same thing: that without supportive family and friends it probably couldn't have happened.

In the scrapbooks that Mum has kept over the years, as mothers do, the first entry is a clipping from the local paper featuring a photo of Ann and me (included in this book). The story records that I ('a Joondanna girl') had been chosen to compete in the Second National Junior Games for the Disabled, to be held in May. The year was 1983, and I was nine. In another article later the same year I was even given a nickname: 'The Joondanna Flash'. 'Louise has a grand prix attitude when she's on the track,' wrote journalist Barney Simpson. Later I also acquired the nickname 'Flipper'. It was around this time that Tuart Hill Swimming Club bought me my first racing chair – at a cost of $400.

I was ten when I went to the National Senior Paraplegic and Quadriplegic Games in Sydney in January 1984. I was the youngest athlete ever to compete there. This was my first trip away without my parents and my mother freaked out. She was really worried that something terrible would happen – that I was too young, that I wasn't independent enough to be travelling so far. The *worst* thing about the '84 trip was that I had to have all my hair cut off before I went. That was horrible. Because I couldn't do my own hair easily I always had long hair almost down to my butt. Now it was all cut off, and there is a funny-looking pic of me (also in this book), sitting with my short hair, showing off some medals that I had won. I survived it all, however – both the trip and being shorn. For me it was the beginning of a great deal of travel in my life – both nationally and internationally.

I competed widely at those Games – in track and field events and swimming. I came back with five medals: two silvers and three bronzes, from both the track and the pool. A week or so later I made almost a clean sweep of medals in the State Junior Disabled Games held in Perth. The following year, 1985, I came home with fifteen medals from the National Junior Games in Melbourne – seven of them gold.

> *Chris Shaw (fellow wheelchair racer, and longtime friend): My first recognition of Louise was in a City-to-Surf race. She would have been about twelve. I was going up this hill and struggling away, and along came this little tyke about so big and scooted straight past me. I've been aware of her ever since – and we became good friends. There's a standard joke at work that I taught Louise everything she knows – which of course is not true. I just know that Ros [Chris's wife] and I are very proud of her.*

All those national titles were an indication that things were getting pretty serious in my sporting life. Sport and I had always got along together well. I had a fighting spirit which backed both the ability I had and the hard work I was prepared to put in to achieve success.

My coach, Frank Ponta, believed I had a lot of natural talent to start with. I was pretty much an all-rounder, good at most of the sports I tried. I had a very competitive nature back then, as now. My desire to win whenever I competed was there from day one – and was as strong then as it is now that I am a professional athlete. But I always did a lot of training too – and it was the combination that paid off. From my earliest days in sport I learned some good messages about training hard, about being resolute and disciplined. I was probably quite young when I picked up the message that if I was going to make something of myself in sport, then there was a price to pay.

When I was little and first started training, I probably enjoyed that more than anything else in my life. The thing about training was that from the beginning I could see the tangible benefits of the effort I was putting in. I was getting faster and stronger, and better, and that made the training more fun. I have always been patient too, never expecting instant miracles. Perseverance is the trick. People who start on diet and exercise routines to lose weight often give it away if they can't measure any tangible benefits after three weeks or so. The message is: stick with it and the results will come. That has always been my belief.

People have asked me since: did I know then, back in the '80s, that sport for people with a disability was going to be something really big in my life? Something that I wanted to do? I honestly don't know about that. It was something I enjoyed, sure – to go to the Nationals and do really well. I'm sure I did think back then, 'I want to do more of this – to train, and get faster and better'. I know it was a good feeling. But I was a kid, and I had no lofty ambitions. I'm not sure I had even heard of the Paralympics at that time. Thoughts of becoming a professional athlete had not even begun to form.

And anyway, all of that was about to take a back seat, as a much more immediate hurdle suddenly loomed, and I began to wonder whether my life would ever be the same again . . .

CHAPTER 4

# THE WORST YEARS OF MY LIFE

The sports involvement I had grown to love as being so important in my life departed completely in 1987 and 1988. It happened because it had to. My spinal condition (scoliosis, the progressive curving of the spine) was worsening, and during a difficult period when I was growing up I had three major operations, which took me away from the sports fields and the swimming pools for two full years. It was the worst time ever. Sometimes I wondered if sport would ever be part of my life again . . .

The purpose of the operations was to insert metal rods in my back, to correct and straighten my spine. They are there to this day, and I'm not letting anyone touch them. My back is not straight now, but I seem straight to look at. I was supposed to have two operations back then, but in fact needed three . . . because one went wrong.

In the first operation, they cut me from the front, deflated a lung and put one rod in, fixed by eight screws. Doctors told me that this was the worst of it, that this first operation would be the most painful, the one I would have most trouble with. I could live with that in the hope that things were going to be better for me down the track.

Two weeks later they did the second operation, cutting me down the back this time and inserting a second rod with a hook on the end. That was the easy one, they told me reassuringly. But from the word go it never felt right, and I was in a lot of pain. It hurt. Badly. If this was the operation that was supposed to be less painful, why was it hurting so much? The medical staff didn't believe me. There seemed to be a view that I was whingeing. But I knew there was something wrong.

Several weeks later, they put me in a plaster cast, took a few X-rays . . . and sent me home. Within two hours there was a phone call: the X-rays showed that the hook had come loose. 'I cannot believe this,' I said. 'I cannot believe this . . . '.

I think it nearly killed my mum. 'I can't handle this . . . I can't handle another month here,' she said when the doctors sat her down and told her there had to be another operation. But it happened . . . they operated again.

> *Karen Long: Lou was so happy when she was allowed to go home. It was just before her birthday. A couple of hours after she left hospital, she rang me, devastated. The second operation had not worked and now they had to do a third to fix it up. So back she went.*

I was fourteen. In fact, I 'celebrated' my fourteenth birthday in hospital. It wasn't one of my best birthdays. The operations I went through were pretty revolutionary at the time, and I suppose everyone was treading carefully, uncertain as to how I would get through. I have probably been sicker in hospital with other things over the years, but I remember that period most sharply of all. They were the last major operations I was to have.

Sustaining me was the thought that if I was patient (and apart from when I'm training, I'm not very good at that), it would turn out all right and I would be able to get back to what I was doing and be as active as I had been. That was why it was all so hard. I had been very active up to that point in my life – and suddenly it had all stopped dead. It was so frustrating. As I've already said, when people have told me I *can't* do a particular thing, I have always been inclined to go straight out and do it. Now, I was immobile . . . and pretty helpless.

For a long time after the third operation, I couldn't even sit up. The process of having the three operations took almost four months; I was in hospital for virtually all of that time and nearly always on a striker bed. You lie on your stomach and they fix another section on top, and flip you over like a toasted sandwich every few hours. I stayed on that bed for what seemed like forever, not allowed to move or get up. I could watch TV, via a mirror they had set up. I had a game based on Rubik's cube too. And Mum, Karen and I used to play Yahtzee all the time. Only right near the end of that period was I allowed to sit up.

I was in there so long that of course I had my good days as well as my bad. I didn't like the hospital food, and most nights Mum would bring me something from home. This was one of the things I looked forward to the most – the sight of my mum coming into the room, with something wrapped in tea towels to keep it warm. It would be a roast, or a chicken dinner . . . something home-made. Occasionally it was McDonald's. When you're stuck in hospital for a long time you look forward to little treats like that.

The same thing applied to Karen's visits. I'd be looking at the clock and thinking, 'She'll be here soon'. And she always was. She used to come after school every day, and at weekends too. She'd ride over on her bike. Today I still find it hard to believe she did that. She could have been out with friends who were a lot more mobile and active than me. But she was there for me all the time. That's really what friendship is about, I reckon.

She was always bringing me flowers; her dad worked for the council and he would pick flowers for me during the day. The hospital had a nap time from 1.00 to 3.00 p.m., or something stupid, and quite often Karen would come at 12.55 with some flowers. Everyone at the hospital knew her and she'd say, 'Can I just put these in water? Then I'll go outside and wait'. But she'd stay in there with me. They'd turn the lights out and now and then the nurse would come in to check on me. Karen would be there wrapped up in a curtain or something with her feet sticking out and we'd be giggling and carrying on. They *must* have known she was there, but they just let it go.

Being in hospital is rarely a fun time, but Karen was there so often to brighten things up. When I was first allowed back into my wheelchair at the hospital she would take me around – at about 100 miles an hour! I could hardly sit up in the chair then, but we really pushed the limits. She helped me get through, no doubt about that.

> *Karen Long: In that time in hospital I think Louise experienced every emotion, from passive acceptance to inconsolable frustration. It was a very difficult time for her. For months she lay there, unable to move, except for her arms. We passed the time by chatting and playing games.*
>
> *When Louise was finally able to sit up, complete with a chest-to-hip plaster, it wasn't long before we were off, racing around the hospital in a chair. She always wanted me to push faster. But the plaster frustrated Louise no end. She was unable to effectively push her chair and when she got back to school she was lent an electric chair to get around in. It was awful, and so slow ... too slow for Louise. We tried everything to make it go faster, and then one day we broke it. Somehow we had managed to wreck the motor.*

We still talk about those days, but about the lighter things, the really good days. Like: 'Do you remember that night the jelly fell on the floor?'. (We always laughed about that because it was one of those jellies that had gone wrong. It hit like a brick – and just stayed there, solid as a rock.) We never recall the sad things or the bad days. But that's life, I reckon. Over time you tend to block out the painful memories and just remember the good ones.

\* \* \*

After what seemed an eternity, I had stabilised enough for them to send me home, encased in a plaster cast that reached from my neck to my hips. I was in that for two months, then in another different cast – and all of it right through the Perth summer, which is really hot. It was horrible.

It was a long road back. For more than three months in hospital I did absolutely nothing – just lay there and wasted away. I was as weak as a kitten. My bicep was the thickness of a wrist. So after they finally took the brace off for the last time my progress was slow – but steady.

After all that I had to wear a plastic brace. 'You'll have to wear this for three months,' they told me when it was first put on . . . and I was counting the days.

I always clung to the positive thought that it was all going to be worthwhile – that in the end it was all going to be worth it. I would lie there and think, 'I'm not going to have a sore back any more. I'm not going to have to wear a brace!'. And this was a big thing, considering I'd worn a plastic brace since . . . well, it seemed forever. Then I would go back in great anticipation and they'd say, 'No . . . it's going to have to be another two months'.

The third time I was told I had to keep it on for even longer, I just snapped. I went really ballistic in the surgery and they had to call the nursing sister in to calm me down. That day I called the doctor everything under the sun. 'You're a liar . . . and you're making me do this!' I shouted. I hated it so much.

\* \* \*

It was two years before I had made enough of a recovery to take up sport again. The funny thing is that I don't remember a lot of what went on during that time – the two years I had away from my sport. Probably I don't remember a lot of it because I don't want to. I don't know how I ever stayed away from sport . . . or how Mum managed to keep me away. I couldn't do anything; I wasn't even allowed to swim. I was kept in the dark by the doctors a bit, too, about what was going on. They didn't want me to get too upset. I sustained myself with the thought that I *would* get back into sport one day. I took everything gradually, one step at a time – and that helped me keep going. When I look back now I don't know how I did it. Sport is such a huge part of my life now and absorbs so much of my time.

*Rita Sauvage: The two years off sport were absolute agony for her.*

\* \* \*

When I got back to school I was put in the lower classes, and struggled trying to catch up on the twelve or thirteen weeks of work I had missed. All of it became pretty frustrating. I was not a natural student – that's about the best way I can think to put it – and I had to work very hard for the results that I did manage to get. I completed my studies at Hollywood High to Year Ten level – and I found the going pretty tough most of the way. But I had really good friends and I have plenty of good memories of my schooldays overall.

After completing Year Ten at school I went to TAFE and did office and secretarial studies for a year and a half. But I never did get to go into the workforce full-time – although I did work part-time for a while at a few places, including the Western Australian Wheelchair Sports Association – a job that gave me the flexibility to train and compete. The sporting events that progressively overtook my life meant that I have never had a traditional nine-to-five job – although I think I work as hard as anyone. And all the things I learned at TAFE a decade ago would be outdated now thanks to the galloping new technology. It was just the way my life turned out.

\* \* \*

# LOUISE'S MEDICAL RECORD, 1973 TO 1987

## OPERATIONS, PROCEDURES AND PROGRESS

**18/9/73**
Seen four to five hours after an elective caesarean section. Bilateral dislocated hips. Spiral fracture of left femur, bilateral club feet. No movement below the knees.

A diagnosis of neurogenic arthrogryposis initially – subsequently shown to be diastatomatomyelia with fibrous band rather than bony peg at the Lumbar 1 level. Gallows traction.

**21/11/73**
Bilateral ETAs (elongation of trendo achilles) plus medial release on the left.

**21/12/73**
Open reduction left hip (F. B. Webb, Jack O'Connor Senior Registrar).

**25/3/74**
Open reduction left hip and psoas tenotomy.

**28/11/74**
Open reduction left subtalar joint, subcutaneous ETA on right.

**11/2/75**
Left salter pelvic osteotomy.

**4/75**
Removal of pins. Fracture of right femur following fall, treated with plaster.

**27/8/75**
Postero-medial release right foot and ETA, posterior release flexor contracture right knee.

**9/75**
Further open reduction of left hip and derotation osteotomy of left femur.

**11/75**
In above-knee callipers with band tops. Flexion contractures of knees improving.

**12/5/76**
Plates removed from left femur. Lateral displacement osteotomy of right os calcis (callansun).

**1/7/77**
Thoracic 11 and Lumbar 1 – partial laminectomy. Fibrous band found tethering cord at Lumbar 1 level.

**23/8/77**
Child becoming difficult about wearing long-leg calliper.

**3/78**
Greenstick fracture of distal left tibia, treated with plaster.

**10/6/78**
Right lower femoral osteotomy to correct flexion deformity right knee.

**1/11/78**
Louise showing strong preference for wheelchair life aged five.

**14/3/79**
Removal of plate from right femur.

**16/6/80**
Long-leg calliper on the right, below-knee calliper on the left.

**1/10/80**
Chiari osteotomy left hip.

**8/11/80**
Right salter osteotomy plus Sharrard Ilio-psoas transfer.

**21/5/81**
Removal of pins from both hips, Fremantle Hospital.

**3/81**
Above-knee, ring-top callipers and back brace.

**12/6/81**
Walking very well in callipers.

### Christmas 1981
Louise has opted for wheelchair life, aged eight. Flexion deformity of both knees, right more than left.

### 30/8/83
Growing like a weed. Competed very successfully in recent Games for the Disabled. Hips were good. Small feet. Crutches given away completely.

### 30/1/86
Two-and-a-half-year break. Very active in her wheelchair. Able to hop onto examination couch without any trouble at all.

### 4/8/87
Modification of Dwyer anterior spine fusion, followed by posterior spinal fusion with Harrington rods.

### 9/87
One of the Harrington rods which had pulled out was replaced. She had a spinal fusion in effect from TL2 to S1. Her scoliosis curve had reached 100 degrees. There was a very good correction with the spinal fusion.

### 3/4/97
Last seen in relation to her right knee.

## SUMMARY

Eighteen operations carried out by F. B. Webb, including five major operations to the left hip, but only one major operation to the right hip. One spinal operation carried out by Michael Lee. Two major spinal operations carried out by Jack O'Connor, fusing spine front and back, and one minor readjustment by Jack O'Connor.

In addition, serial hip, foot and knee plaster changes, several under anaesthetic – but beyond counting.

\* \* \*

Looking back now over this list of operations prepared by Dr Webb, I don't even know what half of them were for – let alone remember having them done. I was very young for most of the surgery I have had in my life. I just know that the hospital became my home away from home and that the people there became like a second family. What was done was certainly done in my best interests at the time – to prepare me for life in the years to come. It was all long ago – although I have hundreds of scars to remind me of those years.

As I write these words I know that there are still a couple of operations I could get done. For example, my right leg doesn't straighten, and I wouldn't mind getting that fixed up one day. I have pretty poor circulation in both legs and a few years back the right one was continuously purple and blue, worrying me to the point where I thought I should do something about it. But a specialist in Melbourne who examined me said it was OK for the time being, and told me not to worry too much. To straighten it via an operation would mean that I could no longer bend it all the way back to get into my racing chair. The alternative would be a long, slow process of gradual traction – and that doesn't appeal much either. So until they figure out a new way to do it, I'm not going to get it done. I am pretty happy with the way I am now – and my motto in that regard is: 'If it ain't broke, don't fix it'.

What happened during my time in hospital, and afterwards, is pretty much in line with my theory about life: that you just deal with the things that come up. Or do your best to. The fact was that I was born with a disability – and I have had to make the best of it.

CHAPTER 5

# WORLD CHAMP...
# AND STARRY-EYED!

As you have probably worked out, I did get back into sport. But the operations I had had, the rods that had been inserted in my back, changed things forever.

In 1989, when I was still at school, I won a place on the state side for the Fifth National Junior Games which were being held on the Queensland Gold Coast, and made my return to top-class competition. The Games took place during an Australia-wide pilots' strike, and it was quite a battle for us even to get there from Western Australia. At one stage we were going to travel the whole journey by bus, which would have been a nightmare. In the end Qantas stepped in and we were flown to Sydney, then we had to get a bus north for the last 1000 kilometres. That was bad enough: I had three chairs – my racing chair, my day chair and my basketball chair – plus all my luggage. Multiply that by thirty – the size of the team – and you can get an idea of the difficulties. I'd never even contemplate long trips by bus any more. Plane travel is tough enough – and I have done plenty of that back and forth across the world over the years.

At those Nationals I still did everything: I competed in track and field, played basketball and swam. But I was different now. The operations I had undergone had changed me, certainly slowed me down in the water. I couldn't do breaststroke as well as I once had, couldn't arch my back. I wasn't the swimmer I had been in '87 before the surgery.

I challenged myself: 'You're not going so well in the pool . . . let's see how you go on the track'.

> *Frank Ponta: She had lost all her zip at swimming and I said to her, 'Look, swimming is going to be out for you – have a go at field events and track and basketball'. She had been a very good swimmer – she would have made the Paralympics as a swimmer. After the operation she didn't know what she was going to do, and it was then I said I reckoned she should give the track a bit of a go. So we got an old wheelchair and she jumped into it, and away she went.*

I had been gone from competition for a couple of years by this point and there were new people on the scene, including a girl named Deann Johnson, who was rated fastest Australian junior wheelchair racer on the track. 'You won't beat her,' people were saying.

Well, I did beat her, despite what everyone had said. Looking back, it was a sort of early watershed moment in my sporting career. I was sixteen, and reaching the stage where I needed to specialise more. I knew I couldn't keep up forever with all the different training required for the different sports. It was then I decided I would make track racing my future in sport . . .

> Frank Ponta: *She started off sprinting, but I could always see that her main thing was going to be middle distance or long distance. At the end of all her races she was so powerful.*

At this stage, though, I was still competing in basketball, a sport that I much enjoyed. And when I went to Canberra with the rest of the Western Australian squad the following year, 1990, for the Senior Nationals, I was both a track racer and a member of the basketball team. I didn't swim.

> Rita Sauvage: *She loved playing basketball. But [before her surgery] her back would often play up and I generally had to rub her after each match – it ached so much.*

I was involved in quite a scene in a basketball match over there in Canberra. I used to get very angry on court; I have never liked losing, although I accept that with a little more grace these days. In a match against South Australia I got really fired up . . .

> Frank Ponta: *There was a real blow-up. A couple of fouls went against Louise and she just did her block, which wasn't really like her. She hated me, she hated our captain, she hated the umpire, she hated the opposition . . . We were a point in front and ended up losing the game. I had to take her out of the match. 'You're off,' I said. 'If I can't have discipline from you, then you can't be part of it.' She came back later and apologised. 'Yeah, I know,' she said to me. 'I did the wrong thing . . . I'm sorry.'*

It was always going to be more satisfying for me to be involved in an individual sport, much as I enjoyed basketball – I love being really loud on court. In a team sport like basketball, I had to rely on four other players . . . and they had to depend on me. At least in an individual sport I could only blame myself if something went wrong, or if I hadn't done the work.

It was on the track that I really made my mark at those Games in 1990. I did really well – won my races and recorded personal best times. As a result of what I managed to achieve at the Nationals, I was picked in my first Australian senior team – to compete at the World Championships for the Disabled in Assen, Holland, in the northern summer.

I have no clear memory of the circumstances of being named in the team – even though it was a momentous event in my young life. I was still in Canberra after competing in the Nationals, and my name would have been read out well down the list, considering that it starts with 'S'. I remember only my reaction: 'Oh my God! I'm going away with the Australian team!'. Aided by a $500 donation from the Tuart Hill Swimming Club, I was on my way internationally . . .

* * *

It was the first time I had been overseas without my parents – an experience I would go through countless times over the coming years. Travelling to distant places is what I have to do in my life, but it is no enjoyment. I hate packing, dislike the travel itself and I am generally a bit paranoid about my chair, about handing it over to someone else for the duration of the trip. I also get out of my routines when I'm away . . . often don't eat as well as I should. Maintaining my weight has been an ongoing struggle – and especially so when I travel overseas. Away from home you often don't have access to the foods that you normally eat. You just have to make do.

One of the worst aspects of travel is the plane trip itself. And it's not just the difficulty of getting on the plane – you're always first on and last off. There can be a lot more. To use the aisle chair requires someone else to push you. You lose your independence – and I really hate that.

I think anyone in a wheelchair is also acutely aware of hydration levels when it comes to plane travel. When you're up there on a jumbo, travelling twenty-four hours to London or whatever, going to the bathroom can become a major operation and a real pain. Domestically it has often proved just as big a problem for me – if not bigger – considering that the planes, up until a change of policy in December 1999, did not carry aisle chairs. I have to dehydrate when I am preparing to fly any distance – which is not good for your body, since you are supposed to keep your fluids up to counter the natural dehydrating effects of flying. I prepare carefully, and essentially 'dry out'. These days I am very aware of when to drink and when not to drink. Dehydrating when you are flying makes you feel pretty poor . . . really drained. Add that to the jet lag and you inevitably get there feeling less than great. Then as soon as you arrive you have to begin the process of rehydrating. I'm used to it now, though.

But flying is not always negative. Although it can be a pain often enough, there are some compensations. Very occasionally a flight can be special when you are unexpectedly shifted up front. I recall one particularly memorable United Airlines flight when a few of us were called up to first class and they cooked individual meals for us. I had a steak that was one of the best meals I have ever eaten on a plane.

Travelling is a hard, sometimes lonely life. But it is what I do. The friends I have made along the way help make it bearable, and enjoyable enough to keep drawing me back. In fact there is such a network now that it's like having a 'second family' – familiar faces, good friends I can hang out with on the circuit. The travelling I have done, the opportunity to meet different people and experience different cultures, has made me a broader person (and I'm not talking about weight!). My tolerance levels are higher now . . . I don't judge people the way I perhaps once did.

People ask me what is my favourite country, considering the amount of travelling I have done. Well, I really like Switzerland, a country I have been to a number of times – but Australia will do me without any doubt.

\* \* \*

The huge amount of travel I have done also sits easily with my broader philosophy: that I have never felt for an instant in my life that being in a wheelchair should stop me from spreading my wings and flying – almost literally.

Just because I sit in a chair doesn't mean I can't do this, or I can't do that. Yet sometimes it seems that half the world still can't comprehend me living on my own, or driving a car, or getting in a taxi that isn't a disabled taxi. People ask me how I manage at home . . . how I can possibly do this, or do that. Well, I mean . . . you find a way. Nothing is impossible. Sure, there are some things I don't do – like hanging up pictures, or changing light globes – but you either get someone to do it for you . . . or you find a way to get by. I don't impose limits on myself.

I've probably done a lot of things that many able-bods have never tackled. I have flown, swum with sharks and stingrays, been to Africa to experience the magnificent wildlife. And all those things have added an extra element to a life that has been intensely focused on success as a professional athlete for these last ten years or so. I believe that you need that balance – that even when you are strongly committed to something important you need to get away . . . to taste different experiences.

I did a scuba-diving course some years ago, and have been on dives in the ocean. Probably best of all was a promotional appearance I did one day at Underwater World in Perth, organised by the Western Australian Disabled Sports Association. It was so peaceful down there, swimming with the sea creatures, with sharks and stingrays gliding past. It was a truly amazing experience, especially for me, because I am not as limited in water as I am on land. I am at home in the water. 'You feel as if you're floating in space and you don't have a care in the world,' I remember saying at the time.

One day in Perth – or over Perth, to be exact – I 'flew' a Tiger Moth, a tiny, seemingly frail plane. I was in the front seat, with the pilot behind, and we zoomed down low over my house. Then he let me fly it for a bit and it was terrific.

Over Mission Beach, Cairns, another morning I did a tandem skydive with my cousin Jacqueline. I was strapped on in front of an experienced skydiver – and it was just awesome, the rush of air and the silence way up there. I also went white-water rafting while I was in Cairns, which was great fun too. Up in north Queensland, I headed into the rainforest at Cape Tribulation and scuba dived and snorkelled at the Barrier Reef.

I like to try different things, although of course there's a limit – things I can't do, or won't do. For example, I won't bungy-jump, because of the rods in my back, although I probably could if I really wanted to. The fact is, though, that I would prefer to have my back in one piece. I suspect that many people stay within their comfort zones, rarely stepping outside those self-imposed limits to challenge themselves – but that's just not the sort of person I am.

\* \* \*

I was almost seventeen when the Assen World Championships were staged – specifically a track athlete by this point, somewhat starry-eyed . . . but delighted to be there, racing against the best in the world. The whole thing was a real eye-opener for me – to see such a gathering of people from different countries (forty-eight in all) and different cultures, all with disabilities. Just to go into the dining hall was amazing – to see the blind athletes, to see people eating with their feet because they had no arms . . . and to see all the people from all over the world who competed in our sports.

I'll just give you a snapshot at this point of the blend of different disabilities in international wheelchair racing. In my sport and disability group there are four classes, which were then known as T1, T2, T3 and T4, although now they are differently named. I'm a T4 (now T54), which is the highest classification – meaning the highest level of functional ability. Then it's down to T3 (slightly less ability), then T2 and T1 (the quadriplegic classes). The T3s and T4s are separated on the track for the 100, 200, 400 and 800 metres; above that we are all combined for the 1500, 5000 and 10,000 metres, and for road racing. Road racing can be anything from 10 kilometres up to the full marathon (42 kilometres). At any distance over 1500 metres – and in some cases over 800 metres – wheelchair athletes race faster than able-bodied runners. These days I predominantly do the 800, 1500 and 5000 metres and road racing. I have only ever done one 10,000 on the track in my life, 1994 – and that was to get out of training! I'll never do one again.

Across the board in sport for athletes with a disability, classification divides all competitors into one of six disability categories: amputation, cerebral palsy, intellectual disability, vision impairment, wheelchair athletes and *les autres* (the others). Competition structures and methods differ for the different sports. In the terminology of sport for athletes with a disability, I am a 'gimp' (an old term from war times, I think) – that's someone in a chair. Sport for athletes with a disability has its own language: gimps, crips (which mean the same thing), amps (amputees), blinkies (blind athletes) CPs (cerebral palsy sufferers) and IDs (intellectually disabled athletes).

\* \* \*

The Assen Championships were a mixed blessing for me – a good example of the blend of agony and ecstasy that sport can sometimes be, but another real turning point in my career.

I was entered in two events: the 100 and 200 metres. I made it to the final of the 100 metres – traditionally track's 'blue riband' event – and ended up winning in world-record time (18.1 seconds – two seconds better than the old record!). My reaction was: 'Oh my God, I can't believe this!'

I progressively chipped away at this record and by 1992 had lowered it to 16.72 seconds, a time that stood until the 1996 Paralympics.

Then when I came out and won the 200 metres as well, everything was so cool.

After the 200 I rang home, as I had after the 100, to tell my parents the news. I was over the moon. But I returned from the phone conversation with my folks to the announcement that I had been disqualified – for coming out of my lane! I didn't recall doing that, but I took it on the chin. 'I suppose I must have,' I told the press. It was quite a blow. In an instant I had learned about the other side of competition – the despair of having something you wanted snatched away from you. It was a hard lesson.

But although there were disappointments, the trip to Europe in 1990 was good for me in so many ways. It stretched well beyond the World Championships – to England for the Stoke Mandeville Games, held at the place where the framework for regular sport for athletes with a disability was laid down in the immediate post-war years. These Games were another success for me, bringing gold in the 100, 200 and 400 metres, plus two relays.

Then I headed back to Holland for the Bloemen Marathon ('bloemen' means 'flower'), which is like a Tour de France for wheelchair athletes, running over eight days and involving stages of 20 to 30 kilometres a day, hill-climbs and criteriums. (These are short course races around a circuit, usually held at the end of the stages.) At the end of the day's racing we would stay in the town, or take a bus to the next one – and start it all again the following day. I raced Bloemen a couple of times (1991 and 1993) and won a lot of criteriums in those two years.

It was in Holland that I first saw Connie Hansen, the awesome Danish wheelchair racer who was rated the best in the world. The ultimate. I decided over there that I wanted to have the recognition that she had . . . and to be the fastest in the world.

CHAPTER 6

# THEY SAID I'D NEVER MAKE IT!

It was at the Assen World Championships that I made the big decision about what I wanted to do with my life. Although there would be gold medals and world records in the years ahead, I have never forgotten that moment as a sixteen-year-old when I realised I wanted to become a full-time athlete. A TAFE student at that time, I came home from Europe and told my family and friends what a good time I'd had – and that basically I had made up my mind to turn professional.

I can tell you I was very much discouraged, on three grounds really: (1) that I was in a sport that didn't get any media coverage and didn't have much profile; (2) that I was female; and (3) that I was an athlete with a disability. I remember my dad and others saying, 'When is she going to stop all this training and get a job?' And obviously it would have been a lot safer to accept their point of view – to focus on something else and be satisfied with being no more than a mediocre athlete.

But here I am, years later, a professional athlete, and managing to make money out of my sport. I guess the road I took proved a lot of people wrong. You've already seen that it's in my nature to go against what others say, and at sixteen, on the verge of seventeen that's just what I did. My belief – then and now – is that just because someone hasn't done something before doesn't mean you can't do it. I was so young when I went to those Games, and like most people of my age I didn't really know what I wanted in life. But I'm happy that I chose the right path – well, the right path for me anyway. If I hadn't done that I'd probably have been sitting with the careers counsellor at Hollywood High ... still not knowing what I really wanted to do ...

\* \* \*

The main thing I remember about that time – about making my bid to become a professional athlete – is writing a hell of a lot of letters seeking sponsorship support – and yep, being rejected many times. It wasn't easy. My sporting career had been a financial struggle up to that point. Just about the only help my family and I had received was from my local association, the Western Australian Wheelchair Sports Association, and from Tuart Hill Swimming Club. It had almost all been down to my parents, their finances stretched thin as they tried to keep up with the growing demands of my career.

But my European campaign, from Assen onwards, had had the effect of putting me on the map internationally, and opened new doors. In December 1990, the Australian Institute of Sport flew their representative Peter Hugg across to Perth. At a meeting held at the Observation City Hotel on Scarborough Beach, he told me that they would sponsor my career in sport. This was a wonderful breakthrough. I really was on my way now. I had had success both at home and overseas – and my sights were set high. I had also been named the Western Australian Disabled Sports Association Sports Star of the Year.

To celebrate I went off and got my driver's licence and bought myself a car – I had been saving up for years.

> *Rita Sauvage: Louise had a car at seventeen, a Pulsar, and that made me redundant – so I went and played bridge. I had some lessons and have played ever since . . . much to Maurice's disgust.*

> *Maurice Sauvage: When Louise started out driving I was scared to go in the car with her . . . she really used to put her foot down. She drove four or five times across from Perth to the east coast and I used to worry about her. Louise will not stop – she'll keep on pushing and pushing. I'd tell her, 'Don't drive at night-time when you're tired'. But, you know, with Louise it's impossible to stop her!*

> *Ann Sauvage: As soon as she got her car, we didn't see her.*

It was also around this time that I hooked up with a new coach, Jenni Banks. Jenni was working for the Western Australian Disabled Sports Association when I first met her. She was working with a small group and I joined up.

I think Jenni and I grew together in the sport. She learned along the way . . . and so did I. She had a degree in Human Movement and was very knowledgeable; she put a great deal of thought into training and into technique. And she kept right up to date with what was happening internationally, with the changes in chairs and technology. Her training programs were so expert, and so good. I think it was Jenni and another coach, Kathy Lee, a good friend of mine, who really put wheelchair racing on the map in Australia. Between them they took the sport to new levels. There was a time when they were really the only two wheelchair coaches in Australia, and much respected for what they did.

The really hard, disciplined training work that has become the basis of my life crystallised in Perth in the early '90s under Jenni's coaching direction. In those days a squad of us would be out along the Swan River, working the cycleways and the freeways in Como and South Perth, pushing around Perry Lakes Stadium. And it was then that hill work became part of what I do – specifically the 'horror hills' of King's Park, the beautiful park that looks down over Perth city. We'd labour up those hills, then belt down the other side. In a racing chair it's quite possible to reach 60 kilometres an hour or more.

Building the mix of upper body strength, speed and endurance I needed for success in my sport was down to the one great secret of just about all success in life: unrelenting hard work. On a program scientifically tailored to the needs of my sport, I started training twice a day, six days a week, as I still do today. It was the same thing, winter or summer, hot or cold, wet or dry. It was never easy – but it was what had to be done. Sometimes when I was out there on a cold morning at 6.00 a.m., pushing against the wind and rain for 25 kilometres all alone, I would ask myself the question, 'What am I doing here?'. There wasn't a week that went by when I didn't quietly say that to myself. Training was very demanding and very repetitive. What has always motivated me is winning – and I long ago accepted that you can't do that unless you put in the work.

> *Jenni Banks: She always had killer instinct. There were times when it seemed she was at death's door – yet still turned up for training. I would have to send her home again. She has shown that there's nothing a kid with a disability cannot do.*

\* \* \*

There have been several breakthrough moments in my career. The first had been when I decided to become a professional athlete. But the first quantum leap was when I seriously began to think about the Paralympics.

Like all sporting careers, mine had been one of stepping stones – from junior days up to state and then national level. Travelling to Europe, I had tasted what it was like right at the top – and I had enjoyed the experience and done well. From late 1990 I could almost reach out and touch the Paralympic Games, just two years away. Various awards that I won – from companies and sports associations, recognising my achievements – only helped whet my appetite a little more. 'Sports Star Aims for Olympic [sic] Gold', read a headline in the *West Australian* of 28 October 1991, above a story that revealed I had my eyes 'set on gold' at the Barcelona Paralympics of 1992. '"People think that because you're in a wheelchair it is not real sport and you're not a real athlete"', I said in the article. '"But when they see what we do they soon realise . . ."'

My commitment was absolute. Training those six days a week, I set about doing what I had to do to get ready for Barcelona. The hard work paid off beautifully when I set a new world record (31.82 seconds) in the 200 metres at the National Wheelchair Games held in Adelaide in April '92 – beating the time I had established in Victoria a little earlier (32.64 seconds). Working hard, doing 100 kilometres a week on the road track and three days a week in the weights room of the Curtin University gym, I gradually got myself ready for the challenge of Spain . . .

CHAPTER 7

# BARCELONA – OLÉ!

Everything about the Barcelona Paralympics of 1992 was brilliant. Those Games were a memorable experience for everyone involved. I was just thrilled to be there, to be part of an Australian team. I had plenty of pinch-yourself moments, barely daring to believe that I was actually there doing what I was doing.

A naive kid at the time (I was still a teenager), I felt right throughout the Games that it was a magical time – and I just went with the flow. By then I had moved up in the world equipment-wise – and was racing in a $3500 custom-built Swiss 'Kuschall' chair that I had shopped for myself.

I remember those Paralympics as a wonderful experience in a city that was really buzzing. It all took place in a sort of ongoing carnival atmosphere that had spilled over from the Olympics. The Athletes'

Village, the facilities, the food, the way they looked after us – I don't think anyone could have asked for more. We stayed in apartments right on the waterfront. Sure, I would like to have seen more of Spain, and sure, I would like to have taken part in the Opening Ceremony (I didn't, because I was to compete the next day), but these things happen.

The organisers in Barcelona really seemed attuned to the needs of athletes with disabilities. The Spanish have a great set-up to support their athletes: they run a special lottery from which millions of dollars are poured into sport, with plenty of it reaching sports for athletes with a disability.

The Spanish people were wonderful in the support they provided to the Paralympics. They made it. For me it was all just awesome.

\* \* \*

The history of the Paralympics traces back more than half a century now – to the Stoke Mandeville Games, begun in the aftermath of World War II. The Stoke Mandeville Games were begun by Dr Ludwig Guttman as part of a rehabilitation program for soldiers injured in the war. They were first held in 1948 in Buckinghamshire, England.

In 1960, games for athletes with a disability were held in Rome, a competition that later became known as the first Paralympic Games. The Paralympics are now held each Olympic year – the peak event of competition for athletes with a disability. Meanwhile, the Stoke Mandeville Wheelchair Games have continued each year, although in 1997 their name was changed to the World Wheelchair Games. In 1999 they were shifted for the first time away from their traditional home and held in Christchurch, New Zealand.

Since the Los Angeles Games of 1984, there had been an opportunity for wheelchair racers to compete at the Olympics as well as the Paralympics. Two track events were held for athletes with a disability: a men's 1500 metres races and a women's 800 metres race – but they were only demonstration races, which meant that the medals did not count towards the final tally. Racing in the women's 800 metres demonstration event had not been an option for me, however. The qualifying heats had been held in New Orleans and getting over there had been beyond my reach financially. So while my main rivals raced for a place in the Olympics, I stayed home and prepared myself for the Paralympics.

The first event I raced in, the 100 metres, will always be very special to me when I think back on my career. But the video tape of the race – its quality fading now (and I must do something about that) – doesn't really give that impression. I had raced a world-record 16.72 seconds in Switzerland the month before. But in the final didn't look very happy at all as I came across the line, 10 metres or so in front of the field, in 17.37 seconds. We had raced into a stiff headwind and my start had been horrendous. Mainly, I think I was just overwhelmed.

This was my first ever Paralympic gold medal, and for me it was the greatest thrill of those Games. It didn't really sink in until I was up on the dais with the medal around my neck and the strains of the Aussie national anthem ringing in my ears. 'This is fantastic,' I thought. 'I just can't believe I'm here.' Back home, as I found out later, the Sauvage phone at home in Joondanna was ringing off the hook – every time they hung up, it rang again. It was quite a day for the Sauvage family: I had won my first Paralympic gold, Ann had landed her first job as an accountant and Dad won a fifth-division prize in Lotto – twenty bucks! The first news of my win in Barcelona reached the household via a circuitous route: through a phone call from Dad's cousin in Queensland. He'd seen the race on TV. Apart from the nightly ABC bulletins from the Games, there wasn't any TV coverage at all in Perth. By the 2000 Games in Sydney, sport for athletes with a disability had come a long way in that respect!

Most of the girls I raced in Barcelona are now gone from the sport. Monica Wetterstrom from Sweden finished second and Daniela

Jutzeler from Switzerland third. Tragically, two years later, Daniela was killed – hit by a truck while training, soon after the 1994 World Championships. The news was shattering.

From the 800 metres final only one other girl is still racing: Chantal Petitclerc from Canada, with whom I was to grab unwanted headlines at the Sydney Paralympics of 2000. To watch video coverage of that 800 is to realise how much wheelchair racing has changed – how much more tactical it has become. We think about our races a lot more these days. The Barcelona 800 metres final was all over the shop, with no-one working together. In that race I gave away far too much ground; I was back last at one stage, gave the favourite Connie Hansen just too much ground – and couldn't quite pick her up in the straight. I came a close second – beaten by 0.22 seconds in world-record time.

Connie Hansen was then pretty much state-of-the-art in the wheelchair-racing business. I had raced her in competitions prior to the Paralympics, but didn't know her well. This was awesome in its own right – that I was there racing alongside, and against, my idol in the sport. She was a tough competitor, very focused, she kept to herself a lot. It was always as if she were playing mind games with me. Towards the end of the competition over there we talked a little more; I guess she saw me more as a respected rival by then.

The 200 metres race was sweet consolation for my second placing in the 800. In the 200 final I became the first female racer to break thirty seconds for the distance (29.03 seconds), setting a time that lasted until the Sydney 2000 Paralympics.

When all the track racing was done, I competed in only the second marathon of my life. The first had been in Adelaide earlier that year to qualify for the Paralympics. The course had taken us past the Adelaide Zoo, and the strong smell of the animals wafting out of the zoo was a clear signal that you had completed another lap! I finished that first marathon in under two hours, which seemed to shock everyone – although I admit I did draft with the guys along the way.

Drafting, being tucked in behind another competitor, gives you a bit of a break – and in a pack ideally everyone takes turns at setting the pace, then dropping back. But it doesn't always work like that. On the circuit there are wheelchair racers who don't do their share, who won't take a turn up front when they should. They are quite happy to sit behind and let others do the work. I get angry about that, and so do a lot of athletes. Those sorts of competitors tend to get yelled at a fair bit. People are going to respect you so much more if you at least go out there in front and have a turn – even if you're struggling, and even if it's only for 200 metres. I always make sure I do my share. And when I'm ready for a break I'll say, 'I'm done ... C'mon, someone else'. It's an unwritten law of road racing that the slogging work up front is shared around. And the international standard is that you can draft only within your own category.

I had been drafting in the men's category in Adelaide, but the opposite happened in the Barcelona marathon, when a guy got into the middle of the women's group. He copped plenty. One girl in particular, Daniela Jutzeler, was abusing him, hitting him and shouting, 'Get out! Get out!'. Eventually, showing good judgment, he did.

Conversation is part of marathon racing. Well, it is for me, anyway – although some people don't talk at all. But it can get a bit boring out there and there's certainly some talk that goes on – and especially if we are working together as a pack up front. Then it will be: 'It's your pull ... I'm done' or 'Good pull!' (after someone has pulled into the wind) or 'C'mon ... let's go ... Let's pick it up!'. Or when there's a surge on it's 'C'mon ... Let's go now ... Go, go, go!'.

I had never really thought of the marathon too seriously when I was considering my program in Barcelona. Then suddenly on a hot summer's day I was out there in the middle of it, a novice pushing in a pack of eight of the top racers in the world and sort of freaking out at the thought. I was up with the pace until about the 30-kilometre mark, then I dropped off the pack and finally finished sixth.

The race really flattened me – my second ever marathon at the end of two tough weeks during which the tiredness had progressively accumulated. At the end of the marathon I cramped up badly – I couldn't even get out of my race chair. The thing was that I hadn't really trained or prepared to be competitive in a marathon. The track races were my goal. But it's a fact of wheelchair racing that athletes mix up their distances – they do things that able-bodied runners would never consider. In that regard we're more like cyclists – who can mix track and road – than able-bodied track athletes. There are wheelchair racers who only compete on the track, but there are many, like me, who do both. Up until Atlanta I was still racing 400s on the track (plus the longer 800s, 1500s and 5000s) and mixing that with marathons on the road – although I had dropped the 100 and 200 metres by then.

The effects of the Barcelona marathon didn't stop me going out partying that night after the Closing Ceremony, to celebrate what had been a very good Games for us Aussies. I went to bed at sunrise, then was up again a couple of hours later to go shopping in town. I was just running on whatever I had left. I guess the adrenaline was still pumping.

The Games had been a wonderful success for me – I had three golds, a silver and a sixth. And even the two races in which I had been beaten, the 800 metres and the marathon, had produced new Australian records for me. Priya Cooper's three gold and two silver in the pool made her the most successful Aussie competitor at either Games, Olympics or Paralympics.

To win gold medals and to accept the praise that went with that, the publicity labelling me the best in the world – for a girl from Perth who had started out with no giant expectations in sport all those years before, the reaction was: 'Yeah, right!'. I was only eighteen – and suddenly all this was happening to me.

* * *

Gold-medalled and starry-eyed, I came home from Barcelona to the sort of public attention I had never even dreamed of. The celebrations included a ticker-tape parade down George Street, Sydney, which was a wonderful boost for sport for athletes with a disability, helping to lift our profile. That was a terrific day. Everything was laid on for us. The night before the parade the team got together for a dinner and a party aboard the *Fairstar*, moored at Circular Quay. We were all staying on the boat and it turned out to be a massive night.

By then I was attracting some personal attention in the major dailies. In the *Sydney Morning Herald*, Michael Cowley wrote: 'Louise Sauvage – name doesn't ring a bell? Don't despair. Amnesia has not set in. Chances are very few people outside her sport would have heard of Sauvage, yet her Olympic [sic – Paralympic] achievement ranks as high as those of [Kieren] Perkins and co'.

When I first started competing seriously in the early '90s I am sure most people looked on wheelchair sports as just a fun activity, or perhaps as a form of rehabilitation. That idea has faded progressively in recent years. The truth is that we are professional athletes in every respect. We neither expect nor give any quarter to our opponents. The 1992 Barcelona Paralympics, with the attention and interest they created back home, were a turning point for our sports.

After the Games I was awarded an Order of Australia Medal, something granted to all the gold medallists from the Paralympics. We were proud for ourselves – and proud for our sport. And my mum was just stoked. She just couldn't believe it. I heard the news that I would be receiving an OAM, but probably the importance of it didn't quite sink in with me. It sure did with my mum, though!

Back home in Perth my parents organised a big party for my nineteenth birthday, setting it all up before I got home, then telling me at the last minute. This night sticks in my mind, considering that I didn't have parties for my eighteenth or twenty-first birthdays – mainly because so many of my friends had left Perth by then. It was a bloody freezing night . . . but I had a ball. All my friends were there, as well as the people from my gym and all the people who had helped me in my preparation for Barcelona.

\* \* \*

But the partying didn't last long. By January 1993 I was back in my race chair, competing for the third time in the Oz Day 10K in Sydney. It was to become a regular part of my life, a challenge and – for the most part – enjoyment every 26 January, run over a picturesque course that takes in the Opera House, Circular Quay and The Rocks. I duelled fiercely – again – with Connie Hansen, and beat her narrowly, becoming the first Australian to win the race.

This first win in '93 was very special – the first time I had beaten Connie Hansen. We were together throughout the race and I couldn't believe I was still there alongside her when we headed for the final sprint. I was still a sprinter at heart back then, and had the speed to edge her out in the race to the line. That finishing speed, stemming from earlier days as a sprint racer, was to stand me in good stead many times in the years to come.

\* \* \*

The Barcelona Paralympic Games represented a crossroads in my career. In the aftermath I honestly didn't know what I was going to do next. I even toyed with the idea of stopping and getting a 'real' job . . . or perhaps going on with my studies. I was still unsure of whether I could earn enough money from racing to make a go of it as a full-time career. But soon afterwards, 1993 presented itself, with its fresh batch of racing opportunities, and I just sort of kept going . . . without ever making a formal decision.

The decision I had just about arrived at, though, was that I had done all I wanted to do on the track. After Barcelona and my successful '92 year, I felt I needed new challenges. On the track there was not a lot of competition for me in the long spaces between the really big events like the Paralympics and World Championships.

So I moved on. I decided I would increasingly focus on road racing, anything from 10-kilometre races all the way to marathons. Basically the decision was made because I knew I couldn't keep training for success in the sprints *and* conquer the road races, which were increasingly appealing to me.

This was, literally, taking the hard road in my sporting life. I knew it was going to be a lot tougher. My training, everything I did, had to change. I knew I had to get stronger – to spend a lot more hours out on the roads, dealing with whatever the weather threw at me. It was one of those 'shifts' that has punctuated my career – from swimming to the track, from the shorter track distances to the longer stuff . . . and now the big move to the road, where there was much more international racing available, and certainly the chance to earn reasonable money if I were successful.

So, my life had been transformed in a single bound via the Paralympics. I guess I knew then that things were never going to be the same again . . .

CHAPTER 8

# NEXT STOP: THE WORLD

My success at the Barcelona Paralympics, and the decision I made in the wake of the Games to tackle road racing head-on, changed my life forever. It was the watershed moment of my athletic career. From a young Perth girl testing the waters of international competition before retreating after each trip into the safe haven of home, I progressively became something completely different: a world traveller.

If I were to become an international wheelchair racer it is what had to happen. Yet this giant step was taken almost in spite of me. After all, as I have told you, I didn't much like travel – hated it, in fact – and I didn't much like the thought of wandering the world alone either. But it was, and is, the way it had to be if I were to be serious about my sport – if I were to grab this as the big chance in my life, as the foundation for a profitable career in the years to come.

The fact is that since 1993, my first year on the international circuit, I have roamed the world, living away from home for four to six months out of every twelve. It has been no easy life. Much of the time I have travelled alone, inevitably down the back of the plane – my two chairs and my bags and I – criss-crossing the Atlantic from the USA to Europe, diving into Asia for a race now and then, tackling with equal commitment the small-town road races and the glittering, big-city championships, in those years when the world's premier events come around. Often a stopover at this town or that is no more than this sequence for me: airport, hotel, race day, hotel, airport. Generally there is not much time for sightseeing ... and there are times when I miss home a whole lot.

> *Tracy Harnett (friend): Louise has never been one to blow her own trumpet about the places she has been, or the races she has won. The only reason I know about a lot of them is that she has a wardrobe full of T-shirts from these places she's been to all over the world. It's the only way you know she'd been there ... and, usually, won. I remember conversations that I've had with her when I've asked her what she's up to. It'll be: 'Oh, I think I'm going to Switzerland on Sunday' ... or 'I'm flying to Japan on Monday'. No fuss. She just does it.*

Because I make my living out of sport, I pick and choose my events pretty carefully, assess prize money, course etc. The money I make in my travels (when successful!) progressively helps me lay down the foundation for the sort of life I want – not that there is any fortune in wheelchair racing, with the prize money ranging from modest to quite generous ... if you keep winning. Most American events are worth between US$2000 and US$4000 or so, but on occasions there are big bonuses if you can break a course record.

The competition factor adds its own edge. I am there as a professional, chasing victory and the spoils it can bring. To win means for someone else not to win – and for all the genuine sportsmanship and respect that exists there is always a mild discomfort in the money side of things. Professional Athletes on a circuit live with that, day to day.

\* \* \*

The American–Canadian circuit is the biggest in the world and goes on almost all year. I have done a lot of the races there over the years. Many of them are colourfully named and genuinely rich in tradition. They are big events in their town's or city's calendar. Most of them have more than a dash of carnival about them.

I travel to the USA three or four times a year these days. As far as the accessibility for people with disabilities goes, it's just the best country in the world. Every restaurant you go to has a disabled toilet, and for people like me it is the easiest place of all to get around in. Flying in America leads the way too. Wherever you go you know they'll be there to greet you and to get your everyday chair up to the door. It is almost never a problem. The old European countries are a bit harder to get around in for a person in a chair, some more than others.

I find America, the place I visit most, a mixed blessing, but then I guess that's the same wherever you go. I find that in the States I have to change my whole vocabulary almost from the minute I arrive there. Otherwise people just don't understand me. Footpaths instantly become sidewalks . . . petrol stations are gas stations. I have become pretty good at adjusting. Because of what I do, the place is part of my life.

Apart from the US, I've raced in Holland, Japan, New Zealand, Switzerland, the UK, Sweden, France and Germany, added to the countless races back home. I've raced in places where Australia seems so very far away as to be almost on another planet. But wherever I am, I am always proud to be doing my bit to represent my country – hoping that any successes I have will add something to people's awareness of sport for athletes with a disability.

My campaigns through Europe, America and Asia provide a mix of memories. The races in total add up to hundreds. Some events gleam like jewels out of the haze – especially so the Boston Marathon, which shines bright in my memories and which drew me back like a moth to the flame, year after year.

It was in 1993 that I started my relationship – a sort of love–hate affair – with the Boston Marathon, the world's greatest road race. The fact is that I was always going to Boston once I made my decision to aim towards road racing after the Barcelona Paralympics. After all, it is the road race that everyone wants to win. It offers the most prize money, the most prestige.

I was nineteen when I first went campaigning in the States, with Boston the centrepiece. Mum was freaking out. I hadn't done a lot in the way of international travelling at that stage, and it had always been as part of a team – but suddenly here I was thrown into the wilds of the USA, alone.

It was quite an adventure, beginning when a guy named Jim Knaub picked me up at Los Angeles Airport and whisked me off to Fresno, California, where I had my first sponsored wheelchairs made for me, by the people at Fortress. They gave me a day chair and a racing chair. It was the first time I had been offered a chair and hadn't had to go out and shop for one myself.

From there it was on to Tampa, Florida, and a 15-kilometre race called the Gasparilla Distance Classic. It is preceded by a sort of prologue, an 800 metres time trial, from which grid positions for the big race are decided. It was a stressful day. For starters they didn't have my name on the list, so a hurried decision was made to add me on – and send me off first, in solid rain . . .

In my new chair, this was the first time I had switched to the kneeling position to race – with my legs tucked underneath. Before that I had raced with them out in front of me, kind of the way it is when you sit in a day chair. But the kneeling position was the new style, the new technique. Around '93 everyone who was serious about road and track racing was going to this position, and now most racers sit that way if they can manage it. These days there is no argument that it is a better position for racing for those athletes who can kneel. It's more compact, more aerodynamic, but it's not for everyone. I really had trouble with it at the start. I can feel my legs, but the movement is very limited, and in my early races my legs would go completely numb. It was kind of scary; I wondered what effect it would have. Now, all these years on, it doesn't worry me at all. And my legs don't go numb any more. You just get used to it.

So there I was on the starting line in Florida, and I suddenly had to kneel and couldn't get into the bloody chair – I'd only been in it two or three times before. They were calling on me to go, and I was still trying to get settled. Talk about stressful . . .

Anyhow, I somehow won the prologue and then – probably against my own expectations – came out in my new chair and won Gasparilla the next day, hitting the front 30 metres out to beat the likes of Connie Hansen and Jean Driscoll (more on her soon). It was an amazing beginning to the campaigns that were to take me back to the US again and again, I no longer race the Gasparilla however. The event lost sponsorship for the wheelchair division some time ago.

\* \* \*

On the plane returning to California, where I was to race in the Los Angeles Marathon before Boston, I was thinking, 'Oh my God, has this really happened?'. It had sort of freaked me out. And I imagined what the people at Fortress might be thinking: 'She's had our chair for three days and she's already won a big race. What's she going to do next?'.

I finished fourth in the LA Marathon that year, and after four goes I finally won it in 1997. As with Gasparilla, I haven't been back for the past few years. The race lost a lot of sponsorship and the original course was shocking. I was invited to compete in 2000 – and I'm glad I didn't go. It poured on race day. But things have been picking up in

LA. The race has a great director in Nan Harman, who puts in a lot of work for the wheelchair division. The course is being changed, and there is good sponsorship for the next few years.

* * *

I flew to Boston after the LA Marathon, not really knowing what to expect. Before I tell you about my first battles in Boston, let me set the scene on race day – and take you to this northeastern US city, and inside the oldest, most prestigious and richest marathon in the world. Boston is a charming place – a city that is both young and old. It's old in the sense of its wonderful buildings, its tradition and style, but young at the same time because there are so many universities and colleges. The city is full of young people. At the time of the marathon each April – Patriots' Day, a Monday – Boston is just mad. The whole town revolves around the marathon. I was to travel there nine years in a row – and could never get over what a huge event it was!

Boston's marathon is a race for both able-bods and wheelchair athletes. People come from all over the world to race Boston. There are generally about 100 wheelchair competitors – limited to that number by the qualifying standards set – and up to 40,000 runners.

The race starts at a little town, Hopkinton, 42 kilometres out of the city, and finishes in downtown Boston. It winds through a series of small towns, the names of which are imprinted on my mind: Ashland, Framingham, Natick, Wellesley, Newton, Brookline, Brighton. The race colours are blue and yellow, and each year you are given a special commemorative shirt sporting variations of those colours. I've got a wardrobe full of them.

The thing I like most about the race is the downhills. I'm good at coasting, you see – that's where I make up a lot of my time, reaching speeds of up to 60 kilometres per hour. The advantage I have over some of my rivals is that I am heavier than them. Anything I might lose on the uphills I make up for on the downhills. Those uphills are what I like *least*. And the road surface can provide its own problems.

There are manhole covers and potholes, and if the winter in Boston has been bad the streets crack and you have to take special care.

Throughout the morning of the race the freeway to Hopkinton is crammed with an endless convoy of buses conveying the athletes to the start. From there the first part of the course is fairly gentle and undulating for about 30 kilometres, and then as it nears Boston it gets tough, via a series of hills – the most famous of which is the notorious 'Heartbreak Hill' on which many Boston Marathons have been won or lost.

The wheelchair racers start fifteen minutes before the runners, at 11.45 a.m. With the men in front we take up grid positions behind a ute – the equivalent of a pace car in motor racing – which eases everyone down the very steep hill, the first section of the course. Years back there was no controlled start and one year there was a massive pile-up on the downhill, wiping out fifteen or so guys. So now it's controlled and you have to stay in grid position and negotiate the downhill with brakes on. At the bottom, the ute takes off . . . and so does everyone else. The guys go ballistic up the next short incline. Then you're out into the countryside and things settle down. The race is on . . .

The Boston Marathon is held in the northern early spring – and before this first trip I had been told that it was almost certain to be very cold there – which it can be – and that I would have to get a long-sleeved Lycra suit. In the past it had snowed in Boston in the week prior to the Marathon. Up to that point in my career I had only ever raced sleeveless, or in short sleeves. But, listening to the expert advice, I got a suit made – and fronted up for one of the hottest Boston Marathons ever!

The suit was all I had with me for Boston – so I had to race in it. And to make matters worse I got the sleeve of the left arm caught along the way and it ended up dragging my arm onto the wheel, which ripped the suit and left me with a massive burn and a huge chunk of skin out of my arm. Talk about a learning experience!

A marathon in the heat, like that first one in Boston in 1993, really takes its toll. How much really depends on how long I am in my chair, how long I am out there. A marathon that takes me over two hours knocks me around a helluva lot more than one under two hours, just being in your chair that extra time. And particularly so in the heat.

I suppose in a strange way part of the appeal of the Boston race is that you never know what to expect weather-wise. For the 2000 race it was bloody freezing and it took me forever to get warm and recover after that. It was a horrible feeling – I just couldn't get warm no matter what I did. I had jumpers and space blankets and rugs on and I was still freezing. Even a mug of hot chocolate didn't help.

In that first attempt at Boston in 1993 I finished third. It was the beginning of my long association with the race . . . and the beginning of my ongoing duel with the great American road racer Jean Driscoll, from Illinois. Everyone knew Jean back then, and as the years went by everyone got to know me too, because of the tremendous rivalry that exists between the pair of us. Everywhere I go people want to talk about the race, and about Jean and me.

> *Chris Shaw: Louise used to come home from those early Bostons [when Jean beat her] and declare, 'I'll get her next time!'*

Jean and I have become friends over the years. We're not great buddies, don't ring each other up on our birthdays or go out for coffee or anything like that, but there is certainly a lot of mutual respect. She was an amazing athlete – so strong and tough. I admire her a great deal. Away from the track we were pretty friendly – happy to do media interviews and appearances together. When it came to race day there was always an edge, however. We didn't sit there and stare each other out or anything, but there would be the occasional comment, designed to unsettle. Once we were out on the track or road, we were as competitive as it was possible to be. We were both there for the same thing: we both wanted to win.

\* \* \*

After Boston I went down to Washington State for the 12-kilometre Lilac Bloomsday Run in Spokane. This is invariably a cold place, but Lilac Bloomsday is a big race, for both wheelchair racers and for runners – probably the largest participation fun run in the world. It's an event with a lot of history surrounding it and is one of the longest-surviving races of its kind.

My main rival, again, was Jean. Her strength was the hills my weakness was the hills. Her body-to-weight ratio and strength-to-weight ratio were always a lot better than mine. She made that race her own and was destined to win there every year from 1993 to 2000. I came second that first year. The race attracts vast numbers of people – and I can remember coming back after finishing and seeing runners at the starting line still waiting to get going! This happened to me a few times at Lilac Bloomsday, although I haven't contested the event for a number of years now.

Like Boston, Lilac Bloomsday is a hard race, with tough hills, particularly one known as 'Doomsday Hill'. It is nicely named. You come screaming down one hill and have to hit the brakes for a right-hand turn at the bottom, which means you have to go from flat-out to almost a dead stop in a very short space of time. Then there's an almighty hill that just climbs on and on. When you reach that it's make-or-break time.

\* \* \*

Next I raced in the Peachtree 10K, a cheering, flag-waving celebration, run on Independence Day, the 4th of July, in Atlanta, Georgia. And yep, you guessed it, we race down Peachtree Road, which all of us heard plenty about during the 1996 Olympics, and finish in a road adjacent to the city's Piedmont Park. It's one of America's biggest 10-kilometre races, with upwards of 45,000 able-bodied starters along with the wheelchair racers.

I won the women's wheelchair division that year, and a fellow Australian, Paul Wiggins, became the first man to break 20 minutes for the wheelchair race. It's evidence of how much faster wheelchair racing has become that the leading men now break 19 minutes in the Peachtree, in their longer, more streamlined chairs – and over a course that has plenty of downhill runs.

I returned from the final leg of my first American campaign in July 1993, a far more experienced road racer and a much wiser person.

\* \* \*

The other sporting highlight of 1993 was the World Championships in Stuttgart, Germany, organised by the International Amateur Athletic Federation (IAAF). This was the first year they had staged wheelchair races as exhibition events on the World Championships program: 1500 metres for the men and 800 metres for the women, like the Olympic demonstration events. It was a great start for me, and amazing to be there with all the able-bodied athletes. I won the gold medal by 50 metres or so and clocked what was a personal best at that stage in my career (1 minute 54.39 seconds).

\* \* \*

By November I was back in Australia competing in the 10-kilometre Melbourne Olympic Dream Road Race, the last race of my Grand Prix Series. It was at that event that I met Shona Casey, who is now one of my closest friends. At the time she was working as a volunteer for the Victorian Wheelchair Sports Association. After the race, with people queuing to get on the buses, I asked Shona if I could catch a ride back to my hotel. There was no problem at all – except that Shona's car, 'Bill', broke down, and the bus had to be called to come and pick me up because I had to be back at the hotel for a meeting! She was horribly embarrassed – but we've been great mates ever since.

> *Shona Casey: I agreed to take her back to the hotel, not knowing anything really about the young woman I had in my 1977 LX Torana; we talked and I asked a lot of questions. She was absolutely unbelievable – so*

*friendly — and she talked as much as I did. My trusty Torana had no idea it was carrying a future sporting legend, so it decided to break down on busy Punt Road, in the middle of Melbourne. I called the RACV [Royal Automobile Club of Victoria] for help – then promptly locked my keys in the car while I called the hotel to get someone to come and pick Louise up. Not a bad introduction! For the next two years, whenever I saw Louise, all I could do was apologise for the breakdown. Who would have thought that a great friendship would start like that?*

\* \* \*

One of the greatest thrills of my career to this point was winning the ABC's Junior Female Athlete of the Year Award for 1993. On the night, they sat me right up front at the presentation and there was a ramp leading up to the stage. I kept thinking, 'I'm going up there!'. And finally I did. Later in the evening I met lots of famous sports people and ended up on the social pages with a friend, Kathy Lee. It was a great night.

The beauty of the award was that I beat all comers, including able-bods. It was a ground-breaking award for me – the first I had ever won where I was in a category that wasn't disability-specific. Since then along the way I have won a few of those. Each time they are very special because they embrace the wider sporting spectrum – and reveal the growing status and recognition of sport for athletes with a disability.

CHAPTER 9

# 'MELT INTO OBSCURITY, MR TUNSTALL'

Even if I was now starting to achieve the same level of recognition as the top able-bods, the XV Commonwealth Games of 1994 in Victoria, Canada, proved that the cause of athletes with a disability still had a long way to go. The Games combined able-bodied athletes and athletes with a disability. But it wasn't the sports stars who stole the show – it was the words of Arthur Tunstall, Australian Commonwealth Games chief. Most likely he now wishes with all his heart that he hadn't said them. His statements earned him headlines all over the world – and especially so back in Australia.

In a television interview and later in talks with Australian media representatives, Tunstall said the presence of athletes with a disability – eleven of them Australians, there for athletics, swimming and bowls – was 'an embarrassment to both sides'. He continued: 'It's got to be an embarrassment because people are going out of their way to assist them and able people are a little bit embarrassed to have them around. I can tell you back in Australia people feel exactly the same way. What I believe is that there should be a disabled Commonwealth Games and that's what I'm pushing for'. Furiously back-pedalling, Tunstall subsequently apologised for his slur – but it was all a bit late by then, with the press back home in a frenzy.

The comments caused a really huge storm. Track star Raelene Boyle described Tunstall as 'past his use-by date' and called his comments 'offensive'. Former swimming world record holder Tracey Wickham made the point that similar comments made by an athlete would have sparked an expulsion from the Games. Then aged seventy-two, the longtime Aussie Games boss had not long been out of the headlines, having recently criticised female athletes for posing for a fundraising calendar.

The 19 August 1994 editorial in the *West Australian* was one of several criticising Arthur Tunstall. 'Melt into Obscurity, Mr Tunstall', urged the headline, above a story that began: 'Australia's Commonwealth Games chief Arthur Tunstall should do his nation and sport a favour. He should pack his bags and come home'. The piece ended: 'The sooner he gets out of the international spotlight and settled into obscurity, the better it will be for all Australians'. The paper accused Tunstall of 'humiliating his fellow Australians' and focused on his 'oafish arrogance'. And so it went on.

And all of this before the Games had even started!

Back home in Perth, I got sick of people asking me why I wasn't over in Canada, and how I felt about that . . . and by the way, what did I think of Arthur Tunstall? The answer to the second question was that I felt a bit strange. Yes, there were some events for athletes with a disability at the Games, but not full medal events – and for male wheelchair racers only! Some discrimination there, perhaps – and an easy answer to why I wasn't there representing Australia. At the 2002 Commonwealth Games in Manchester there will be full medal events for athletes with a disability, covering different sports and different disabilities – and for both men and women. For me there will be an 800 metres.

And as for Arthur Tunstall? Well, I thought of him as just an old official who opened his mouth before he really thought about what he was going to say – and who obviously didn't think about whom he might be hurting with his words. I believed then (and now) that the integration of all athletes was a fair thing and that it was good for us to compete alongside able-bodied athletes, and be recognised as their equals.

If it was a real foot-in-the-mouth performance – well, it had benefits too. In a strange way it worked to the advantage of sport for athletes with a disability – it attracted so much attention. In fact the theory was put forward that no PR manager could have done a better job for us than Arthur Tunstall had done. He certainly brought the presence of athletes with a disability into the glare of the spotlight – and Channel Seven subsequently covered the disabled events at the Games, possibly because of the controversy that his words had stirred up. At least it made people realise we existed – and I doubt he hurt anybody too much. 'We're pretty thick-skinned,' I said in one interview. 'You hear worse than that.' The focus it brought on athletes with a disability was overwhelmingly positive. I bore no grudge. He was an old man who had perhaps said something regrettable.

I met him later at a dinner. Dennis Lillee was there, from memory. I greeted Dennis and then Arthur, standing alongside, swung around. 'Hi, I'm Arthur Tunstall,' he said. 'Yes, I know who you are,' I responded. And that was about it. I really had nothing more to say.

\* \* \*

Even though I didn't get to the Commonwealth Games, 1994 was another big year for me. It was the first time that I was named Australian Paralympian of the Year, an honour I have received four times now.

In January my mum and I were invited to a cocktail party and dinner at Government House, Perth. The special guest was HRH

The Prince of Wales, Prince Charles! My mum was absolutely having kittens – she is a very big royalist. Anyhow, Prince Charles was walking around saying hello to everyone at the cocktail gathering – and then the invited group went in to dinner. We were sitting at a different table from him, but when the desserts were served he came and sat with us . . . right next to my mum. She was quite beside herself, and managed to spill chocolate cake down her front, which made things worse. She sat with her hand over the spot for the rest of the night! But he was so natural . . . just chatting away. He was wearing a tie with little whales on it and I complimented him. 'What a cool tie,' I said. 'Oh yes,' he said, 'that's my Prince of Whales tie'. Yeah, right! He was very pleasant and very interested in us . . . it was quite a buzz, especially for my mum. My success over the years has led to a lot of 'brushes with fame'. I have met the sort of people you usually only dream of meeting: from Nelson Mandela to Marion Jones, from Boy George to the Royals . . . and heaps of others.

I met Prince Charles again soon afterwards at the Oz Day 10K presentations in Sydney. That year I became the first female racer ever to successfully defend the title. Then, in April, I was thrilled to come second behind Jean Driscoll in the Boston Marathon.

\* \* \*

In June I travelled to Europe for the Sempach Marathon ('Marathon Autour du Lac de Sempach'), held in Switzerland – two laps around a beautiful lake. This is a wheelchair-only race, probably the second-biggest wheelchair-only race in the world (behind the huge annual race in Oita, Japan – more on that later). I won Sempach that year, and the local paper wrote of 'la victoire bien meritée' ('the well-deserved victory') and of 'l'australienne très rapide' ('the very fast Australian girl'). I have won it twice (1994 and 2000) and the only thing I don't like about it is that it starts in the afternoon. It was so hot in 2000 that I thought I was going to die – then thankfully the clouds came over.

\* \* \*

In July I went to the International Paralympic Committee (IPC) World Disabled Championships in Berlin. These Championships, in a famous city, provided great memories for me. I won four events – the 800, 1500, 5000 and marathon – and set a new world record in a heat of the 800 (1 minute 51.82 seconds), a record I was to lose in controversial circumstances five years later.

It was awesome to be in Berlin. We went across into East Berlin, visited a section of the Wall that was still standing – and imagined how it must have been before the Wall came down. The stadium where the Games were held, a wonderfully preserved old stone structure, was one of the few places that didn't get bombed during World War II.

In Berlin I saw Connie Hansen for the last time, too. She was pregnant at the time, and no longer competing – but was there as a classifier for the Games. Careers move on – and her life had changed after all the years of success as an athlete. She now has three children, two of them twins. She was, and is, a champion.

\* \* \*

After those Worlds of 1994 I was feeling stale and in need of new horizons. I left Perth and went to live in the suburb of Mulgrave in Melbourne, driving all the way over to the east coast. My mum was very worried about all that – and especially so when I drove across the Nullarbor Plain to get there. I've done that trip a few times now – and I don't think she worries as much now as she did on that first occasion.

The move was basically about needing a change, and also about the opportunity of having different people to train with. A lot of the people I had been training with had left Perth by then. I felt I could ignite my own pushing a bit by moving on. I think it was a bit of a freedom thing, too. It represented independence, since it was the first time I had lived away from home, and like most people in that situation I had a *really* good time. I already knew a lot of people in

Melbourne, including Shona Casey and many people within my sport. Young people of the age I was then will often move a couple of suburbs or across the city from the family home. I went one better, and moved all the way across the country.

In July 1995, while I was still living in Melbourne, I even 'starred' in a couple of episodes of 'Neighbours'. They actually wanted tennis players, but the tennis crowd was out of town so they settled on a couple of wheelchair racers instead – Greg Smith and me. We played ourselves, working on rehearsals and shooting over a couple of days, and had a lot of fun. It was aired in September in Australia, but the best part of it was when my aunty Margaret saw the episodes in England – 'Neighbours' being bigger than *Ben Hur* over there. She got pretty excited and all my rellies and cousins thought it was great. As I've said, being 'high-profile' sometimes brings unexpected bonuses!

\* \* \*

I suppose you could say that the time I spent in Melbourne during 1994 and 1995 represented a quieter phase of my career – though I was still pretty much on course. Life was enjoyable and good, but as you've seen, my training and focus were a little short of the really hard edge they needed.

I went back to Berlin in September '94 and won the Berlin Marathon (billed as the Marathon World Championships). It's a fast, flat race – some of it over a cobbled surface which makes the going difficult. But it's a race with a lot of tradition behind it, running through both the east and west sections of the city and past grand buildings and historic sites. I competed again in '97 and enjoyed racing there the two times – but it was a fairly expensive operation and after the travel expenses and hotel bill were paid there wasn't a lot of reward left from competing.

In November I won the Olympic Dream 10K in Melbourne. The Atlanta Olympics and Paralympics of 1996 were drawing closer, only eighteen months away by then, and I guess all Aussie athletes of ambition were starting to dream. I continued to juggle track and road racing, winning 1995's Oz Day 10K in Sydney, then two road events in the US, the Gasparilla 15-kilometre road race and the Top End Criterium in St Petersburg, Florida. I placed second in the Los Angeles Marathon, Lilac Bloomsday 12K and the Peachtree 10K, and fourth in the 1995 Boston Marathon.

In August 1995 I competed at the IAAF World Championships in Gothenburg, Sweden, in the 800 metres exhibition race. I was the only Australian winner. The fact that it was a demonstration event, and the coverage it received (or rather lack of coverage), suggested that it didn't mean too much to anyone, although I was still very happy to be there representing Australia.

The clearly identifiable lack of interest back then shows how big a step forward sport for athletes with a disability has taken in the last few years, in terms of media and public acceptance. My win in '95 barely rated a mention. The following day one Aussie paper ran almost a full page on the Championships, focusing on Steve Monaghetti's eighth in the marathon and the win by Irish runner Sonia O'Sullivan in the 5000 metres. At the bottom of this long story was one sentence: 'Australian Louise Sauvage won gold in the women's 800 metres wheelchair race yesterday'. That was about it.

The television coverage consisted of a brief flick-over from the men's marathon to the very final stages of my event. My race lasted less than two minutes; the marathon coverage was more than two hours. The TV treatment was very disappointing for family, friends and everyone in the sport waiting up till all hours at home, hoping to see the race in full, or at least a fair chunk of it.

It was very annoying – not so much for me, but for my sport. Back then, though, that was the way it was. A nice story by Ron Reed in the *Herald-Sun* after the Championships called me 'very accomplished, but little recognised' and said: 'Sauvage is the gold medallist whose feat has past almost unnoticed, or been quickly forgotten'.

Of course, athletes with a disability are not the only ones who have suffered from fairly threadbare media attention over the years. I am thoroughly aware that some of our field athletes – shot-putters, discus throwers and the like – get little attention in comparison with people in some of the 'glamour' events.

I remember when Lisa-Marie Vizaniari, the discus thrower, won the athletics Grand Prix points score for 1999. (This is based on a series of track and field meets at major centres throughout Australia.) It was the first time she had won it – and she was understandably very excited. But at the press conference, after she had been asked a couple of questions, the attention rapidly switched to Melinda Gainsford-Taylor, who had made a big comeback but had only finished second in the Grand Prix points.

Lisa-Marie got really angry. She must have wished she could say to them, 'I won ... Shouldn't you be paying *me* some attention?'. She wasn't happy. And as she told me later, 'Well, because I'm not running down the track and not as glamorous as some, I don't get the attention, I don't get as much sponsorship. And I'm ranked whatever in the world ... and she's not'. Her frustrations really came out at that time. I think plenty of athletes with a disability, well used to not being the first choice of the media, understood the point she was making.

\* \* \*

I had done well at the Worlds – not that anybody took much notice – but afterwards I began to look towards an even bigger and more prestigious goal: Atlanta. I was progressively realising, though, that if I wanted to reach my full potential Melbourne was not the place for me to be.

Although the move to Melbourne had been great for my social life, it probably hadn't been so great for Louise Sauvage the athlete. I found I had lost focus on what I was doing. I was having fun, but I was nose-diving in terms of my sport. I didn't train as well while I was over there ... I didn't do gym work, I didn't do the early mornings that provide hard discipline in my life as a professional athlete, and I lost speed. I still pushed six days a week and did a lot of swimming – but being away from the gym meant I lost a lot of my training balance and some of the basic strength I needed. I find the gym work, which is very sport-specific, helps me a lot with the day-to-day things I have to do. The strength phases of the work help make me stronger for the racing, the hill-climbing . . . the speed.

I made a decision that to do well in Atlanta I had to move back to Perth, to get back to my gym at Curtin University and back to the people who were training me. (Jenni Banks was still coaching me via fax machine and phone, and even though she had moved to Sydney in the mid-1990s she guided my program for Atlanta.) It was a case of going back to familiar ground, to where I had done it all before.

I was reluctant to move back home after living on my own for over a year. Two of my great friends in Perth, Chris and Ros Shaw, were then living in Ferndale, which was close to a network of cycleways and to the Curtin University gym. They're a great couple. I had known Chris through wheelchair racing for years. 'We've got a spare room if you want to come over to our place,' they said to me. So I did, stayed eighteen months, trained hard – and got myself ready, dragging together the training program I needed to get me successfully through the challenges of Atlanta.

> *Chris Shaw: I'm not sure Louise's mum was too pleased with the move. She came over and checked us out, checked the house out. There are so many things I remember from that time – how hard Louise works, how focused she is. Probably she has always had the natural ability – but she never backs away from putting the hard work in too. Just about every morning she'd be out early . . . Sometimes I used to go pushing with her. I found it hard to keep up after a while. One day I was in the gym, doing bench presses with the weight up around 75 to 80 kilograms. I was struggling to do one – and Louie jumped in there and went 'whoosh' and did a set of them.*

> *Ros Shaw: I remember rainy, cold mornings when Chris and I would be snug in bed – and Louie would be out there training. It was a happy time – we're just her friends ... and we let Lou be Lou. She's so natural ... she would come along and support us at dog shows [one of Ros's and Chris's hobbies].*

Ros was recovering from a serious accident at that time, and it was often very hard for her.

> *Ros Shaw: Louise helped me through my difficulty. When she first lived with us my speech was a lot worse than it is now. I remember one day we went down to a place to get something for the house, and the guy was having trouble understanding me and didn't know where to look. He turned to Louie – and she said to him, 'Well, it's not my house ... talk to her'. She was saying to him, you deal with it – and she was stressing my independence. She can be very direct – and looking back on that time having her living at home was very positive for me.*

On reflection, that period with Chris and Ros enabled me to get my training preparation back on track for the double challenge ahead. As I observed to the media, one day before Atlanta when I was in heavy training (twice a day, pushing 180 kilometres or so a week): 'It does wonders for your social life. I'm in bed at 8.30 every night!'.

\* \* \*

As part of a pre-Olympics and pre-Paralympics promotion, Australia Post brought out a special release stamp to celebrate the XXVI Olympiad. As the subjects, they chose Edwin Flack, our first Olympic gold medallist, Fanny Durack, the our female gold medallist – and me, in my racing chair, in a gesture of triumph at the end of a race! I was on the $1.05 stamp ... and I was pretty proud of that.

But before the Olympics I had the hurdle of Boston to overcome once more. This year I led for the first 15 kilometres, with Jean Driscoll a minute behind at one stage. But she caught me by the time we reached the hills, and made her move then – as she always did. I was unable to go with her, and she went on to win the race for the seventh year in succession. My second placing gave me some encouragement, though, in the lead-up to Atlanta.

I was in a far better position than I had been in before Barcelona. At least now I was able to compete in the 800 metres demonstration race at the Olympics; back in 1992 I couldn't even afford to get to the trials.

But in terms of financial security I still had a long way to go. At this stage I had just two sponsors, the Australian Institute of Sport and (since 1994) the American company Top End Action, now owned by the larger Invacare Corporation. I was deeply grateful for their support, but to be honest it was a struggle. I'd had a couple of really flat times in '95 and it hadn't been a great year for me – not helped by the move from Melbourne back to Perth. In fact there had been times when I'd been at a fairly low ebb, I was just so glad to be going to Atlanta at all.

Financially, I was getting by, but I really wasn't *making* any money out of what I was doing. The fact is you can't make a living out of being a professional athlete in my sport unless you have some solid corporate support in the background. I really had to think about how I was going to do it if I decided to keep going. That thought was a spur as I trained for Atlanta – to do well and at least give myself the best possible chance to make it more of a 'profession'. I had made a decision at that point in my life that I really couldn't keep going the way I was.

\* \* \*

I trialled in Paris for the Olympics and made it safely through to the 800 metres final. A 400 metres race (which was not an Olympic distance) was added to the program in Paris to give us some more racing experience before the 800 metres semifinals. I came back briefly to Australia from France – then went on to Atlanta for the Olympic Opening Ceremony . . .

CHAPTER 10

# ATLANTA GOLD

Atlanta's Olympic and Paralympic Games of 1996 were a mixture of good and not so good. I'll start with the Olympics, and then in the next chapter I'll tell you about the shoddy Paralympics that the city turned on, and about my disappointment at how poorly they chose to treat the world's top athletes with a disability.

The Olympics, too, were badly organised, as the media were quick to point out at the time. From the very beginning the placement of the Games in Atlanta (both Olympics and Paralympics) had been a worry. I'm sure most people thought Athens should have been the host, because that year was the centenary of the modern Olympics (1896 to 1996), but the almighty dollar and factors linked to the commercial world took over, and so it was Atlanta.

For me the problems started before the Opening Ceremony had even begun. Actually, I was lucky even to get to the Ceremony. First we got lost on the way to the stadium, courtesy of a bus driver who didn't know his way – not an unusual event in Atlanta, as we soon discovered. Things got quite heated on the bus for a while, with people shouting out – and Tim Forsyth, our high jumper, did a good job in keeping the lid on it. 'Don't worry . . . we'll be right, we'll get there,' he said. And of course we did – and in heaps of time considering the long wait we had before finally getting into the stadium.

Then the organisers wouldn't let me come into the stadium with the Australian team – over and down the ramp, which provided such a spectacular entry point. It was too steep, they said. I was annoyed – and especially so when I realised there was a Spanish girl in a chair who *was* allowed to come in with her team – she competed as an archer at both the Olympic and Paralympic Games. Instead, I joined the team when they turned the corner and came onto the track.

Anyhow, I got to march around with the team and stay out in the middle for the Ceremony – and that was just brilliant. (At the Barcelona Paralympics, as you may recall, I hadn't been at the Opening Ceremony, since I had to compete the next day.) It's something I'll always remember. I was out there thinking, 'I can't believe this . . . I'm part of an Olympic Games!'.

I stayed briefly in the Village, then headed out to a training centre some 100 kilometres outside Atlanta. I stayed out there until my race was run, and it was very difficult indeed to be so far away from the centre of things. But in the Village there had been no chance to do any road training at all, and that is my preferred training. To get a 30-kilometre push in you had to do it on the track, which is so boring. But the training centre didn't prove to be that much better – the area was just so hilly, and it was hard to find a decent place to train.

I came back into the city the day after the bomb went off in Centennial Park – and the security was unbelievable. It was terribly difficult even to get back into the Village.

In and out of the Village, it was a frustrating time. I didn't enjoy it that much. With limited access around the Village and the dragged-out wait for my race, things became pretty strained – even between Jenni Banks and me. I just wanted to race. Within the Olympic Village I'm not sure that many of the Australian team actually knew what I was doing there. The awareness of the demonstration races was not high.

Physically I wasn't as well as I would have liked, either. I was battling a cold and sinus problem, which didn't help. I think it had a bit to do with being forever in and out of air conditioning, the Atlanta ('Hotlanta') days being consistently 30-plus degrees Celsius.

On top of the cold, an old problem recurred: a chronic wrist injury that gives me a hard time when I have to do a lot of pushing in my everyday chair, as I had to do in the Village (and anywhere else I went over there, for that matter). I have to be very aware of the injury when I travel anywhere to compete, because it's become a fact of my life. When I'm back home in Sydney, I don't push my everyday chair a lot – only in day-to-day things, such as around the shops or supermarket. Most of the time I drive – but when you're away, in an Olympic Village or at some other international competition, you can't drive, and pushing is the only way of getting around. So my poor old wrist just got worse and worse as I made my way around hilly Atlanta. In the end I had to wear a brace.

Even the race had its frustrations. To go from the warm-up track to the main stadium we had to get out of our racing chairs and get on a bus. This was not an easy operation – not ideal at all. Before any race it takes time to get settled, to get 'right' in your chair.

Race morning was warm but fairly yucky, with heavy clouds hanging low and rainwater on the track. Showers threatened as we did our warm-up laps. I was especially careful about applying the glue to my gloves; the last thing I wanted to do was to miss a push in the wet. I apply a product called Klister, a substance that provides more grip between my gloves and the push rims of my chair.

There seemed to be very few Aussies at the stadium. Jenni was there, of course, and so too was Aussie sports physiologist Dr Jeff Simons and I really appreciated his presence. I kept looking out for some green and gold in the crowd – and finally I spotted a bunch of guys from the Australian team, close to the front with an Aussie flag, screaming and yelling. That was really fantastic. It gave me quite a lift in this stadium far away from home, where I knew not too many people would be cheering for me.

The two wheelchair races – men's and women's – were run in the middle of the morning heats and semis, not with the other finals, which were scheduled for the evenings. But the crowd was still a big one – one of the biggest I had ever raced in front of, although the final nights of the 1992 Paralympics in Barcelona drew amazing crowds of 70,000 to 80,000.

We raced on a wet track – American Cheri Becerra going out hard, with Chantal Petitclerc chasing. Starting from Lane Five, I was always up close to the lead, or in the lead – and that was exactly as I had planned it. I wanted to be out the front throwing up the spray, rather than back in the field catching it. In the end I did most of the work, but that suited me, especially so when I decided to surge because I thought that the two Americans Cheri Becerra and Jean Driscoll might be working to box me in.

When we turned the corner into the straight for the sprint home I was narrowly in front, out in Lane Three and feeling strong, although we were all pretty much together, and several of us had a chance of grabbing the gold. Peter Fitzsimons of the *Sydney Morning Herald* covered the race and wrote of the entry into the straight: 'They [Cheri Becerra and I] entered the bend tight, with another American, Jean Driscoll, coming hard at them also – three machines within inches of each other, absolutely motoring, with all three athletes leaning into the curve to counter the centrifugal force. Out of the bend Sauvage took over, still feeling strong on the reserve power she had built into her arms, lungs and heart over the past four years of solid training'. Jean finished second and Cheri third.

It was a tactical race more than anything else; we all knew the time would be slowish (1 minute 55.62 seconds) on the heavy, wet track. With 15 metres to go I knew I had it . . . and I was smiling. When I hit the line I was so happy, just stoked. I had no idea who had run second or third at that stage, and I didn't care. I was so excited. I did a lap of honour and everyone was screaming and yelling.

Jane Flemming interviewed me afterwards and I think I told her that for me this was the ultimate. Right then, I wasn't even thinking Paralympics – I had been so focused on this one race. I stayed trackside to watch the men's race, to give Aussie teammate Paul Wiggins a cheer (he ultimately finished seventh). It bucketed down just as they started, as it had been threatening to do all morning.

The media asked me at my press conference whether I felt I was out there representing Australian Paralympians. 'I was there representing Australia,' I told them. 'I am an athlete and that's all I want to be. I don't want anybody's sympathy.' And when people asked me later whether it was 'strange' racing at the Olympics, I told them no – that I was there to demonstrate my sport, and even though many of the athletes around me were more famous than I was, I knew for sure they were no more committed.

Back home, my mum and dad saw it all on TV. Financially it hadn't been possible for them to travel to the Games – and instead they were up at some ungodly hour of the Perth morning, sitting there in the lounge room in Joondanna hoping that Channel Seven would show it. And they did!

The 800 metres medal ceremony was held that night. As I headed happily back to the track through the mixed zone (the area close to the track where the media get their quick 'grabs' after an event), one of the Australian reporters said to me, 'You know, this will probably be the only time the Australian national anthem will ever be played at this track'. That made me feel so proud. So did the presentation itself, as the Australian flag was slowly raised and the strains of 'Advance Australia Fair' rang out. It was something I'll never forget.

CHAPTER 11

# ATLANTA BLUES

The Olympics had been OK, but at the Atlanta Paralympics I felt like a second-class citizen for the first time in my life. The Paralympic Games appeared to be no more than an afterthought for the city in the wake of the Olympics.

For months leading up to the Paralympics there were concerning signs. We were hearing rumours back in Australia – and strongly – that the Americans didn't want the Paralympic Games and were trying to get out of hosting them. The story was that they were desperately trying to shift them somewhere else, because they realised Atlanta couldn't provide what was required. And as it turned out, the city produced something that was definitely inferior to what it should have been.

After the Olympic Closing Ceremony, I left the Village, stayed in a hotel for a couple of days and then went to Tennessee to meet up with the Australian Paralympic athletics team. When I came back to Atlanta with them I was horrified to see what they had done to the Village. It was a totally different place from the vibrant centre it had been during the Olympic Games.

The Village for the two Games of 1996 was the University of Georgia, a huge place that should have worked perfectly well for both events. During the Olympics, I lived in dormitory-style accommodation with the Aussie team, and the facilities were good. There was a little train that ran around the place, and a choice of dining rooms. I only went to the big dining hall once because there were just too many people there, too many able-bods, and it was a bit of a battle getting around. I usually went to a hall that was quieter than the main one, and it was fine. There was an International Zone that had all the facilities you could wish for: a choice of cinemas, a bowling alley, shops, restaurants, little cafes, Internet places, hairdressers, florists. There were even live bands – one night Hootie and the Blowfish came in and played a concert. I don't know who was more excited – them to be there, or us to have them there! It was a whole self-contained world – and I thought it was all pretty unbelievable. There were heaps of things to do, and I had probably never experienced anything quite as extravagant.

When I came back a few weeks later for the Paralympics the whole thing had changed. The Australian team was put on the opposite side of the campus to where I had stayed before, and housed in apartment-style accommodation. There were twelve to an apartment, each containing two bathrooms and three toilets, and two to a room – the tiniest rooms you have ever seen, with no real space to put our wheelchairs or any of our gear.

And just about all the 'extras' that had been there for the Olympics had gone. There were no cinemas, no shops . . . even McDonald's had disappeared. Our International Zone for the Paralympics was a little area with maybe eight tents in it: a hairdresser's, a shop to buy merchandise, the real basics. For meals there was just one main dining hall which smelled increasingly unappetising as the days went by – and which featured a lot of repetitive food. It seemed to me that everything had been downgraded.

I was aghast. 'I can't believe they're treating us like this . . . I can't believe they have done this,' I thought. 'The United States is supposed to be such a great world leader, a great country, where everyone is treated equally. How could they have got it so wrong – and not even seemed to care?'

I probably took it harder than just about anyone else – because I had seen the contrast. Sure, it was fair enough to shrink the size of the Village. The numbers were down from 10,000 at the Olympics to under 5000 for the Paralympics. But the changes were so pointed, so dramatic . . . so *dismissive*. In Barcelona in 1992 everything that had been in the Olympic Village was still there for the Paralympics. All the facilities – the movie theatre, shops, bowling hall, dining hall – were modified so they were accessible for the Paralympic athletes. But in Atlanta they just closed everything down, and squeezed us into one area. Security was nowhere near as thorough as it had been at the Olympics. Even the American athletes were ashamed of what their country had turned on!

It seemed that the two organising committees for the Olympics and Paralympics didn't work together at all. The story was that after the Olympics had ended all the keys to the apartments that would house the Paralympic competitors were placed in a bucket – and handed over unnumbered. So all the locks had to be changed. Phones were ripped out, leaving just the exposed wires – so they all had to be reconnected too.

The only thing that didn't change was the transport. It was a nightmare for both Games. A fifteen-minute trip to the track could take up to an hour and a half – depending on which driver you got. I'm sure Sydney learned a lot from Atlanta's blunders. For example, I understand they put in all the ramps in the Village in the *first* place – instead of having to rush them in at the last minute like they did over there.

But on the bright side, at least Atlanta was a city where public access was very good for people with disabilities. You could catch any bus, any train... do just about anything you wanted with comparative ease. And if there was anything that came close to saving the Games it was the attitude of the volunteers, who were so friendly and helpful. The 'southern hospitality' there is all that people say it is. There is a great warmth about people in the south of the US. If you wanted to get something done, and you gave someone a smile and a pin... they'd give you the world!

For all the problems, there wasn't much we could do but accept the way things were in Atlanta. And that's exactly what we did at the Paralympics of 1996. Despite the hiccups, there was a great atmosphere within the Australian team. I was there to compete and after my initial disappointment at what had been done I quickly got my mind back on track. My attitude was this: 'I am here to race... things here are the same for everyone. It doesn't matter'. Focused and as ready as I was ever going to get, I managed to carve out a very successful Paralympics, in front of crowds that were disappointingly thin after the tremendous support given by the people of Barcelona. Once it got going, my own program consisted of full-on racing and lots of pressure.

Of my track events, the toughest was the last – the 400 metres, run only an hour or so after the 5000 metres final. I had won the 5000 in a world-record 12 minutes 40.71 seconds and was all hyped up and excited, doing interviews and soaking up the feeling. And drained, too; the 5000 metres is a tough race, and was especially so in Atlanta's heat. Then I was told I had to do a drug test, but I couldn't do it before my next race. That stressed me out. And all the while the clock was ticking, reducing the time I had to get myself back in the right frame of mind for the 400, to build my physical and mental energy levels, to try and cool down then warm up again.

It was rush, rush, rush. Everything was happening so fast. I got out of my racing chair and had a cool-down of sorts, via cold towels – a technique we had used in pre-Games training in Darwin. It feels pretty horrible. You're hot – and suddenly they put these cold towels all over you. It's a shock, I can tell you.

The call room was the final stopping-off point in Atlanta, as it is at all big meets – a quiet place where people either (a) don't look at you or (b) try to stare you out. I'll always just sit there quietly and go through things in my head, knowing that I've put in the work, that there's not too much more I can do. I focus on getting myself positive, telling myself, 'This is it. This is my race. This is what I have trained for'.

It's a difficult place, the call room, because you usually feel sick and nervous and horrible. My method is to work on deep breathing, on calming myself down and concentrating on what I am there for and what I have to do. Essentially, I go through my race plan, go through my start, go through everything in the hope that it will all work once the gun is fired. I try to have a plan ready for every possible situation. I run over it all in my mind a hundred and ten times! Then I do it all over again.

When it comes to nerves before a big event, the degree is the important thing. I think that as an athlete if you weren't nervous on the big days . . . then there'd be something wrong. But if the nerves are too stretched, then that can definitely wear you down too, drain you of energy. A little dose of nerves before a big race is a good and necessary thing. It gets the heart pumping. I get my share – but I have become better at controlling it, and better at making positive use of the nervous energy.

But yep, I'm a great one for stewing over things; too often I've kept myself awake at night, going over things endlessly in my mind. I perhaps go slightly overboard with that sort of mental preparation. I use visualisation, picturing where I want to be in a race – particularly the last 200 metres. I have a lot of mental imagery related to upcoming races. And I use key words, a technique that gives you the ability to change your frame of mind. Key words can be very useful if you are anxious or worried. They can be very helpful before a race, getting you into the right mind-set.

So the 400 was a tough one, so close to the other race, and a very hard race in its own right, because 400 metres is very short for me these days. In retrospect, though, having the other race so close was quite a help – because I was still really pumped up from that when I went back onto the track. I had a really good lane (five) because I was one of the fastest qualifiers – and I just went out there and said to myself, 'Let's go!'. I really attacked the race, and won it – in a pretty good time, a Paralympics record of 54.96 seconds, carrying me almost two seconds clear of silver medallist Chantal Petitclerc.

What I search for in a race is clear space. Back in '96 I probably wasn't quite as confident about racing from the front, pulling the whole race. Now I am quite happy to do that. I know I am strong enough. It doesn't bother me if someone comes around me in a race. I know I have still got it in me to win. It comes with time: getting stronger, more experienced, more confident, more mentally tough.

I raced the marathon on the final day of the Games. By that stage I had been away from home for something like two and a half months and I was pretty much exhausted, both physically and mentally. On race morning I was up at 4.00 a.m., for a 7.00 a.m. start. When the race began Jean Driscoll went out hard and broke away from everyone and I pushed with a couple of the other girls, an American girl and a Japanese girl who ended up second. In the end, I knew I couldn't do it. So I ended up pushing the marathon at my pace, encouraging the other girls – and coming home fourth.

I was stuffed at the end of it – but happy. I had four gold medals, 400, 800, 1500 and 5000 metres, plus the one from the Olympic Games, and was just so glad it was all over. When the media asked me about the future I replied, 'When you're here you think it's definitely worth it, but then you get home and have to face the real world. It's a long time to keep going . . . four years. I just don't know yet. There's no fortune in what I do . . . I get by, that's all'.

After the marathon I did something pretty stupid . . . the sort of thing you do at the end of a Paralympic Games, I suppose. I went out partying after the Closing Ceremony, and stayed up for twenty-seven hours or so. We Aussies had something to celebrate: forty-two gold medals in all, and second spot on the ladder behind the Americans. We went to an Irish pub at Buckhead and kicked on for ages. One of the best things about that night was catching up with people from other sports – like the players from the men's basketball team, who were as high as kites on the euphoria of winning gold. I didn't drink a lot, because I was still dehydrated from racing the marathon and the alcohol would have gone straight to my head. I was desperately tired, but I stayed up to help look after a teammate who was the worse for wear. Just about everyone else was tanked. Close to sunrise, four of us headed across the road to a cafe for breakfast. I was probably the only semi-sober person in the place.

When we got back to the Village there were all sorts of dramas. Some of the athletes had been booked on a flight to go back to Australia that morning. They had known about that before they went out – but it sure hadn't stopped the partying. Team officials were trying to round up people to get on the buses to the airport and there were tears and last-minute rushes to try and pack bags. It was a riot. Being reasonably sober, I was one of the people on the phone at seven o'clock in the morning, trying to change airline tickets. Around me there were people in tears. It was hilarious and terrible at the same time. It had been quite a night . . .

Finally it settled down a bit and I managed to grab a couple of hours' sleep before I got up to help my roomie, Christie Skelton, to get up and packed and on her way. She got the wrong bus and came back after a while. Eventually she managed to find the right bus, though – and off she went.

By the next day I was one of the only athletes left in the Village, the only one from our apartment of twelve, and all of it was a mess. Masses of Aussie uniforms were left strewn everywhere – showing how little people thought of them. It was to be so different in Sydney in 2000: there we had really smart uniforms, plus the same Nike gear that was given to the Olympic team members.

The chaos continued to the end. A group of us, including a few of the equestrian girls, a friend of mine Jodie Worrall (a staff member with the equestrian team) and Sandy Blythe, the captain of the Rollers basketball team, hatched a plan to fly across to Los Angeles early and spend some time at Disneyland before flying home. We thought we were being really smart, really cool ending the trip this way. We had it all planned: the bus to Anaheim etc. But mechanical trouble with the plane in Dallas on the way pulled the rug right out from under that one. In the end, having sat around in an airport bar in Dallas, we only just got back to LA in time to catch the plane home. It was a stupid ending. Sandy and I sat there sharing one beer, drowning our sorrows – we knew we had a long flight ahead . . .

\* \* \*

The aftermath of the Games, though, was terrific. I received the $15,000 bonus offered by the Australian Olympic Committee to all gold medallists at the Olympics (although gold-winning Paralympians received nothing). I was named Australian Paralympian of the Year for the second time. I soon realised my profile as a sportsperson had lifted – even more so than after Barcelona. The TV audience had been bigger than at Barcelona, and the Paralympics were a great success for the ABC, which had taken a risk by deciding to provide wide coverage. I had more public recognition than ever before and the awareness of our sports was greater. To be put on a pedestal with the likes of Cathy Freeman, Kieren Perkins and Susie O'Neill was such a giant step. I don't think most people realised how big a deal that was – to be recognised just as an 'athlete' for what I had achieved in the sporting arena, regardless of my disability.

> *Ros Shaw: It's Louise who has been the role model, the front-runner of everyone involved in sport for people with disabilities. As soon as someone says 'wheelchair athlete' people think of Louie. If any able-bodied athlete had done what she has done – winning over all distances, road and track – they'd be an absolute world superstar now.*

When I first started out to tackle the challenge of high-level sport I was patronised to an extent – not really treated the same as other sportspeople. In the beginning my story was in the 'human interest' pages of the newspapers. But since Atlanta I've been covered in the sports pages . . . which is good, and the way it should be. The sports pages are the place where all elite athletes deserve to be. The media can be a great help in raising the profile of our sports, educating people who don't really understand or recognise our sports because they have no knowledge either of the skills required, of the sports themselves, of the disablities catered for in various events – or of the huge amount of training and effort that goes into competing at the highest levels.

But the gap between able-bodied sport and sport for people with a disability was still a wide one, even if it had closed a little on what it had been four years earlier. We had come a long way in terms of funding and support – and today we have come further still, thanks to steady progress and the exposure from Sydney's Games. Yet if things have improved for us, the support of able-bodied sport has, at the same time, gone to another level again. And it really makes me angry when people say, 'Oh, the Olympics and the Paralympics . . . they're the same.' They're not when it comes to levels of support – and my belief is that the gap will never close. They are two different events, with their own separate identities; our dream is no more than to be accepted on the same level as the able-bods.

\* \* \*

Within a short while after the Games a couple of new sponsors came on board – National Australia Bank and Qantas – and said they would like to involve me in their plans. The timing was perfect – I've already told you about my shaky finances before the Games. The new sponsorships, added to the old, made life much easier. I appreciated the support more than anything because it came from people and companies who believed in me. Back in '92 I was successful as well, but not a lot came out of that with regard to gaining sponsorship. But my profile had lifted a lot in those four years, and now everyone's sights were set on Sydney 2000 – Paralympics as well as Olympics. In '96 after Atlanta people believed in me and said, yes, we will take her on board and include her in what we do. That was wonderful; I was such an untried commodity really, but they were prepared to take the risks that others wouldn't. I appreciate that, and just hope it has proved as good for them as it has for me.

The new sponsorships, the fact of the 2000 Games being at home in Sydney and my genuine love of my sport were behind my decision, quickly made after Atlanta, to press on. 'If I'm going to do this, I'd better do it right,' I said to myself. 'I'd be mad not to go on to Sydney.'

And so I did – peering down that long, straight road to something four years ahead and pledging that I would give it my best shot.

CHAPTER 12

# THE LONG ROAD HOME

The year that followed the Atlanta Games, 1997, was another significant one for me both personally and professionally. Not only did I compete in some important events, including one of the most exciting races of my life, the 1997 Boston Marathon, but I also acquired a new place to live, a new coach and my first manager.

I have told you about how my profile suddenly soared after Atlanta – and I began to feel I was in need of some professional help in managing my career. The requests started rolling in: corporate guest-speaking opportunities, school speech days and plenty more. It was all becoming too much. I didn't want to be thrashing out corporate deals. And I certainly didn't want the media and everyone else coming direct to my home number.

Karen McBrien was someone I had known for quite a time through the Oz Day 10K, with which she had been involved for years, and via her work in other aspects of sports for athletes with a disability, mainly in the area of event management. We had talked at length about my career during the Oz Day 10K promotion of '96.

Then in January 1997 I flew to Sydney and Karen and I had another long conversation about possible future plans and discussed the necessity of a move to Sydney if my career were to continue to grow. Karen agreed at that point to come on board as my manager. I flew home to Perth and sorted out my things, and my life. She and I travelled to the Boston Marathon of that year in April, and the next month Karen flew across to Perth and joined me for the long drive to Sydney. I had taken the step that I knew I had to take.

As a friend (and my manager for four years), Karen has made a big difference to my life. As my manager she took a lot of the day-to-day pressure off me, allowing me to do what I had to do as a professional athlete. She dealt with everything to do with my commitments to sponsors, public appearances, media demands and various commercial contracts.

Of the members of Team Sauvage, Karen probably had the most complex role – trying to juggle the business side of the operation with my competition and training obligations, and also helping me to preserve my sanity in a crowded life. She helped me find balance – which was not easy, especially in the months leading up to the Sydney Olympics and Paralympics. I love staying in Australia and training here and being in a routine – but there is also a lot more pressure when I am home, many more demands on me and my time. Overseas that side of things is great. There is no hassle; I don't take a mobile phone – and I find I can just get on and do what I have to do.

Karen has extremely good personal skills – she's a person who can talk to anyone and is quite happy dealing with anyone. I'm sure she found it easier saying no to requests than I did. I'm a bit of a softie in that regard. If someone wants to meet with me, and I *know* I don't really have the time and shouldn't do it ... well, I'll probably do it anyway. It's hard – I like to do the right thing and it's nice when people want me to be there and do stuff. But a good manager provides a buffer, gives you that breathing space. And Karen did that.

I was very happy to have had her represent me as my first manager. I know that she always had my best interests at heart. To have a good manager is an essential part of the operation when you become an elite athlete these days. You need someone in the middle ground, someone who can assess everything that comes in – then act on those things to your best advantage.

I am now, I suppose, a Sydney girl, well supported by the people around me, and living in my own place in a mid-western suburb not so far out of the city.

The reason for my move to Sydney was straightforward: to be on that side of Australia to prepare myself for the 2000 Paralympic and Olympic Games, experiences I so much wanted to be part of. Sydney was the place to be for sponsors, for opportunities and for just about everything else relating to my career. It was the only place in Australia that had a wheelchair track and road program (through the New South Wales Institute of Sport). I was also coming over to the east coast every couple of weeks anyway – an expensive exercise. Getting out of Australia – to the competitions I regularly tackle in the US and Europe – is an easier exercise from Sydney too.

The shift to this big, bustling city with its attractions – and drawbacks – was not an easy one for me. It was a lot harder than the move to Melbourne. Suddenly I was about to land in a city of four and a half million people – the biggest in the country – not knowing as many people as I knew in other places, and confronting traffic and road systems that I just wasn't used to.

Training in Perth, with its small community, was a friendlier experience than it is at times in Sydney – although Centennial Park, one of my main training centres these days, is a harmonious sort of place. On our runs along the Swan River in Perth, people walking their dogs would inevitably greet us, take an interest in how we were going. We'd see a lot of the same faces. I wondered how Sydney would be. In a newspaper interview before I shifted east, I expressed exactly how I felt: 'I'm a bit scared about the move,' I admitted, 'but I think it will be OK once I get over there'.

It was tough at the beginning, kind of lonely – although I don't have a massive life outside my sport wherever I am. 'Uncertain' might be a better word to describe it – that was how I felt about so many things in Sydney to start with. But this was going to be my home for all the right reasons to do with my career – and I had to work through it. So I did . . . and the more I get to know the city and its appealing places, the more I like it.

When I first came to Sydney I lived at Winston Hills for a time, sharing with Karen McBrien in a house adjacent to the M2 freeway. Then we moved closer in, to a rented house in West Ryde, and after a year or so of settling into Sydney life I bought the semidetached villa that has been my home these past four years.

So after five years, it's OK. But I found Melbourne a much more user-friendly place and enjoyed the eighteen months I had there, spanning 1994 and 1995. It's a city of some style. I knew more people down there; I liked the 'feel' of the place – it moves a lot more. Sydney can be a harsh town at times, but I needed to live in the hub of the Australian sports world, and I have come to terms with that. It's a city that can bite hard at times – as when thieves broke into my home and ransacked it in July 2000, a terribly unsettling event. But the truth of modern living is that something like that can happen anywhere.

On reflection the move has paid off, for sure. It's been beneficial to me as a person – and to my career as an athlete.

\* \* \*

Apart from getting my living arrangements sorted out, I was in need of a new coach in 1997 as well. Jenni Banks and I had parted company after the Atlanta Games . . . we both sort of went our separate ways. I was still in Perth then, and basically coached myself for a time.

About halfway through 1997 Andrew Dawes, from the New South Wales Wheelchair Sports Association, started to do my gym programs. And when it became too demanding for me to work out track and road programs he came in to help me, agreeing to take over my coaching on road, track and gym around November of that year.

We've been working together ever since, devising my programs. The mix has been very good. I had been doing it myself for quite a while, but Andrew, although fairly new in the sport, brought up-to-date technical knowledge with him. We have grown together as a coach-athlete 'team' since it kicked off at the end of 1997.

I was an experienced athlete by the time I met Andrew through New South Wales Wheelchair Sports. Andrew had a similar background to Jenni's. He was coaching at a junior level at the time, but was very interested in my sport and hungry for information about it. He no doubt learned a lot from me in the early stages – and I have enjoyed and responded to his coaching. It's been a very good partnership.

> *Andrew Dawes: Louise shaped me as a coach. The ethos I have developed as a sports coach has largely been through the work I have done with her. She is such a committed, hard-working person, a perfect role model. If I am regarded as a hard taskmaster in my coaching now, it's because of what I have learned from her career. Louise's commitment to training is unfailing and constant – the getting up at 5.00 a.m. . . . the fact of never missing a session.*

\* \* \*

Moving across the country and assembling a new Team Sauvage didn't stop me from putting together a gratifying list of achievements in the sporting arena that year. On a rainy Australia Day I raced against Jean

Driscoll, in a duel that attracted a lot of attention considering her achievements in Boston. But, proving that nothing is ever certain in sport, Jean got a flat tyre along the way, I won clearly – and she pushed the last 8 kilometres with the flat, for second place. After I had won that race I told the media: 'I love the Oz Day 10K; I like to call it my own event.'

But if the Oz Day 10K was regarded as mine, there was little argument that the Boston Marathon belonged to Jean.

The Boston Marathons of the years 1997 to 2000 add up to a story about as dramatic as sport can get. People who hear me talk about the saga of my long-running duel with Jean Driscoll up and down Boston's hills each April are generally pretty amazed. Two years in particular, 1997 and 1998, turned out to be epic races; surely no Hollywood scriptwriter could have produced more drama. For me they were also the turning point after years of chasing Jean to the finishing line . . .

The 1997 Boston was the first that I had competed in since the Atlanta Paralympics of '96 – and my fifth Boston Marathon to that point. By then the 'unbeatable' Jean, Queen of the Boston race, was my nemesis, absolutely. She had won all five of those races; my best results had been seconds in 1994 and 1996.

My preparation for the '97 race had been excellent. I was still coaching myself at the time, at home in Perth – and I'd done a lot of hard training to improve my hill work and a lot more kilometres than I had ever done before. I came to the race feeling as good as I ever had. Perhaps only athletes understand this – but sometimes you feel just about invincible.

As I've told you, my new manager Karen McBrien joined me on the trip, and it was good to have her along. I didn't have to worry too much about the media leading into the race – most of the attention was on Jean and I was able to ease into it without too much fuss.

But the night before, I just couldn't sleep. I was really hyped up, and something of a mess. It was the first time that Karen had travelled overseas with me. She had never really seen me before a big race . . . let alone shared a room with me. She was a bloody mess too.

She couldn't sleep and I couldn't sleep and we ended up having a big pillow fight in the middle of the night. She was really worried about my not getting any sleep before the race . . . but that was just me. I never sleep much before a big race.

The nerves got me, as usual, in the hotel lobby on race morning, and there were various trips to the loo. But I was feeling OK when I got on the bus for the trek to Hopkinton, my confidence boosted by the fact that I had beaten Jean Driscoll in the LA Marathon the previous month – the first time I had won that race. In Hopkinton we would set up each year in a big school hall: check our chairs and organise water bottles, race numbers and microchips. Yeah, microchips. There's one affixed to each chair and to a shoe of each runner and you're scanned along the way to pinpoint your position in the race.

I was usually one of the last to leave the hall each year. More often than not it's quite cold in Boston on race day – although I told you about the unseasonably warm weather in '93! But each year I tried to reduce the time I spent just sitting in the racing chair out there as much as possible, the warm-up area being pretty limited – a narrow stretch of a very congested street, invariably crammed with people.

The path to the starting line at Boston really revs you up for the race, as competitors go one by one through deep lines of spectators. Everyone is yelling and screaming and the atmosphere is great. But on the starting line it's generally a chilly wait of fifteen minutes or so as the American anthem is played and some speeches are made. Then it's into your grid position. I would always wish the other girls 'Good luck' or 'Safe race', and mean it, even though I was only there for one reason: to win. I remember wondering at the start of the '97 race whether this was to be my year. Then it was the gun, and we were away . . .

I raced in a pack of five or six up front early, with all of us working together, taking turns to push from the front and then drop back to draught for a while.

On a hill 10 kilometres into the race Jean Driscoll and I took off. By the time we had got to the top and then descended the other side, the rest of the girls had dropped off. And that's the way it was for the rest of the race – just the two of us, working together, taking turns at the front. Jean had traditionally been stronger than me on the hills. Her disability is spina bifida – and like me she hasn't got a lot of weight in her legs. She's smaller than me up top, but very, very strong.

There is a point 30 kilometres or so into the race when you go down a hill, then make a right-hand turn at a fire station. After that it gets hilly . . . and tough. And each year I would think the same thing when I got to the fire station: 'OK, here we go!'.

In '97, it was the same pattern as before. Into the hills Jean started to edge away from me, gradually pulling clear. It had happened year after year. This time it was the same . . . yet different . . .

Jean Driscoll would have been about 600 metres ahead when I *really* got mad that April afternoon. 'I've done all this hard work . . . I'm just not going to let it happen again,' I said to myself. So I put my head down and pushed as hard as I could. There was no way I was going home for the fifth year in a row having to tell people the same story: that she had beaten me on the hills.

This time, I kept her in view, and on the downhill runs made up ground, as I always do because of my size. With about 7 or 8 kilometres to go, at the bottom of a sharp downhill, I rocked up alongside her with a big grin on my face and announced myself back. It was probably the first time she had had someone alongside her at that stage of the race. Even then, I had won the race as far as I was concerned, because I had overcome what was the hardest part for me: the hills. I could hang on for the next 7 or 8 kilometres without a problem – there was no way I was going to let her win now.

We kept working together to a point in the race where there is a very steep downhill. At the bottom of the hill trolley (tram) tracks cross the road diagonally. I was just in front as we came ripping down the hill, and she was doing her utmost to catch me. Across the trolley tracks I took a better line than Jean, and in a fateful moment a wheel of her chair caught in the tracks . . . and tipped her out! I can still hear the clatter and crash behind me at that instant. I looked back over my left shoulder and she was in the air, heading for the road. We had been travelling at something close to 50 kilometres an hour.

Right there, the Boston Marathon was mine for the first time. Jean had taken a chance, taken a precarious line – and had paid the price. Shaken, she climbed back into her chair, with some help, but by then I was long gone, and she was struggling with a flat tyre. I won by seven minutes in 1 hour 54.28 minutes. I told the media: 'It's the one race I have wanted for so long. It's on a par with my medals in Atlanta. But it's almost not fair . . . I feel really bad for her'.

Jean, who thankfully escaped with not much more damage than scraped elbows, explained her position too: 'I set up for the tracks every year, but I've never had anyone around me going over that part of the course. This year I had some competition, so I tried to be a little bit more aggressive and I got caught in the track'.

The win was a huge breakthrough for me: I had stayed with Jean, the 'Marathon Woman', on the course she knew so well – and I had finally come first. Everyone seemed shocked that I had beaten Jean. I felt great, and I had no trouble convincing myself that I deserved to win – and would have won anyway. In fact the win felt as good as the four golds I had captured in Atlanta the year before. I went away with a trophy and US$10,000 in prize money – of which 37 per cent was taken out in US taxes!

But I felt a little empty too . . . with some anger mixed in with that. I had wanted to race Jean all the way to the line and beat her. Some of the locals were saying, 'You only won because Jean crashed'. That guaranteed one thing: that I would come back the next year for sure and prove the point. My stubbornness made absolutely certain of that.

Celebrations inevitably follow the Boston race, and since I had won I shouted dinner. I had hardly eaten all day, and I was really hungry. Karen and I went out; she was as high as a kite after my win. 'I'm going to have champagne,' she said. 'Even if you're not going to celebrate, I am.' I knew that a glass of champagne would have bowled me over – so I ate just about everything in the place instead, cutting loose for once from my usual diet restrictions. I stayed in New York for a while after the race, and it was a bacon, egg and cheese bagel for breakfast every morning – then nothing until afternoon tea, when I'd have a slice of cheesecake.

\* \* \*

Apart from Boston, I won several marathons and road races that year. I've already mentioned my win against Jean in the LA Marathon in March. Then in July I won the Peachtree 10-kilometre road race in Atlanta for the first time since '93, the year I began doing the American circuit.

In September I competed in the World Championship 10-kilometre Road Race, otherwise known as the Riverside Rumble, in Wilkes-Barre, Pennsylvania. The Riverside Rumble is a wheelchair-only race, and a big one, and it coincides with my birthday in September, so it's a race that sort of sticks in my mind. Wilkes-Barre is a quiet town – even McDonald's closes at 6.00 p.m.! But on race day people turn up in large numbers. It's one of their big days of the year. The race used to be for US athletes only, but in 1997 they opened it up to international competitors and I ended up winning it three years on the trot ('97, '98, '99). Then I raced the historic Berlin Marathon later the same month, for the second time – and won.

In November each year Oita, Japan, hosts the biggest wheelchair-only marathon in the world, and one of the biggest road races. There's both a half-marathon and a marathon, and there'll be as many as 600 chairs. The first part of it can be a nightmare. It's a grid start, with seedings done on times and everyone jumbled up and out of their classes, lined up across a six-lane road. Keeping an eye on your main competitors is usually impossible the way it's done. Within a kilometre the road narrows to two lanes, at which point you make a left-hand turn. And it's right here that all the bingles happen... It's amazing. At this point there'll be large crowds of people all lined up on the median strip with their cameras, shooting the great charge of wheelchairs coming towards them. It's an incredible experience – thousands of cameras flashing as you head down to the left-hand turn, hoping that you're going to get around. You just keep your head up and hope for the best.

I've raced Oita three times ('95, '96, '97), although not in recent years. It's a big event ... but a frustrating one because of the way it starts. I'm glad I raced it, though. Oita is closer to the 'real' Japan than places like Tokyo, because it's not a big, overpowering city. They certainly look after you well; the visiting racers get put up in top-class, western hotels and are treated like gods. It is immaculately run in the Japanese manner, very orderly. On race day it's 'Hurry up, hurry up ... Wait ... Hurry up, hurry up ... Wait' as they set it all up. In 1997 I came third.

In December I also won the Honolulu Marathon. I relaxed the next day, snorkelling in Hanauma Bay. After my victory the media asked me about the famous annual Hawaiian Iron Man contest. 'I'm probably mad enough to try it,' I told them. Hmmm, I'm not so sure about that now! Honolulu was always good fun, and like the Riverside Rumble, I won it in 1997, 1998 and 1999. Because the race is run just before Christmas there's a nice festive feel to it, with the lights up and everyone in a happy mood.

\* \* \*

That year I also qualified for the 800 metres demonstration race to be run at the IAAF World Championships in Athens in August. But a week before the race I was still sitting at home, wondering if I was ever going to get there. After all, the meet had already begun.

In growing panic, I spoke to Athletics Australia, who told me that the Greek organisers of the Championships were handling everything. So I waited ... and waited. Four days before my race I still hadn't heard anything – and took to the phone, talking to athletes who were competing over there, trying to find out how they had organised their trips.

Right at the end, Athletics Australia booked me a flight with Qantas; on the same day came the belated news that the organisers had, at last, booked me a flight too – with Olympic Airlines. 'Just take our flight . . . we'll sort it out later,' Athletics Australia told me.

So at the last minute I made it to the World Championships. Just one ticket was provided, so there was no chance of a coach or anyone else going with me. The local organisers met me at the airport and took me to the hotel where the Australian team was staying. I was happy to get there and see some familiar faces at last.

They had a room there for me, which was fine – but no team uniform. I ended up with one of the men's throwing suits, a pair of black tights, a huge jacket that didn't fit me and a few T-shirts. Oh, and a nice sportsbag – which I still use today. Even though my event was only a demo, I still felt like something of an afterthought. It wasn't too bad . . . but it would have been nice to have felt more a part of the team. It didn't feel quite right.

Tanni Grey (now Grey-Thompson), representing Great Britain, whom I knew well from competition and from time she had spent training in Perth, was there with one of her coaches, Vicki Goosey – and I was very grateful for their presence. They really helped me out. I was pretty much alone. The rest of the Australian team was there of course, but I didn't really know a lot of them.

So I hung around mainly with Tanni, against whom I was to race – and together we battled to overcome the vagaries of the Athens transport for the event. It seemed they had only one wheelchair-accessible bus for the whole of Greece – and we managed to catch it only once. But the athletics facilities generally were great – they had four top-class tracks within 200 metres of each other. I spent some time, too, with Nova Peris-Kneebone and her little girl Jessica and then-husband Sean. I had known Nova since 1996, when she was living in Perth and a member of the Hockeyroos.

The trip turned out to be quite an enjoyment, even though I only had four or five days there in the end. I won my race in the quickest time I had recorded for a couple of years, 1 minute 52.11 seconds, ahead of Chantal Petitclerc and Tanni. After the race I did some touring around Athens with a group that included some of the British team and Chris Cohen from the International Paralympic Committee. We did the real tourist bit: up to the Parthenon in Athens, through the markets – generally having a good look around the ancient city that, all being well, will host both the Olympics and Paralympics in 2004. I'd never been to Athens before, and I loved the great sense of history that was everywhere. Despite the bumpy start, I was really happy I made it to those Championships.

\* \* \*

As the year ended, in recognition of my achievements, I was named not only Australian Paralympian of the Year – for the third time – but also Young Australian of the Year (National Sports Category). Since this was an award open to all Australian athletes it was a particularly high honour – and another triumph for sport for athletes with a disability.

On a more glitzy note, *Cosmopolitan* magazine also picked me in a group of '30 Most Successful Australian Women Under 30'. I made the list again in 1998 and 1999. The first time I did it, I thought it was one of the best things I had ever done – my first full-on photo shoot, and with the whole glam hair and make-up bit.

When my mum bought the magazine and first leafed through it, she couldn't find me! She picked up the phone: 'Are you sure you're in it?' she asked. Then when she sent the photo to my rellies in England later the response was: 'My God . . . is that *her*?'.

The party was held in the restaurant down at Sydney's Domain, opposite the Art Gallery of New South Wales. The sponsor was a champagne company and the current Bachelor of the Year was invited along – Scott Miller, the butterfly swimmer. Helen Razer and Judith Lucy entertained the crowd . . . everyone drank too much champagne, me included . . . and it was heaps of fun. Glamorous, hey? Being a sports star is not *all* about hard work!

CHAPTER 13

# THE GREAT RACE

Looking back on the following year, 1998, everything I managed to achieve finished up in the shadow of a truly extraordinary and unforgettable event: the now famous 'photo finish' Boston Marathon.

On 26 January I had tightened my stranglehold on the Oz Day 10K, with Jean Driscoll absent this time: I won by four minutes, racing alone throughout. But this meant little compared with what lay ahead in April: the unfinished business between Jean and me...

In '98 my coach Andrew Dawes joined me in Boston – and for the first time I got to stay in the big flash hotel that is the home base for the event's top brass. I was, after all, the defending champion. At breakfast on the Saturday (the race was the following Monday), they presented me with number 101 – and it was a real honour to get it for the first time. The defending men's wheelchair champ gets number one (since they start before the women on the grid) – and 101, signifying pole position (the women's number one spot on the grid), is given to the defending women's champion from the previous year.

This time round, I had a lot more media and promotional commitments to contend with. Talk about the 1997 race still raged in Boston. Should they have covered the trolley tracks? people asked. I met Jean Driscoll at one of these media events – and it sort of freaked me out. I don't really know why. It was kind of stupid. But the hype about the race, about the upcoming rematch between the pair of us, was truly unbelievable.

My training build-up hadn't been as good as the previous year, and now there were all these distractions. I wasn't feeling too great about the whole thing at all. I had been struggling with my ongoing wrist problem, which had affected my preparation and reduced the mileage I had done in training.

Things got worse on race morning. Andrew pushed me over to the wheelchair athletes' hotel – from which the buses for Hopkinton departed. On the trip out I felt sick all the way . . . really horrible. The culmination came in the school hall, when I threw up all over the place, which was so embarrassing, so awful. I hadn't thrown up before a race for five years or more. I was just so nervous . . . I felt so sick. I had to take my Lycras off and rinse them – and if you've ever tried to get wet Lycra back on . . . it's disgusting! But with a little help from some friends, I eventually got myself back together again. It really was a nightmare lead-up to the race.

> *Shona Casey: I have watched her race on many occasions and seen the nerves that almost consume her before she takes to the start line. I am aware of races before which she was physically sick. But no-one ever knew. She just went out and kicked butt. I still get goosebumps of excitement watching her race.*

Anyhow, I made it to the start and the race turned out to be the same formula as every year, with Jean and me working with a pack for 10 to 12 kilometres. By the time we got to the fire station before the really tough hills, she and I were out on our own – again. But going up the hills, it happened again. I just couldn't go with Jean . . . I didn't feel strong enough. Minute by minute she edged away from me, to the point where she was a kilometre in front.

In the past, I had had a recurring mind-set: if I couldn't see Jean when she broke away in a race, then I couldn't catch her. My mind would tell me, 'If you can't see her any more there's no way in the world you're going to catch up with her'. And I would sort of give up, take a relaxed attitude and settle for second place.

But in 1998, I kept pushing. Hard.

After a few kilometres of not catching a glimpse of her I pulled to the top of a hill and finally there she was: still far away, and right at the bottom racing away – but at least, briefly, in sight. I could see the fluorescent yellow top she was wearing, and the red lead vehicle. So I kept pushing and pushing – not having any inkling that from about 5 kilometres from the finish she was starting to cramp up, unable to muster the sort of speed she had had before. Slowly, gradually, I made up ground on her. The fact of being able to see her and of knowing that I was gaining on her drove me on.

Near the end of the Boston Marathon the crowds thicken behind the barricades. There is a right-hand turn and then a left into Boylston Street – the finishing stretch. At the left-hand turn I was 40 or 50 metres behind Jean Driscoll . . .

Before then I had read many times of marathon runners 'hitting the wall' and the pain barriers that long-distance athletes manage to break through. They were things I had never thought much about, or believed in, but I got to that final left-hand turn on this afternoon in April 1998 – and something very weird happened. Suddenly I couldn't hear anything, couldn't hear any of the screaming and yelling that was going on around me. Suddenly I was in a strange, quiet zone. Every single thing was switched off – except what I was focusing on. I couldn't feel my arms or hands, couldn't feel the blister that had been throbbing away on one hand – couldn't feel any pain at all. It was like I was in another world, another dimension. My focus was only Jean ... and the finishing line, too close now it seemed. It felt as if everything had sped up. Everything that happened in the final seconds of the race took place in some sort of huge blur. I was on some sort of weird automatic pilot.

From that final left turn into Boylston, it's about 700 or 800 metres to the finish line. The road is wide there, probably four or five lanes wide – and all I could see ahead was Jean, and the finish line with the big banner standing out above the road, bright in blue and yellow ...

All of it was hurtling towards me ... Jean, the finish line, the sign. I wanted to push it all a little further away. I had no sense of what I was doing. But I know from watching the film later that I was pushing hard, finishing fast.

People told me later that the commentator had announced Jean as the winner as she neared the line. 'And here's Jean Driscoll, coming in for her eighth victory ... a record for the Boston Marathon!' The words are captured on the American tape of the race. At the time, though, I didn't hear a thing ...

The photograph of the finish that appears in this book tells the story of what happened better than any words can. It shows Jean, her arms rising to break the tape for the expected victory – and me whizzing past her, half a chair length in front after 42 kilometres! I was behind her, then up alongside ... then past!

Afterwards, pandemonium reigned. Everyone was crying out, 'Oh my God ... oh my God!' and the commentator was asking, 'What's happened, what's happened?' I race in an Invacare suit, and a lot of the guys wear those as well – and many people thought that it was one of the male competitors who had come flying through. I went over to Jean and we congratulated each other. I don't know what was said – I think we were both in shock. She couldn't believe it ... and I couldn't believe it. How crazy it was – that a marathon race of 42 kilometres had come down to the last 2 metres!

At the finish line I just sat there, totally drained. Andrew didn't have accreditation and he was trapped behind the fence. We exchanged a few words of mutual disbelief through the barrier. It was a frustrating experience for him. He couldn't get near the finish line – and had only been able to watch the last bit of the race on a big screen.

> *Andrew Dawes: The '98 race was one of my biggest thrills in sport. I chose not to go out to the start – so I could be there for the finish. It was a bit frustrating, watching on TV with 90 per cent of the coverage focused on the runners. There I was, sitting in my motel room, trying to get updates. On the first hill Louise was with Jean, by the second there was a bit of a gap – and by the third Jean was gone again. I was sitting there thinking that maybe the quest was lost again.*
>
> *With about fifteen minutes to go, I made my way down towards the finish line. The crowd was huge – and I went about 400 metres up the road to the first place I could get near the fence. Then Jean comes through and I think, 'Damnit!' ... Then Louise comes through 150 to 200 metres behind, with only 400 or 500 metres to go. I thought, 'That's not too bad, the time is pretty quick ... this is a pretty good second'.*
>
> *From where I was I couldn't see the actual finish and I walked through the crowd to meet Louise, to see if she'd got through all right. The next minute there's this image on the screen of Louise going across the line. I couldn't believe it – that she'd actually chased Jean down, and won.*
>
> *I grabbed a guy next to me. 'What happened? ... What happened?' I asked. I honestly thought that what I'd seen might have been some old footage. But he told me that*

*Louise had won... and I was absolutely astounded. When Louise passed me she was at least fifteen seconds behind and they were travelling at 26 to 28 kilometres an hour, with only 400 to 500 metres to go. It was just amazing. Every time I have watched it since I get a tingle.*

Then it was on to the ceremony – the medal, the wreath, the national anthem – and later, back at the hotel, the press conference to try and put it all into words. The aftermath of the race was something of a blur too. The winner's wreath on my head, they took me through the big recovery tent where rows of stretchers are set up annually with drips over them, and space blankets at the ready – a sight that unsettled me the first year I raced Boston. They were obviously expecting some customers!

Physically and mentally I was terribly drained by the race, and it took me a long while to recover. I rang Mum; Andrew had already rung Karen and conveyed the news to Australia.

'What's wrong with you?' my mother asked when I got through. She couldn't understand how I could sound so bad after a race. I told her I'd won. 'Well, that's really good,' she said, 'but you sound terrible'.

After the call I just sat there for a long, long time – and they replayed the finish over and over again on TV. 'I can't believe that... It's mad,' I thought as I watched that last second of the race. I just sat there saying, 'Wow!'.

That night I went out with Dawsey and Ben Lucas, a New Zealand racer who had stayed with us – and we really enjoyed ourselves. At two o'clock the next morning I was still on the phone talking to journos who had called from back home. Then I was out early for a 10-kilometre push. It's hard, but I generally do that after a big race – I find it helps me recover.

I have never again (so far) experienced whatever it was that came over me in the last stage of that race. I went to another level – to somewhere I had never been before, to a place where nothing in the world was relevant but what I was doing. It was very strange. There was a sense in it of me being detached – of looking at myself from outside my body.

I still have a clear image in my mind of the last 100 metres of the race, although everything happens so quickly in what I recall. I am aware of the crowd, of the movement of the lines of people, of the clapping and shouting. Yet everything is so quiet. It is just incredibly freaky.

\* \* \*

Four months after my win in the Boston Marathon of 1998, and the completion of other racing commitments in the US, I made my way to London and on to Birmingham for the IPC's World Championships, the event that alternates every two years with the Paralympics. En route, I stopped off to race in the Swiss National Championships in July and broke my own 5000 metres world record – by six seconds! At that time I was holder of four individual world records, the 200 metres, 800 metres, 1500 metres and 5000 metres – although the 800 was to be gone before long.

In Birmingham, the Australian team caused a big hoo-ha when the decision was made that the allocated accommodation wasn't suitable. Our move to a hotel caused a huge drama. 'Who do they think they are?' people said of our team, and 'So, we're not good enough for you?'. It was pretty uncomfortable – but sort of in tune with the entire running of the Championships, which hit all sorts of hurdles due to the way they were run and due to a continual squabble over classifications. It was an interesting experience! Many countries did not bring full teams, the result of which was that some of the best female athletes in the world weren't there. That was frustrating for me; I like to race against the best competition.

But for all that, it was a big success for the Aussies. I was one of the co-captains of the team and certainly proud of the successes we achieved. Personally, they were a great championships for me. I won six gold medals: the individual 800, 1500, 5000 and marathon, plus two as a member of the relay team (the 4 x 100 and 4 x 400) along with Christie Skelton, Holly Ladmore and Angie Ballard. We Aussies finished with sixty-four medals in all, to beat Great Britain (on sixty-two) to the top of the table.

Both relays were thrilling races. In the 4 x 400 we gave the British a huge start at one stage, but Angie made up a lot of ground on her lap – and we ended up winning clearly and breaking the world record by eleven seconds. I was to learn later that my last lap in the 4 x 100, in which I came from behind to win over the Americans, inspired artist Evert Ploeg to paint a portrait of me for the Sporting Archibald Prize, sponsored by the Sydney *Daily Telegraph* in 2000. I enjoyed the experience and columnist Jeff Wells later wrote of Evert's painting as 'a fine piece – she radiates indomitable strength'. I liked it a lot, too.

The pressure on the relay team was added to by the fact that filmmaker David Goldie and his crew were there making a two-part documentary on the four of us – subsequently shown twice on Channel Seven in 1999 and later as a two-parter on the ABC before the 2000 Paralympics. It was called 'Three Seconds from Glory'. The making of the film made life a bit uncomfortable – as if we were 'special' or something.

My mum and my aunty Margaret from Leicester were there in Birmingham for the Championships – it was the first time that Mum had been present to watch me compete in an international competition overseas. I looked for her when I was out on the track. It was fantastic knowing that she was there. She was in the crowd most days and was interviewed by a TV crew at one point. She enjoyed every second of it, I think.

> *Rita Sauvage: I had tears in my eyes watching her. I feel as if I reap some of the rewards, through her reflected glory.*

\* \* \*

One example of this 'glory' was an article by Mike Carlton that appeared in the *Sydney Morning Herald* on 22 August, six days after the Championships ended, full of praise and support for me and other athletes with a disability:

> *Let's hear it for Louise Sauvage, champion athlete, holder of four world records, winner of no fewer than 24 international gold medals and one silver since 1990, and the Australian Institute of Sport's Athlete of the Year in 1997.*
>
> *Scorching along in her wheelchair, aged 24, Louise blitzed the field at the International Paralympics Athletics Championships, in Britain this month, in everything from the 800 metres to the marathon. The rest of the team was up there with her, beating 54 other countries with a tally of 64 medals including 30 gold.*
>
> *By any standard it was all guts and glory, putting our disabled athletes bang on target for a stunning triumph when Sydney hosts the Paralympic Games in 2000. The only fly in the ointment is the sour, rotten lousy, miserable, tight-fisted, penny-pinching, cheese-paring, scrimping, scraping, mingy, stingy Federal Government, which is obstinately refusing to come up with the money so desperately needed to help prepare the team.*
>
> *This financial year the Australian Sports Commission has $25 million to spend on training and development of its Olympic Athletes Program. The Paralympians were offered just $1 million, or 4 per cent of that, to be doled out between 280 athletes and their coaches, in 18 sports. The rest of the cash goes to able-bodied Olympic hopefuls, an act of discrimination as blatant as you could expect to see. The Sports Commission is spending more on minor sports, such as volleyball, than it is on the entire Paralympic squad.*

*The Australian Paralympic Committee estimates that it needs another $1.5 million from the Feds this year, hardly an earth-shaking sum in the grand scheme of things. It has pleaded its case to the Sports Commission and the Federal Minister of Sport, Andrew Thomson, in meeting after meeting and letter after letter, only to be snowed in by a blizzard of red tape and snivelling excuses.*

*Last month, after weeks of cap-in-hand negotiations too tedious to describe here, it managed to squeeze another $250,000 from the Feds – take it or leave it, thank you and goodnight.*

*It is an utter disgrace. These people might be in wheelchairs, or they might have artificial limbs or, in some cases, they might have intellectual disabilities, but the Paralympic Committee argues – rightly – that they train as long and as hard as any able-bodied athlete to compete at world-class level.*

*To which I add what should be the bleeding obvious, that they are taxpaying citizens like the rest of us and are therefore entitled to a fair and equal share from their Government. And it's not as if there's a shortage of money in Canberra at the moment. Peter Costello announced a surprise-surprise Budget surplus of $1.2 billion only a week ago. In one of the more blatantly political rorts of our time, the Howard government has found $15 million of public money to bang the drum for its election campaign tax promises. No penny-pinching there, then.*

*Somehow, our Paralympians will make it to Homebush Bay in 2000, where they will again scoop the pool and where, no doubt, politicians will rush to bask in the reflected glory of gold, gold, gold. I do hope Andrew Thomson will not be around to show his face. He ought to be thoroughly ashamed of himself.*

Then something else happened one afternoon in October that made me feel even more appreciated than all Mike Carlton's rousing words could. It was a strange day. I knew something was up – but I didn't know what. The story I had been given was that I was filming a TV commercial with New South Wales Olympics and Paralympics Minister Michael Knight. Karen McBrien was with me at the Olympic site at Homebush, and I was asking a million questions as they did my hair and put on the make-up. I'm such a practical person; I need to know what's going on. I must have driven Karen mad, as I realised later.

At the last minute I almost ruined the whole thing. 'I've got to go to the loo,' I said, pushing off and heading towards a tunnel in the stand – causing a huge panic, as I later found out. I wondered why people were so agitated. 'Don't worry . . . I'll be back in a couple of minutes,' I said.

So the filming of the 'commercial' began. Something still didn't seem right, but they had teleprompts and everything, so we pressed on. Suddenly someone was tapping me on the shoulder and I was trying to ignore it and not stuff up my lines. Finally, I turned around. It was Mike Munro . . . and he said: 'New South Wales Olympics and Paralympics Minister Michael Knight . . . now, you've always been a bit of a Louise Sauvage groupie, haven't you?' And Michael Knight answered: 'Oh, I've been out at the airport at the crack of dawn to see Louise when she has come back with yet another swag of gold medals. She is an amazing competitor. She is not a person with a disability – she is an elite Australian athlete who happens to have a disability. She is a marvellous icon for sport – all sport. And I just can't wait to see her compete in 2000 with the support of Australians behind her. She will win a swag of gold again.'

And so it was on . . .

Thanks to a giant conspiracy by family, manager and friends, I had become a subject on 'This is Your Life'! The rest of the day was a blur: back home to get changed, then on to the studio. I remembered words I had uttered to Karen when we were talking once and the subject of 'This is Your Life' had come up: 'I am not going on that show, because I am not done with my life'. But now I was on it.

The show was great, an enjoyment for sure – although I sat there the whole time thinking, 'Who are they going to bring out next?'. Well, there were all sorts of people, like one of my old schoolteachers, Mrs Twining, and sportspeople such as triathlete Emma Carney, track athlete Melinda Gainsford-Taylor and Shelley Taylor-Smith, the openwater long-distance swimmer. From Karen Long, my best and oldest friend, there was a message, to say she couldn't come. At the end, of course, she turned up, bringing with her Doggie, the little toy dog that has been with me since I was three, and is a very prized possession. Doggie has travelled the world with me, survived an experience in a hotel laundry after being swept up in the sheets by a cleaning lady one day – and also journeyed safely through the American postal system. His travelling days are now over, however. I have retired him.

After the filming of 'This is Your Life' there was a big party at the studios and then it was off to the ANA Hotel with other guests of the show for cocktails in the top bar. There followed a week of some upheaval, with the family staying on in Sydney for a few days, and me desperately trying to get organised in my new place. I had only just moved in and there was barely any furniture. When I bought my house I had bedroom furniture and that was about it – so it was a challenge to gradually find the things I needed.

Unfortunately there was some bad blood in the wake of the screening of 'This is Your Life'. There were phone calls: 'Why wasn't Jenni Banks on the show? She made Louise who she is' ... that kind of stuff. Heated words were exchanged, to and fro – and Karen was blamed for the fact that Jenni was not one of the invited guests.

Then when the show went to air they edited out the things my sister Ann had said – and she was upset. I kept getting this sort of negative feedback and having to say, 'Look ... I had nothing to do with it!'. Karen and I had 'words' – she was upset that I apparently hadn't appreciated all the work she had done. But of course I had – and the good things far outweighed the bad. It was just disappointing for all that bad blood to eventuate out of something that was supposed to be a celebration.

I was disappointed for Ann. We are not mega-close, but we probably get along better these days than when we were younger. Geographically we are not a close-together family – with me living my life way across the other side of the country. We see each other only in small doses. But Ann and I do a lot of business stuff together; she's an accountant and helps me out with lots of things. When I go home it's good. We hang out together, and Mum and Ann and I will head off for a day at the shops.

\* \* \*

The relay wins in Birmingham back in August had really put Angie, Holly, Christie and me on the map – as a team. In November we became involved in one of the most tiring things I have ever done: a fundraiser and awareness-raising campaign for the New South Wales Wheelchair Sports Association, the Byron to Bondi Challenge.

As the name suggests, it involved pushing 845 kilometres down the coast in stages from Byron Bay to Bondi – setting out each morning to take turns at covering the kilometres of that day's schedule, and fulfilling obligations in the towns we passed through. All the way down there were school visits, dinners and fundraising events. We met literally thousands of people, and I don't think there's any doubt at all that the promotion introduced many new people to wheelchair sport and raised the awareness of others. I have no doubt that some people would have travelled down to support the Paralympics in 2000 because of their involvement with us two years before.

But oh boy, it was hard work, something that I would have to be paid a *lot* of money to tackle again. The distances covered weren't a problem – they were in line with our normal training programs when it came to kilometres. But the routine of getting up every single morning at 6.30, packing up and getting on the road to battle the traffic, the flies and the hills, knowing that your day was going to extend to 11.00 or so that night, owing to the planned dinner in this town or that – it was bloody tough. Almost every night meant a different hotel, in a different town, although there was a welcome two-night stop in Port Macquarie at about the mid-point. I flew back to Sydney at one stage during the campaign to attend an awards dinner, adding to the load.

The whole thing took us two weeks, and when I finally saw Bondi I thought, 'Thank God for that . . . I'm so happy I'm going home'. I was thoroughly sick of it by then. Because my profile was the highest of the four of us, I found myself in constant demand all the way down, although the four of us did our best to share the duties. I think I sat next to almost every town mayor in New South Wales at some stage on the trek! The whole thing was a 'challenge' all right . . . but I guess very positive and worthwhile in the big picture, too.

The year ended on a positive note, when I was named Australian Paralympian of the Year for the fourth time – and for the third year in a row.

CHAPTER 14

# WIN SOME... LOSE SOME

In 1999, with the Sydney Games almost in sight, I experienced the high of my third straight Boston Marathon win and the low of losing my world 800 metres record in circumstances that still make me very angry today.

When I won the Oz Day 10K in January – although being a little below peak form – Heinz Frei, the champion wheelchair racer from Switzerland, took the men's event. That was a thrill for me; I have always looked up to Heinz as one of my heroes and role models in sport. Just before the Sydney Paralympics, when the *Sun-Herald* asked me to name my hero, I picked Heinz. He is just a great athlete – the fastest in the world over a number of distances. He's awesome. I respect him and look up to him so much.

I put Connie Hansen on the same pedestal. Connie was the fastest in the world when I started out and I wanted to be just like her. I thought she was great and the respect she had in her sport was amazing. I was in awe of her in those early days.

I said years ago that I look up even more to the people in my own sport than I do to the able-bodied champions. And that's the truth of it.

I like mixing with sportspeople, finding myself on the same wavelength as just about all of them, and enjoying their company. I've met heaps of them: Steve Waugh, Cathy Freeman of course, Pat Rafter, John Eales and plenty more. And George Gregan – he's really cool – I had lunch with him one day in Melbourne.

I like Emma Carney and Reen Corbett a lot. And I suppose I envy them for what they do. I would love to be a triathlete or an ironwoman. And I think the world of Shelley Taylor-Smith – she is one of the strongest people I know, mentally and physically. She is a brilliant person, with an underlying toughness and a great attitude to life. She has jumped many hurdles, and I admire her a lot. She came on the 'This is Your Life' program they sprung on me – and so did Melinda Gainsford-Taylor. I like Mel a lot too. She has been so supportive of me and my sport for a long time.

> *Shelley Taylor-Smith (on 'This is Your Life'): We're both from Perth, we're both from the same swimming club and we've both got broad shoulders from swimming days. She has been such an inspiration to me and whenever I am in Perth swimming, the first thing I see when I touch the finish line is Louise. And I have always been there to support her when I can too.*

I have probably always been in awe of Cathy Freeman – and I wonder if she thinks I'm a bit rude. I tend not to talk that much when I do meet up with her. Half the time I just don't know what to say. It's like, 'Oh my God, it's Cathy Freeman!'. Sometimes I wonder what she must think of me. I must apologise to her one day.

I've had a fair bit to do with the swimmers, and find them a really good bunch. Daniel Kowalski is a special favourite, such a nice guy. He always has the time of day for you. I get the impression that Daniel would go out of his way to do anything for anybody. I just wish so much that he had won a world or Olympic 1500 metres title in his career. Susie O'Neill is kind of quiet, and nice – and I've also met, and enjoyed meeting, Sam Riley, Geoff Huegel, Kieren Perkins and Ian Thorpe along the way. Ian is just brilliant – a marketer's dream. He's good looking, so articulate – and he's only nineteen. The world is at his feet.

I've also had the opportunity to meet plenty of famous people outside of the sports world. Madonna remains someone I really want to meet. She is unbelievable – and so smart. I'll catch up with her one day.

I was always especially keen to meet Jimmy Barnes, and I've done that a few times now. I'm a great fan of his. The first time I was so overawed I could hardly speak. I got to sit next to Jimmy at the 'One Year to Go' Paralympic countdown launch in Sydney on 18 October 1999. As a Paralympic Countdown Ambassador, I had the opportunity to select a track for the special CD that was being put together – and I picked his 'No Second Prize', a sentiment that suits my philosophy about sport.

At one stage at the function he was bowing down and kissing the ground in front of me! My God! Anyhow, he asked me if I'd like to go to lunch that day, so I went with him and a group of people – Jimmy's wife Jane and one of his daughters and Mandawuy Yunupingu from Yothu Yindi and Joshua Busteed from New South Wales Wheelchair Sports – to the Malay Restaurant in George Street. It was great, even though I barely spoke – I could hardly understand what Jimmy was saying, with that accent of his!

\* \* \*

The year 1999 also brought the final addition to my coaching and management team. Gary Foley, a masseur, personal trainer and running coach by profession, started to work on my track programs. Gary had already been assisting me in the boxing and medicine ball work that has increasingly become part of my training. His involvement in my track programs took some pressure off Andrew, who was now a national coach, with other athletes to look after. Gary is my masseur, too, and a big help in keeping me fit. He and his family have been very supportive of me. He has also worked a lot with me on my mental preparation for racing, and on race tactics. It has probably been an ongoing learning experience for both of us. He hadn't worked with wheelchair athletes before – but he's hooked on it now! The balance of Gary and Andrew is good, and I'm fortunate to have them as part of 'Team Sauvage'.

\* \* \*

April meant the challenge of another Boston Marathon. I had major problems with my left elbow in the lead-up to Boston in 1999. Both my elbows are full of arthritis, but I also hyperextend on my left side – that's my pushing technique – and it's that side that gives me the most trouble. In '99 the elbow was causing me a lot of grief, and for a time it looked as though if I wanted to compete in Boston, I wouldn't be able to train. It was a catch–22 situation: if I kept doing the kilometres I needed to do, then my arm would be too sore for me to race.

In the end Andrew and I made a compromise decision that I would train with my arm heavily strapped for the three or four months before the race – strapped up *every* time I trained, whether it was gym, road or track work. Firm strapping tends to give me enough support to get through. But the downside was that my skin became very intolerant of the tape and I ended up with blisters all over my arm. Finally I had to use special, non-allergy-causing tape *under* the ordinary tape – a laborious process every training session, and a real pain in the bum.

Anyhow, I made it to Boston – and when I got there fairly early to do some media stuff, I decided I really didn't want to be there that particular year. Boston is a difficult place for training if you happen to be staying in the heart of the city. It's so busy that it's very hard to find any decent long kilometres where you can do an uninterrupted push. There was big media focus on local favourite Jean, who said she could feel the fire within – and believed a historic eighth title was going to be hers.

On the Saturday before the race, just like the year before, Andrew and I organised to be dropped out along the marathon route, then came home the last 10 to 15 kilometres along the race course – Andrew on a bike, and me in my racing chair. Mentally, I found that very helpful, reacquainting myself with the terrain, reminding myself that some of the hills weren't *quite* as bad as my memory told me. The training run certainly helped to get me into a better frame of mind than I had been in.

The '99 race was just about the usual formula – although this year the breakaway group numbered three, with a Swiss competitor Edith Hunkeler, a good racer and a really nice girl, joining Jean and me out in front. She was with us until the fire station – and then she dropped back, and it was down to just the two of us again.

For the first time ever in the Boston Marathon, I stayed with Jean through that tough, hilly, 'make-or-break' section. She let me pull the entire final section of the race and didn't show any inclination to go to the front at all, just tucked in behind. That was fine by me. I am always quite happy being in front, in control.

Notwithstanding the etiquette of wheelchair racing – that the job of setting the pace should be shared around – I had no problem with having Jean sit behind me in the latter stages of that race. Towards the end of a race I am always quite happy to be in front dictating the pace. And both Jean and I are very fair racers – we had done our share of work throughout that race, as on every occasion we met. Her choice of tactics near the end of the 1999 race was simply about trying to win the race. I would have been equally happy to have her out in front too; I would put money on myself nine times out of ten to win a sprint finish against any female racer in the world.

Two or three hundred metres out from the finishing line of the '99 Boston Marathon, I put in an effort and started my sprint. Jean pulled out from behind to try and sprint with me, but I held her off in another desperately close finish, and won by about the length of the chair, coming home with another trophy for my mum's mantelpiece. The Boston Marathon website records that we were given the same finishing times in both 1998 and 1999: 1 hour 41 minutes 19 seconds (1998) and 1 hour 42 minutes 23 seconds (1999).

> *Andrew Dawes: The 1999 win was probably even more satisfying than '98 – because Louise stuck with Jean up the hills. After '99 she had proved herself as a Boston Marathoner. Jean had the easier ride that year, sitting behind Lou over the last 3 or 4 kilometres. She is amazing – she takes on Jean Driscoll in the Boston Marathon, then switches to the track for the Olympics to take on the best racers there.*

Back in the hotel Andrew watched the race on TV – with Karen hanging on the telephone line from Sydney, for the entire race! It must have been a circus. At different stages Andrew was doing push-ups in his hotel room as I was working up the hills, doing his best to will me along, and cradling the phone at the same time. Near the end, Andrew was saying, 'I can't look . . . I can't look'. He had turned to the wall. Meanwhile Karen was screaming down the phone from back home, 'Look at the television! . . . Tell me! Tell me!'.

A statement by Jean in the *Boston Herald* the next day showed how much the race had meant to her. Jean said: 'It's frustrating. I had a God-inspired fire in my belly this year and I came out here believing I would win. I came down Boylston [Street] believing I was going to win. I think when you compete at this level, you believe you are going to be the winner. I wanted No 8 so bad. I was hoping to do to her what she did to me last year. Just as I was trying to come around for my sprint, she went into her sprint. My hat's off to Louise. She's very talented'.

The men's event featured a clear leader and clear winner in '99, so a major part of the coverage was on Jean and me battling it out. The closeness of the Boston races and the huge media interest in the unbelievable rivalry that had built up between the two of us have brought a considerable bonus for women's wheelchair racing.

\* \* \*

But the sweetness of this third Boston victory turned sour in July, with the frustration of losing my 800 metres world record in a situation that was way beyond my control.

The record of 1 minute 51.82 seconds, which I established in a heat of the IPC Championships in Berlin, had stood since 1994. The record, and the 800 metres race, were very special to me. The 800 is not quite a sprint – but I am strong enough and confident enough to know that I can race it any way I want, out in front throughout if I have to.

In 1999, I had travelled to the US to compete in some lead-up races, heading towards the eventual goal of the US Nationals, which were to be held in Atlanta. At the Nationals, the plan was for a meet of two and a half days, with the first day consisting of the usual preliminary rounds. But on the second day Atlanta was struck by unbelievably bad storms: thunder and lightning and rain that just hammered down. The day's competition was cancelled.

Subsequently organisers announced they were going to compress the program, and that in all events they were going to run separate timed heats – and the fastest heat winner would take the title. The problem was that I was drawn in a slow heat, a race missing the fast girls I needed to push me along. I was really mad about that, and made quite a fuss: 'I should be in the race with the fast girls . . . there's no point my coming all this way to race by myself,' I told them. I was really causing some grief – and finally my coach Andrew advised me, 'Just leave it alone'. I was angry at that . . . angry at the whole thing . . . but I ended up, reluctantly, just going with the flow.

So I finished up in a race in which there was basically only one other competitor who might go with me. In the following heat were the world 400 metres record holder Cheri Becerra and my main rival, the Canadian Chantal Petitclerc.

My heat was a solo journey, and I won clearly – in an OK time. But in the next heat, as I had feared, Cheri pulled the first lap in world record pace, leaving Chantal with the chance of bringing it home hard, which she did, for a new world record.

After that, I was really furious – angry that the heats hadn't been run as seeded races, angry that my world record had gone without my being able to defend it, angry at the coaches and organisers who had allowed it to happen, angry at Andrew – who wasn't very happy with me in return. All I had wanted was to have been able to get the chance to defend something that had been mine for five years. To be robbed of that chance in the way it happened was cruel and unfair. I made sure that everyone of note there on that day knew *precisely* what I felt about it all.

Later we went out and raced the 1500 – and I raced it angry, and won. It didn't make me any happier. I had lost a world record in circumstances that were patently unfair. Chantal had the world record – but I knew that if I had been in her heat, benefiting from the pace set by Cheri, I would have been there at the end. If she had beaten me fair and square, I could have lived with that. And if she had broken the record when I hadn't been there, that would have been OK too. But to lose your world record while you watch on helplessly from the sidelines . . . that was bloody awful.

In the cooler aftermath, I worked hard to take positives out of what had happened. It certainly made me think a lot more about what I wanted to do and what I wanted to achieve. It provided an extra spur for me to train harder, although with the Sydney Games only a year away the greatest incentive of all was clearly in view anyway.

The Atlanta affair left me with a fierce determination: to get the record back. It was a new goal for me, and I need those in my life.

The events in Atlanta 1999 provided a sour ending to a US trip I hadn't enjoyed too much anyway. The truth was, I hadn't really wanted to be there in the first place. I hadn't been pushing too well before I left, and to be honest I didn't feel that I belonged too comfortably in the group I travelled with.

\* \* \*

But another high succeeded the low of losing my world record. Being named in December 1999 as Australia's Female Athlete of the Year was one of the greatest thrills of my life. After all, I was picked from a field that included Cathy Freeman, Susie O'Neill, Karrie Webb, Anna Wilson and Zali Steggall. My God!! On the night, at the Regent Hotel in Sydney, it was indeed a fantastic surprise and an overwhelming honour. My mum was there, and she was so proud and excited – and when my name was read out and there was a standing ovation from everyone in the place ... well, recognition doesn't get much better than that. I had a great night, and went home glowing.

The next day, however, a storm broke – with claims that my selection had been in the realms of the 'politically correct', hints and outright declarations that I had only won because I was an athlete with a disability. 'Female Award Good Cause for Road Rage', read the headline in the *Daily Telegraph* above a story that described my award as 'a decision that is certain to cause controversy'. In the *Sydney Morning Herald*, Richard Hinds called me a 'deserving winner' – and then wrote: 'But does her being a worthy winner mean she was the *right* winner of this year's award? Not in the year of Karrie Webb'. (In 1999 Karrie had won six times and recorded twenty-two top ten finishes. She had earned her first Rolex Player of the Year Award, become the fastest player in Ladies Professional Golf Association history to cross the $3 million and $4 million marks and set an LPGA scoring record with a 69.43 average.)

My phone started ringing from early that morning – and rang all day. Mum was getting ready to head back to Perth and was keen to have lunch down at Doyle's at Watson's Bay for a last look at the city. I had training to fit in before that ... and the phone just never stopped. It was a tough day – and especially disturbing for my mother to have to listen to me virtually defending myself over and over again. I really don't know how many people I spoke to. But I do know that it was exhausting, and at the end of it I was absolutely drained.

By then, though, there was a lot more positive than negative. Friends and sponsors and people who knew me, and some others who didn't, really rallied round. 'You deserve it ... so much,' they told me.

When I finally dropped Mum at the airport, I still had an interview to do with Channel Ten, for 'Sports Tonight'. I got home at eleven o'clock. Late that night I was left there trying to convince *myself* that I did deserve the award – and that it was OK to accept it. I kept telling myself, 'Look, you didn't pick it ... it was voted on by more than 200 different people'.

So my emotions were mixed and the aftermath of the award was a real struggle – but despite the controversy there was a lot of pride too. To me this was the one to win. I had been nominated four times previously, and not won – even though I had been named ABC Junior Female Athlete of the Year back in 1993. At those times I would say to myself, 'One day I'm going to win this'. Very, very deep down I had really wanted to win this national 'all-in' award ... to become the first athlete with a disability to do it ... to show everyone that anything is possible. That was the beauty of it for me and, I hope, for all the other athletes with a disability out there: to be able to take my place alongside great sportswomen like the line-up of that year – and to win!

From today's more distant perspective, I like to think that, even though the controversy caused by the award gave me an uncomfortable and stressful following day, the overall effect was a wonderfully positive one for athletes with a disability. Sometimes I think there's been too much focus just on me – but at least now one of our own had been named female athlete of the year. That *had* to be special.

> *Shona Casey: Louise said to me one day that she felt guilty at the fact that she was getting more attention than any other Paralympian. She is a selfless person... But the fact is Louise is a bright shining light for her sport, and has evolved into a true leader – no longer being quite the meek and mild young lady I first met in 1993. These days she doesn't have any trouble expressing her opinion!*
>
> *We have a special bond... I can sense from her voice when things are right in Louie's life – and I know how high her individual expectations are of herself. She is a trusting, loyal friend to those who know her well, independent and determined. I don't think there's been a time when I have watched her up on the dais accepting the awards that have come her way that tears haven't welled in my eyes. It's just a feeling of being wonderfully proud of her, and of what she has achieved.*
>
> *Chris Shaw: Her mind is so focused, so strong. She comes across as very modest, which she is... but she doesn't take any nonsense from anyone. When we go somewhere and facilities [for people with disabilities] aren't right, she'll point it out. She is not backward in coming forward. In that way Lou is a leader, and something of a crusader.*

It is probably a result of my own success, and definitely a result of the rising profile of sport for athletes with a disability, that I am now a publicly recognisable figure. I'm sure I'm not in the Ian Thorpe or Cathy Freeman league – but to go to the shops now is usually to have people come up and talk, or stare. Lunch in a restaurant very often brings with it requests for autographs. I hoped from the start that the attention meant I was reaching people, perhaps changing their views about athletes with a disability, which has always been a very big issue with me. I am always appreciative of people's interest in me and support for me.

Funny thing is, I don't much notice people staring at me any more. You almost get used to it. Television guarantees there is no real anonymity for prominent athletes any more. In one way it's positive. Sometimes I think, 'God, I must be doing something pretty good . . . something more than other people'. Sometimes, though, it just wears me down . . . and I hanker for some peace and quiet.

I guess every famous sportsperson feels like that at times. The fact is that one of the prices you pay for being an athlete is that you are tired a lot of the time because of the training you do, and because of the disciplined, programmed sort of life you have to lead. Probably the majority of people never quite understand that – just how hard sportspeople train, just how much they give up in their lives. It can be a harsh business: there are so many people who train with immense dedication, making vast sacrifices in their lives – and then never get close to the high-level success they chase.

Having said all that, I go to some wonderful events, meet some really great people along the way, and have some wonderful times. And now that I have management support to help sift through all the requests, I have the chance to say no – nicely – when I'm feeling too worn down. That was something that was always a problem for me before. 'You're too nice . . . you can't say no,' Karen used to say. And it was true – I couldn't.

CHAPTER 15

# THE GATHERING STORM

My preparation for what was to be probably the biggest year in Australian sporting history, Olympic and Paralympic year 2000, was a bumpy and worrying ride. In the first few months of the year I was beaten in both the annual Oz Day 10K in Sydney and the Boston Marathon – two events I had worked so hard at making my own. Then, I had to break in a new chair, something that's never easy for me. Getting used to a new chair, finding the position that is just right for racing, can be a very difficult task. My neck is always a problem – having the chair at just the right height is essential to ensure that it doesn't cause me pain.

To tell you the truth, three or four weeks out from the Sydney Olympics, in my eleventh year of representing my country internationally, I was feeling like crap. Ask Karen McBrien; she can tell you that at times I fell pretty low, even questioned whether everything I was doing, or trying to do, was really worth it. Things had just not gone well.

For starters, my racing campaign in 2000 had kicked off with that loss in the Oz Day 10K. Heading into the event I knew I had a new and difficult opponent that year: the Japanese athlete Wakako Tsuchida. She clocked a very fast time, faster than me, in the Monday prologue – and the thought nagged me that it was going to be very tough this year. Wakako was a bit of a mystery; she hadn't competed in the 1996 Atlanta Olympics or Paralympics, or the 1998 World Championships in Birmingham. It turned out that she was a top-line Winter Paralympian who had switched sports. 'Don't worry about things you can't control,' my coach Gary Foley told me. So in the end I didn't worry – just went into the race to race my plan and to try and win for the eighth year in a row. And Wakako proved to be just as tough as we thought she might be . . .

It turned out to be a great race, with a pack working together up front – and everyone taking turns at doing some work. To her credit, Wakako Tsuchida did a great deal of the work up front, and after the hectic finish in which she held me off by a metre or so I told the media: 'It was great to race her because she led from the front. Finally someone was willing to go to the front and have a go. In previous years people have drafted off me.' And that was it: she deserved to win because she did most of the work.

Deep down, though, I was pretty disappointed. I am always an over-cautious racer, inclined to take the safety-first approach rather than take a risk. I made a really bad last corner – a left-hand turn, in which I swung far too wide. The others cut in tighter and stole almost two lengths on me and I just didn't have the time or the distance available to catch them, particularly as there was other 'traffic' (some of the men) to negotiate on the downhill run home. I got cluttered up among other competitors and only just caught Holly Ladmore for second place, just behind Wakako. With a clear run to the line, I'm sure I would have won the race. But she had earned it after the sort of race she had run – and I was happy for her.

There was a great fuss because I *hadn't* won. Holly was crying her eyes out, and I was there, gulping down my own disappointment and consoling her at the same time: 'Holly, it's all right'. 'No,' she said, 'it's not all right . . . you got beaten'. At fifteen, Holly had pushed a great race – her best ever. And here she was in tears . . .

I suppose people were especially upset because they saw the annual Oz Day 10K as belonging to me – just the way it was with Jean Driscoll and the Boston Marathon. And in truth, it had been 'mine' since 1993, providing an always-positive start to my year. There had been some good and keen races along the way. But now, in 2000, I had been beaten.

A few days later I breathed a little easier when I beat Wakako in a 14-kilometre international road race staged at Parramatta, outspeeding her in the final sprint to secure the Summer Down Under crown, an award that covered a sequence of races on both track and road. I won all the races on the track that year.

\* \* \*

But a couple of months after that came another loss – in Boston – after my three successive victories in the big race, which had effectively broken the stranglehold Jean Driscoll had held on the event.

Injury again gave me a troubled build-up to the race in 2000 – but a different injury. This time it was my neck, a chronic thing to do with the joint and the muscles tightening to the point where they can't be released. It's very painful. When it is at its worst, as it was over there, I can barely move. Increasingly I have difficulty flying because my neck gets really bad when I am on long flights.

In Florida before the 2000 Boston race I had been in bad trouble. It was only the work of Alan Thomas, one of the Aussie Paralympic team masseurs, who lives in Florida, and his wife, Sheila, that got me through. The treatment they gave me left me as sore as anything for two days but at least freed me up, gave me some movement – and effectively got me to the starting line. But I wasn't happy within myself. I had been away from Australia for quite a time by then, and I hate that. The long flights are a drag, as I've told you, and I felt that more acutely than usual in 2000. I went to Boston not feeling as confident as I had at times in the past and not really happy with my preparation. But I was there, ready enough to race, and I gave it my best shot.

This, however, was Jean Driscoll's Boston – her eighth victory. A group of four leaders had become three . . . and then two when we hit the hills. I stayed with her – but about halfway up Heartbreak Hill Jean got away and built a break on me that I could not peg back.

It was both a good luck and a bad luck race for me. A couple of kilometres from the finish of a race run into a strong headwind I knew something was wrong with my chair, something was loose. It felt weird and I began looking down, checking everything I could. Then I noticed that the spring unit that holds the steering together was cracked almost the whole way around. I knew it was going to go and I didn't know how long I had. From that point, I just wanted to finish – and I did, twenty-four seconds behind Jean, who later declared herself 'scared stiff' that I would catch her again, as I had in '98. Five metres past the finish line the steering unit on my chair snapped completely in half.

The equipment problem was no excuse. I had lost the race before that happened. But I was also very, very lucky: if the steering had snapped on one of the downhill runs I hate to think how I would have finished up. I could easily have been road kill! I consoled myself with the thought of that fortunate escape, but I felt disappointed about the race. I felt that I had let people down.

> *Tracy Harnett: One of the many terrific things about Louise is that whatever takes place in a race she never makes excuses – and to me that's the mark of a great athlete. Whatever happens she will never blame injury or the weather or whatever. She's just a great, great person.*

After the race Jean was going absolutely ballistic at having won her eighth Boston – a record. She had been trying for that for the past four years, and her joy was understandable.

For me, the night was quiet. In the previous three years, when I had won the race, my phone had run hot all night. I would get twenty or more phone calls: people ringing to say congratulations, and members of the media ringing for a talk. This night I received three. It says a lot about winning and losing in sport, I guess.

For me, there is an element of the movie *Groundhog Day* in the Boston Marathon: the same event repeated over and over again. In the two or three months after some of the races it has been firmly in my mind that I won't be going back, no way. Then suddenly it's April the next year and I'm on the plane for Boston and it's all happening again. There's always a moment when I think, 'I can't believe I'm here. I can't believe it's April and I'm doing this bloody marathon again'.

But I do. (Well . . . I did.)

The race has taught me a lot. It has taught me on the one hand what my limits are – but on the other hand it has taught me just how far I can push myself, just what I am capable of. Deep down I probably never really believed I could do what I did in 1998 – give Jean the start I did, and still beat her. That race was a breakthrough for me, eroding that old belief of mine that if I couldn't see the leader ahead of me then I couldn't catch them either. Awareness of the mental factor has been a continually growing feature of my career in sport, the knowledge that your body will take you just so far – and then the mind takes over. The ending of the 1998 Boston is about as dramatic an example of that as you could imagine.

I was chuffed in late '98 when Jean appeared on my 'This is Your Life'. 'You have done a great thing for our sport,' she said, 'and taken it to new levels. The people in Boston love our rivalry'. I really appreciated those words from her – such a keen opponent, *especially* in the Boston Marathon.

The defeat in 2000 convinced me of one thing: that I had to go back for one last time in 2001. For all my mixed feelings it was going to have to be a case of 'Heartbreak Hill, here I come' . . . again. And I knew that whatever happened then, I would never forget Boston, USA, and its big race.

\* \* \*

I ended up racing three marathons in three months that year: Boston, the Host City Marathon in Sydney and Sempach (in Switzerland). This was a far heavier load than I would normally take on. In a normal year I would race four or five marathons maximum – but in 2000 I was keen to tackle the Olympic course, and doing this meant the extra load of the Sydney Marathon. Long races are draining for wheelchair athletes – not quite as much so as for the able-bodied runners, but they take their toll all the same. Three in three months was a tough program. In fact, on reflection it was probably a very stupid load to take on – something I would never contemplate doing again. But it was my choice and there was no serious opposition from anyone telling me I shouldn't do it. And if there had been, I probably would have raced the three marathons anyway; I'm such a stubborn person. Through it all, though, in the lead-up to the Games I became increasingly stressed, and more and more tired.

\* \* \*

Early in 2000 I also learned the news that I had been offered a 'free ride' into the Olympic 800 metres demonstration race. Australia, as host nation, was offered a single wild card into both of the demonstration track events, the women's 800 and the men's 1500. It turned out that the men didn't even use theirs.

When I was told that I was the 'obvious choice' for the wild card entry, I raised the point that I was also one of the most likely to make it through the trials and qualify – and so why not give it to someone else? 'Nobody deserves it as much as you,' I was told, 'and we really feel we couldn't give it to anyone else. At least this means that if you get sick or injured or something – then you're still guaranteed a spot'. I finally accepted it . . . with some trepidation. The last thing I wanted was people whispering about my getting it handed to me on a plate . . . getting the easy road.

What I *wasn't* told then was that if I did accept the wild card I wouldn't be able to race in the pre-Games trials, to be held in Switzerland – although I would still be able to compete in the other European track meets. This really made me wonder whether I had done the right thing. For one thing, I was going to miss out on the sort of tough racing that can really put the edge on you, get you ready for something like the Olympics. As well as that, the race for the final seven spots would perhaps be very different tactically because I *wasn't* there. 'Damnit,' I thought. 'I would rather have been there to stir the pot . . . to make them race hard'.

\* \* \*

A burglary really rattled me in July and prompted me to install a home alarm system. Thieves got in one day and took a lot of things . . . a video, jewellery, my telephone and plenty more. It was very upsetting and unsettling. As I told journalist Kate Cox in an interview for the Sydney *Sun-Herald*, my house is my own personal space and I don't particularly want people to know where I live and what I have or don't have.

\* \* \*

But if the first half of 2000 is sounding like it was a pretty negative time for me, at least there were a couple of bright spots.

A new and sometimes troublesome element in my life came in the shape of Penny, the small, energetic Tenterfield Terrier who now shares my life. From Sparky in the early days all the way to Punch and Judy we had almost always had a dog around the place back home in Perth. When I moved into my own house I really wanted to get a dog – and my inclination was to go to the RSPCA and get an older one. A friend had told me of a dog with three legs at the RSPCA Centre – and I thought, 'Yeah, that'd be right . . . I'll finish up with a disabled dog!'.

But Margaret Emerton, a friend of Karen's and mine, had opened a pet shop at Seven Hills and we trekked up there one day to check it out. Penny was the only pup left from her litter, and was sitting all alone. For some reason they couldn't sell her. Despite my inclination *not* to have a puppy, I ended up with her, of course – and as puppies do she has brought both pleasure and dismay to my life, doing the usual amount of damage, like regularly digging up my rose bushes as I tried to settle into my new place.

She is already quite famous. The people who run the Lucky Dog Great Australian Dog of the Year Competition saw a photo of Penny and me in the 'Burke's Backyard' magazine and asked me if I would enter Penny, do a photo shoot and help promote the competition. So I did – and was given twelve months' supply of dog food, which little Penny took fifteen months to get through!

Penny goes almost everywhere with me these days – to the physio, on shopping excursions – and I miss her terribly when I go on tour. She's part of my life now, and I love her . . . well, most of the time.

\* \* \*

There were also a couple of huge nights in my social calendar in early 2000 – both a tremendous thrill. On 22 March I was invited to a big meet-the-Queen-and-Prince-Philip dinner in Canberra. I was extra pleased when I found myself sitting down the end with Michael Klim. That *was* a big night, all very formal and flash. The guest list was a sort of who's who of Australian life: the likes of Dick Smith, Peter Cosgrove, Kim Beazley, Ruth Cracknell and lots of stars from the entertainment and sports world. Sir William Deane and his wife were terrific that night, talking about the Paralympics and telling the Queen and Prince Philip all about me. They were very nice, and the Queen chatted away to me about what she had done that day, and that sort of thing.

I had a good ally that night in Dawn Fraser, a friend who has given me great support over the years. We sort of hooked up together. Dawn is such a legend, and a really nice lady. She is very supportive of what athletes with a disability do and has a real understanding of our sports. I always get the sense she would do anything she possibly could to help me. I greatly admire her strength and forthrightness too. She is never afraid to say what she thinks.

It was a once-in-a-lifetime sort of night, going to a dinner like that. Normally I wouldn't be able to do it, because of my training, which always comes first with me. And has to. But this was so special.

An even more lavish function followed in May: the first ever Laureus Sports Awards. At a glittering ceremony in a glittering town – Monte Carlo – I was named World Sportsperson of the Year with a Disability, perhaps the highest honour I have ever received.

I will forever cherish the award, a gorgeous thing in gold and silver, designed by Cartier. And to be named alongside the other winners, who included Tiger Woods and Marion Jones, was just a tremendous thrill ... unbelievable, really, and a further step in my quest to be recognised as the equal of the top able-bodied athletes. I was really up there with the sporting elite: European soccer champions Manchester United, Spanish golfer Sergio Garcia and US cyclist Lance Armstrong were among the other category winners, all of us selected by a panel that included the likes of Pele, Jack Nicklaus, Michael Jordan, Ian Botham, Viv Richards, Martina Navratilova, Edwin Moses and Katarina Wit, members of the World Sports Academy. And all this in Monte Carlo, playground of the rich and famous!

If it sounds like a dream ... well, it was and it wasn't. The whole thing was definitely a mixture of the glamorous and the not-quite-so-glamorous. When a representative of the Australian Paralympic Committee was unable to attend at the last minute, my mum was offered the chance to go with me as my travelling companion. She needed no prompting; she thought she had won the lottery.

I initially had no intention of going. I was about to head off to

Switzerland to get some serious racing in before the Olympics, and *that* was my focus. But it was suggested to me firmly that there was every reason that I should be there.

So Mum and I flew to Nice, via Singapore – and suddenly found ourselves in the midst of something that was a very, very big deal. Until I received some pre-ceremony paperwork over there I didn't realise just how big a deal it was. The town was full of celebrities: film stars, stars of the international stage . . . an amazing line-up of people. A fleet of Mercedes was continually whisked here and there, ferrying the guests around – us included. We did the tourist bit – went to the Royal Palace of Monaco, had a look at the Grand Prix set-up and went out sailing on the Mediterranean aboard a lovely yacht (Monaco's two ports are full of huge yachts!) on a most enjoyable day.

But, as I discovered, Monaco, like most of Europe, is not such a friendly place for people in wheelchairs, and I ran into lots of problems. I took my racing chair with me, hoping I'd get the chance to do some training, since I had big races coming up in northern Europe. But when we arrived at the airport, they picked us up in a sedan car and my chair wouldn't fit in. The driver promised they'd send it straight around to the hotel. We arrived in the morning – and by the next day the chair still hadn't turned up, and didn't until the following day. It had been sitting in a van. I was really worried about the whereabouts of my chair, and furious at the delay – especially when one of the guys nominated in my category in the Awards got to go training with Marion Jones on a track somewhere nearby! Monte Carlo proved generally difficult for someone in a chair, pretty inaccessible really. Inevitably if I had to go up in an elevator there would be stairs leading to it . . . and no ramp. I don't like being carried anywhere and I got annoyed at not being able to go where I wanted to go.

The presentation ceremony for the Awards was done in the style of the Academy Awards – running from 8.30 p.m. to 11.00 p.m. It was a wonderful thrill to win – and afterwards people were congratulating me and making a real fuss. 'Now for a bite to eat and a celebratory drink,' we thought. There were different restaurants at the place where we were – but they were all full. Mum and I were with Dawn Fraser and her daughter Dawn Lorraine – and Dawn was getting more and more angry and frustrated.

In the end I just couldn't stand it any longer. There were people milling around everywhere and I was stuck in the one spot and couldn't move. 'Let's go back to the hotel,' I said to my mum – and so we did. There, having just been named the world's number one sportsperson with a disability, in Paralympic year 2000, I celebrated on a single muesli bar, and a couple of packets of snacky things that Mum had brought with her.

Notwithstanding the hiccups, I'll never forget the night. When they read out my name, my mum just burst into tears. I much enjoyed the company of Dawn and Dawn Lorraine and we also hung out with US athlete Brian Frasure and his partner. I met some incredible people: I shook hands with Nelson Mandela and Prince Albert of Monaco, and chatted with Marion Jones (as you can see from the photo in this book!) and John Eales, with whom I spent some time at a very ritzy cocktail party held the night before. Ashley Judd was there and Samuel Jackson, Jon Bon Jovi, Sylvester Stallone, Dennis Franz from 'NYPD Blue', Naomi Campbell, Danny de Vito and Boy George. This was genuinely what the media like to call 'a star-studded occasion'. I can report that my mum was not impressed with Sylvester Stallone, who was much smaller than she had expected. All the while I kept thinking, 'This is mad ... me in the middle of all this, socialising with people I have never thought it possible that I would ever meet. And in Monte Carlo!'.

> *Rita Sauvage: As far as Ann and I are concerned we have reaped a lot of benefits from Louise's life in sport, attended her trophy nights and so on. Now, I had been to Monte Carlo. She has given us all a lot of joy and pleasure in a lot of ways.*

> *Karen McBrien: It was typical of Louise, who can be such a tough self-critic at times, that she was not happy with her acceptance speech at the Awards that night. The fact was that she had made a truly wonderful speech – as I realised when I saw the video coverage later.*

I have a house full of trophies now, and so does my mum across the other side of the country – and the awards won, the honours bestowed and the recognition given are very greatly appreciated. But to me, nothing beats the raw triumph of winning in the 'field of battle' through my own hard work, ability and determination. The victories gained doing what I do – racing in heat and cold and rain and wind in different countries against the best wheelchair athletes in the world – have always meant the most to me. To cross the line first in an Olympic Games, a Paralympics final (especially in Sydney!), a World Championship, a Boston Marathon . . . those are things to rejoice in, I can tell you. The 'glittering prizes' like the Laureus Award represent the icing on the cake, I suppose – overall recognition that perhaps you have achieved something worthwhile.

\* \* \*

Meanwhile, the lead-up to Sydney 2000 certainly brought its share of controversy for sport for athletes with a disability. In August a 'glamour' calendar for 2001, featuring athletes with a disability, had been launched, designed to help boost finances for the Paralympic movement as the Games approached. Columnist Miranda Devine wrote an article about it in Sydney's *Daily Telegraph* that basically seemed to state that she thought athletes with a disability shouldn't be presented in a 'glamorous' way. Here are some excerpts from the piece:

> *The calendar is gorgeous. From January to December, it is all sex, youth and perfect bodies clad in nothing but shimmering body paint and sequins. Pouty lips, tawny brown skin, long red nails, smoky eyes, jutting jaws.*

*Pecs to die for. It's the Body Beautiful, not an unfamiliar notion in 21st century culture. It is the altar at which we worship.*

*But this calendar is for the Paralympic Games. And nowhere is there a hint of disability. Wheelchairs, missing limbs, prosthetics . . . not a sign. The message is digestible disability and make sure you look cute too. Only the cover photo, of world-champion racer Louise Sauvage, gives a clue that the calendar is more than a lovely cheesecake, with the spokes of a wheel (a wheelchair? a bike?) in the corner of the frame.*

*But, considering we live in an era when supermodels are chastised for presenting impossible body images to young women and launching a thousand eating disorders, why would the Paralympic Committee be travelling down the same route? We can get calendars of beautiful people any time. Calendars of barely clad athletes are a dime a dozen.*

*Isn't the whole point of the Paralympics that the athletes are people who have triumphed over adversity, who have lost limbs, become paraplegic in car accidents, who were born with cerebral palsy, who spend their lives in wheelchairs? Surely the Paralympics represent the triumph of the human spirit over the imperfect body. Why then would the Paralympic organisation market itself on the attractiveness of its athletes and the illusion of physical perfection?*

*In many ways it is a greater achievement to be in the Paralympics than in the regular Olympics. What could be more inspiring than these heroic tales of human strength and courage: Sauvage, born with the spinal cord malformation, myelodysplasia, who has gone on to win seven gold medals in wheelchair racing . . .*

> By hiding their disabilities, the calendar does a disservice to the athletes and trivialises their achievements. These are more than gorgeous flesh. The calendar's deception is hand in hand with the apparent drive within the organisation now for recognition as elite athletes above all else. Sure, but what about those of the 4000 disabled athletes coming to the Paralympics in October who don't look so gorgeous? What's the message to them? Hide your disability and tough luck if you're not beautiful.

Devine's views generated a huge storm. I was overseas at the time with other Paralympians – and our attitude was pretty much: 'Why should we fuel the fire for her?' Whatever she wrote was her opinion, to which she was thoroughly entitled – although it soon became obvious that many people didn't share it.

Two days later the *Telegraph* ran a response from my manager Karen McBrien:

> It was with great concern and regret I read Miranda Devine's article (DT 14/8/00) regarding the recently launched Paralympic 2001 calendar. Having had a close association with athletes and people with disabilities for more than 11 years, I believe I have a greater understanding, knowledge and appreciation of members of our community who just so happen to have disabilities. I do not need to see David Hall's wheelchairs or Amy Winters' missing lower arm to acknowledge them as people or successful athletes. Ms Devine may like to note we do not run away from their so-called disabilities, we do not even try to hide them. The fact is their disabilities are just a part of our lives, as are many other elements that make up our community. Having a disability does not dictate that this must have an

> *apparent and visual impact that society should and must acknowledge in every circumstance. Louise Sauvage, who is featured on the front cover of the calendar, was born with her disability. She has been quoted only too often as saying: 'I do not see myself as being any different from other members of the community. This is the way I have always been, and I do not believe my life has been any harder than many people who faces challenges every day of their life. Each one of us faces challenges in one way or another and I think I've had a very good life and I know I've done everything I've ever wanted to do without a second thought.'*

I echo Karen's sentiments – I certainly didn't share the views of Miranda Devine. After all, why say what she said about us when so many other able-bodied teams and individuals had been involved in the same sort of thing? What is the difference? I am not hiding my disability. Was she saying that only the 'beautiful people' should do such things? Hello! Let's look at the able-bodied athletes on the Australian Olympic team. Not everyone looks like Tatiana Grigorieva, you know! Anyhow, all of it was publicity for our calendar and for the Paralympics . . . and that had to be good.

Later the media did their best to embroil me in another controversy that flared up when it seemed that Paralympians were to be billed $1085 each for accommodation in the Paralympic Village, while members of the 650-strong Olympic team were being given free board. The issue caused a huge, brief stir in the papers, with the media thundering down on our side and pointing out the unfairness of it all.

But my choice at that high-pressure time of my life was to stay right out of it. I figured I had enough to do, trying to prepare for the two challenges that lay ahead. Chances were that media and public pressure would sort it out pretty quickly anyway. It wasn't that I didn't think it was an issue – it's just that I decided I wasn't prepared to carry the load at this time. I had enough to do, getting ready to race at the Games.

I took a call at home from a journalist and told him, 'Look mate, I am not going to get involved. There are plenty of Paralympians who might share their point of view on it – but I'm not going to. Sorry'. They were keen to embroil me because I happened to be one of the higher-profile athletes, and involved in both the Olympics and the Paralympics.

As it turned out, basketball captain Sandy Blythe chose to have a say on it, and hit out strongly in the *Daily Telegraph*, calling the situation a 'farce'. He wrote: 'How in heaven's name can Australia as a whole – being a community that beats its chest and trumpets how it really is a land of the level playing field – allow this to happen?' 'Counting the Cost of Shame' was the headline on a strong and supportive *Telegraph* editorial alongside the Blythe article.

After all that it didn't happen and was settled favourably within twenty-four hours. Pressured by the media on an issue where they couldn't win, the Government quickly and generously stepped in and picked up the tab. This was an interesting exercise in people power, and in the power of the press. There was such an outcry that the politicians had no choice but to react.

By now it was early August and the clock was ticking towards two of the greatest sporting challenges of my life . . .

CHAPTER 16

# COUNTDOWN!

Just over a month before the start of Sydney's Olympics, I set out on a final trip to Europe – along with fellow wheelchair athletes, also Games hopefuls – as I searched for the tough competition I needed against the best in the world. First we were to compete in the Swede Elite Games in Gothenburg, and then in the Swiss National Championships, in where the Olympic 800 metres trials would be held.

On the August day on which I left Australia to begin the final countdown to the Games, I took on a new challenge: to scrupulously record (via dictaphone) a daily diary for this book. And through the long hours of travel, hard work and anticipation of August, the growing excitement of early September and the avalanche of pressure and competition in late September and October, I managed to keep the promise I had made to myself . . .

## Tuesday 8 August

Today it all begins. We leave Australia to go to Sweden and then on to Switzerland – where people will be vying for places in the Olympic demonstration races. I have already accepted a wild card for the 800 metres so I have automatic entry into that event at the Games – and I don't get to race in the trials. But I am still going to compete in the two track meets.

Training is going well. I had a really bad patch five or six weeks ago and wasn't sure whether I would even be ready for this competition – but I seem to have picked up and everything is going OK now. Lately my speed work is coming together well.

I am really looking forward to competing in Europe – not necessarily the travelling to get there(!), but arriving and doing some racing. Hopefully there will be some of the really fast girls there – and I can achieve what I have set out to do. One of my goals before the Olympics and Paralympics is to try to get my 800 metres world record back, and these are the only two track meets that will give me the opportunity. It's a case of waiting to see whether the conditions are right and the tracks are fast.

## Wednesday 9 August

We are in Gothenburg, Sweden. It's 7.10 in the evening and it's thirty-eight hours now since I left my house in Sydney. Everything is pretty good, although I am really, really tired. I have stayed awake the whole day, so hopefully I can get a good night's sleep. Everyone's luggage has arrived – except for my bag. My racing chair is here, my wheel bag is here, and my day chair . . . but of course my main luggage is not, despite promises that they were going to deliver it.

Later: I suspect the bag is in Helsinki, Finland... which is really great, because I'm in Sweden! Everyone has arrived safely now, but a few of the chairs are a bit damaged, including the steering on mine. I think we can fix it. So everything is pretty much OK – apart from my missing bag. The hotel is not really flash, but good.

## Friday 11 August

When I still hadn't received my bag late on Wednesday night I rang the airline (again) and some stupid woman hung up on me. I was very angry. I waited up until half past eleven, and no bag. Eventually I went to bed – and didn't sleep much. I was up at five, went downstairs – and there was the missing bag! During the night I had worked out in my head my letter to Scandinavian Airlines because I was so angry. I'm tired still, but after breakfast we trained at the stadium, which is only a short walk from the hotel – which is a plus, because it means we don't have to get on buses. Training was pretty good, although by the end it was getting a bit dangerous, with so many guys in chairs out there training. It's a drizzly day, which is a bummer.

In the afternoon our physio worked on my neck and my elbow – my 'trouble spots'. They are not too bad, pretty stable in fact. I went out to tea with the boys to an Italian place and was battling to stay awake. Everyone seems good, except Christie Skelton, who is off colour and didn't train.

## Saturday 12 August

Morning: Competition starts today. I didn't feel so good at training yesterday and I don't know why. My legs felt swollen. It was strange. For me it wasn't a good session at all. In the afternoon we went into town and I pushed my day chair for something like three hours – which was probably not the best thing to do, but we got lost trying to find some e-mail place.

Christie is really sick now. She went to the doctor yesterday, came back and got worse. She is not competing. I feel OK this morning and am looking forward to it. The track is great, although the weather isn't. I am hoping the competition will be strong, although it seems the numbers have dropped a bit.

Evening: It wasn't a great day. In the morning I raced the 1500, a straight final. I just didn't have any speed. It took me something like 100 metres to even catch them after the start. Pretty pathetic. I ended up winning the race but it was kind of a slow time and I am a bit disappointed. Races like that really reinforce, I suppose, how much work I still have to do before the Games.

I came back to the hotel and then returned for the 5000, later in the afternoon. I had a really, really bad stomach ache and was really flat – hardly had any speed again. It was another slowish time, but I sprinted for the finish and won.

My neck has given me a lot of grief today. It started after the 1500. I have been worked on tonight pretty hard so we'll see how I pull up tomorrow. I am used to being worked hard – as long as I am pain-free I don't care.

Christie is fine now. She went to the hospital last night and is on the mend. Greg Smith clocked a world record today, in the 1500. He went under four minutes and it was just so exciting. I am very happy for him; it's his first world record.

## Monday 14 August

Sunday proved a better day for me. I raced the 800 and the 400, with heats for both. In the 800 heat I went out hard and pushed the whole race by myself – and was really trying to go for a good time. And it *was* pretty good considering, a high 1.51 – but nowhere near world record pace as I had hoped. I was really stuffed at the end of it, though; I had given it everything I had. In the final I dicked around a bit and came home two seconds slower than I had recorded in the heat. I also raced my first 400 for I don't know how long. In the heat I clocked about a 57, which was OK. Then in the final I did just under a minute; the wind had picked up unbelievably and it was horrible. I won the race, though.

Greg Smith established another world record yesterday. My God, he is so good. Last night we had dinner at an Iranian restaurant, and it was an enjoyable and different experience. The food was good and I actually had a beer. I think Smithy kicked on – and didn't get home until early this morning.

Today was a rest day and we went into town, to do some shopping. I pushed my day chair forever! The cobblestones here are just horrible to push on. It is a real nightmare in a wheelchair.

I crave vegetables! Every place we go seems not to serve decent vegetables with any of our meals. It would be nice just to have something steamed.

Tomorrow is our second last day here, and it will be good to move on to Switzerland. My neck is still very painful – but I've got a lot more movement in it than I had.

## Wednesday 16 August

My training session yesterday afternoon was pretty pathetic. I just didn't have much speed. Last night we went out for a Thai meal – and it was the best meal I have had since I've been away. Annoying, that, and always the way: just before you leave somewhere you find something really good! Our first group has already headed off to Zurich, and the rest of us are going this afternoon.

## Thursday 17 August

We're in Zurich – well, actually at a place called Delemont, which is almost two hours outside the city.

Yesterday we had a pretty good transfer here, although it was a long trip. We flew from Gothenburg to Copenhagen – and got off the plane in the quickest time ever. It was just amazing. Two guys came to organise things and there were four of us in chairs and we went down that aisle so quickly! We were off in five minutes. We had four hours in Copenhagen – we couldn't find any Internet access, but we had a good dinner, and finally flew on to Zurich, reaching there about 9.00 p.m. I caught up with Kellie Puxty, who had been on a different flight. Kellie, who is from New South Wales Wheelchair Sports, is here on a grant, travelling with the team to learn more about our sport and the organisational side of it.

We got on a bus with some of the Japanese guys and had to travel for almost two hours to where we are staying. It was almost midnight by the time we got to Delemont – and we're staying at a boarding school – but it is totally accessible and there are showers! We had been told there were no showers there and we would have to shower at the track. The rooms are great and everything is fine.

## Friday 18 August

We went training and I saw Jean Driscoll and Wakako Tsuchida, the Japanese girl who beat me in the Oz Day race in January. (I call her Wako . . . I have trouble getting around the name, so she is Wako.) Both of them looked really fast. I had a good session too, then went into town, where I bought some chocky for my neighbours at home.

Back at the track in the afternoon, I saw Chantal Petitclerc, who was pushing really well, really fast. I'd like to know what speed she was hitting. She apparently has a broken leg or patella or something but it didn't seem to make any difference. It is kind of weird to see these girls – and know I am *not* racing against them in the Olympic trials. I am kind of glad about that.

I suppose I haven't been really super-confident about this competition . . . and I'm still not. I am sure when I get to the track and see all these girls again I will be freaked out. But everything, generally, is OK. Last night I attempted to make my gloves. Oh my God, I hate making gloves . . .

To push my racing chair, I use gloves that I have always made myself. I start off with baseball batters' gloves and tape them up and then use neoprene, the wet-suit material, as padding. I then use more tape and another rubber substance, which I sew onto the points where the gloves contact the push rims. It's a fiddly process and I can't say I enjoy it – I detest it, in fact! But my home-made gloves do the job perfectly: they provide good traction and wear very well. I try to make them last as long as I can because I hate making them so much. I just keep repairing and repairing . . . until I can't repair any more.

**Saturday 19 August**

Morning: The trials began last night. Unfortunately Christie Skelton and Holly Ladmore got knocked out in the first round. Christie was very disappointed, because she was beaten by a lot of people she usually beats. But she has been sick and couldn't be expected to be at her best. It's a shame; I think she would have made it through. So far two of the boys have made it through to the next round: John MacLean and Kurt Fearnley. We got home pretty late – me to have some work done on my neck which is really giving me a lot of grief. It was so stiff today it wasn't funny. We had to get up this morning at 5.30 and have breakfast at 6.00 to catch the bus at 7.00 – so I have been awake for a while now and it is not even 7.00. I have two races today: the 800 and the 5000. I don't think anybody among the high-profile people is going to race my 800, because it is scheduled before the other, Olympic trial 800.

Afternoon: It was really, really hot today – over 30 degrees Celsius. My 800 was OK. As I had suspected, I didn't have anyone to push with, so I did it by myself and was going all right . . . then I kind of died in the last 200. Again, no world record. Never mind.

Following on, they ran the Olympic trial races and I was very surprised at a couple of people who got through. I was probably *more* surprised at who missed out. Jean Driscoll was one of them. As a result there will be only one American in the demonstration race in Sydney: Cheri Becerra. I was very nervous watching it all. At times I wished I was out there, but I handled it OK, although it was stressful having to sit there and just watch – for both the men's and women's races. The men's races had lots of dramas and crashes.

After lunch I lined up for the 5000. It was so hot it was just disgusting. We all agreed that we were going to fry out there. I hardly did any work in the whole race. It was like catch-up the whole time and I felt really weak and just so hot. I briefly took a pull at the front and dropped the pace down to around 20 kilometres an hour.

It ended up in a final sprint and I managed to beat Wakako Tsuchida – by hardly anything. And I was just stuffed. I headed off the track and sat in the shade for a while, and could hardly move. It felt like my head was going to explode. I think it's the first time I've ever really had anything like sunstroke. Our team physio, Greg, came to see me, and rounded up some ice and tried to cool me down. I couldn't move, almost literally. Eventually I went back over to where my gear was, got out of my racing chair and basically sat there for two and a half hours drinking, with ice on me. It was just way too hot. I later found out that a couple of the girls had pulled out during the race because of the heat; others were in the medical tent getting ice and treatment.

At night they reran the men's 1500, after a crash in the original race, featuring a French guy and John MacLean. In the rerun John finished third – by two one-hundredths of a second – and so has made the Olympic demonstration race. Kurt Fearnley ended up ninth fastest overall. At the moment they are only taking eight into the demo race for the men. Kurt was naturally disappointed at that – but kind of happy that he is ninth in the world. He might still be a chance; apparently there is consideration being given to taking the field back up to ten – which is what it normally is at big meets.

Tonight, instead of a planned gala dinner we had pizzas and chips and wine to celebrate Smithy's birthday. We were all pretty tired after the early start and the day's racing in the heat.

## Sunday 20 August

I had just one race today: the 1500, run mid-morning when it was still pretty cool. There were two heats; in my heat I was in a group with Madelene Nordlund and Lily Anggreny, and when nobody wanted to take the front after I had pulled the third lap, I decided I might as well stay out there. With about 150 metres to go I really put on the power and sprinted home and won the race. So I'm back at our accommodation having lunch and relaxing – and it's lovely.

## Monday 21 August

Hi, it is Monday morning and we are about to go to Basel, Switzerland's second biggest city. Early on we went for a push and it was really good. It was the first time I have trained on the road for two weeks – and I really like training on the road.

Last night, when we had dinner down at the track, I had quite a long chat with John MacLean, a talk that continued back at our accommodation. I discovered that he doesn't feel very welcome within the team, doesn't feel like he has received much in the way of congratulations after making the Olympic event. I spoke with him about a whole lot of different things.

My roommate Kellie Puxty and I have been eaten alive by mosquitoes for the last week of staying here. It's just been so hot that we have had to have the windows open at night. There are no screens, so we have just tried to cope with the mozzies. Today I counted about thirty-five bites on my left arm alone, and I even have one on my eyelid. At about ten o'clock last night Kellie got out of bed, grabbed her doona cover and started whacking the mozzies . . . on the floor, on the walls and on the roof! She'd had enough.

I tossed and turned till about three o'clock, when a huge thunderstorm hit – with lightning and pelting rain. I got up and watched it at the window. It was amazing. Such a fine day and such a storm. It kept us awake that little bit longer. I was still up early, had a push before it got too hot – and was ready for the trip to Basel.

## Tuesday 22 August

I have been to Basel once before – but today I had the chance to look around and shop. It was great to have a break and get the chance to do that. Tonight the cook at

> the agricultural school where we are staying prepared dinner for us, and it was the best meal ever. We had lamb, which was just beautiful, and later they brought out schnapps and I had one of those – but didn't like it one bit.
>
> Today I think everyone is excited because we are going home. I can't wait. I just want to leave. It's a long haul: a two-hour drive to Zurich, a ten-hour flight from Zurich to Bangkok and then an even longer leg from Bangkok to Sydney. Then the other guys who are going interstate will have to catch their domestic flights.

Bangkok on the way home provided a glimpse of what it can be like when groups of athletes with a disability travel together. My own preference is to travel alone, or with just one other companion. There were twelve of us on that trip, and when we got to Bangkok we headed into the transit lounge for an hour or so. To rejoin the plane, passengers had to be ferried across to where it now stood – a fair way from the terminal. While the rest of the passengers hopped on the buses, we got loaded onto a truck, were driven ten minutes or so to the plane – and then sat there for fifteen minutes or so until they were ready to open the it. At least there were empty seats aplenty on the way home and the chance to get off your butt, stretch out and have a sleep.

On the flight home I wondered whether the trip had been worthwhile – the tough racing I needed had not really been there. I had gone away hoping to reclaim the world 800 metres record that I had lost in such infuriating circumstances. But in Europe I didn't get the chance to race against all the fast girls in the 800 metres Olympic trial – so that hope never eventuated. I doubted even back then that I could possibly do it at the Olympics or Paralympics – the racing at such meetings being much more about tactics . . . and just winning.

### Wednesday 23 August

> It's almost 11.30 a.m., eastern Australian time. I am back home in Sydney. The trip had its hiccups, but I sort of sat

back and let it all unfold around me. In Sydney we were the last people through customs and out of the airport. But I am home now and really happy, and with lots of mail and things to catch up on over the next few days. I have only ten days in Sydney before I head to the Gold Coast for training.

### Thursday 24 August

I managed to stay awake all day today. I woke at 4.00, tried to sleep for another hour, got up and watched an hour of television and then went training – at Homebush. It is just amazing how that place has changed in two weeks. The blue line for the marathon is already down and today there were cops and army people and sniffer dogs and everyone there. It was just mad . . . unbelievable. All of a sudden it looks so much like an Olympic City. There are tents everywhere. It was really something to see all that happening around me while I trained.

Today I also picked up my little girl Penny. She seems to be very tired – but she was pretty happy to see me . . . and I was pretty excited to get her. This afternoon I had a meeting with Karen to go through a lot of things, which was mad but good. I have hooked up one of my new racing frames and hopefully I will try that tomorrow. I also tried a new pair of gloves today. The Games are getting close now.

I had not had the chance to break in my two new chair frames before I went to Europe – so took an old one with me . . . and then unfortunately faced the task of getting acquainted with the new ones back home at a time when the countdown to the Games had well and truly begun.

Nothing was easy. After three training sessions in my new chair I was struggling. My neck was playing up, and so too the old elbow injury that is my constant travelling mate. There was also the challenge of getting training right for two closely scheduled events, the Olympics and Paralympics – of juggling a taper for the Olympics with more work on the track than usual so the taper didn't impact on my form for the Paralympics. All I could do was to keep plugging on – and hope that all of it was just the storm before the calm . . .

### Sunday 27 August

On Friday I trained at Centennial Park really early and used my new racing chair, which was OK, but feels kind of weird. It is a lot tighter than my other one, although the steering is looser than normal. I don't think my position is quite right yet. We'll work on that.

I'm still catching up after the trip, still tired. On Friday night I went to a fortieth birthday party; Penny came too. I wasn't really drinking – I had one glass of wine – but most other people were just totally pissed and it was really funny. Penny ate all the tinsel on the ground and then was in the ice tub the ice trying to eat it, which was also kind of amusing. I had a really late night. I probably shouldn't have . . .

On Saturday I trained on the M2 and felt terrible. I was all over the shop on the hills with my new chair. Not having had much sleep didn't help. Gary Foley came with me on his bike and got a flat halfway, so I pushed the rest by myself. I went and saw about the ramps for my house, which Karen's mum and dad are painting for me. Afterwards I attempted to do my insurance claim for the burglary at my house in July, and also my tax – which was absolutely horrible. I think it is the worst thing in the world trying to do that. Today I'm off to the NRL (rugby league) Grand Final match, Roosters versus Broncos . . . and I'm being picked up in a limo! Karen and I are going to a $650-a-head sports lunch beforehand, and then I get to be part of the handing over of Stadium Australia to the Olympics and Paralympics!

## Monday 28 August

Grand Final day yesterday was a lot of fun. We were picked up in a Mercedes – shame it was such a short drive to Stadium Australia! And the lunch was good. Tim Webster was MC and I sat on his table with Duncan Armstrong and Mark Tonelli and their partners. After lunch I went down to the players' level and out to the centre of the Stadium. There were three Olympic athletes and me, along with David Hall and Lois Appleby, and we accepted the keys to the Stadium. I got the key from Andrew Ettingshausen and Laurie Daley was up there, too.

The game wasn't great – because the Broncos won so convincingly. But I enjoyed the afternoon a lot. Wendell Sailor (the Broncos winger) impressed me. He is built like a brick! After the game, when we were getting into our limo, John Singleton and a couple of his mates got in with us. They were half tanked and gee, they were a bit rude and crude too, but also quite funny.

In the evening I had a commitment at Ryde-Eastwood Leagues Club: to be present when they did some lucky prize draws. I signed so many autographs, and afterwards they bought us dinner, which was really nice.

Today we trained at Eastern Creek and it was terrible. I felt really bad. I had no speed and just didn't feel like I was sitting properly in my racing chair. This was the third day that I have pushed in the new chair, and if it doesn't pick up or get any better soon then I'm going to have to go back to my old chair or try the other new frame out. I really don't have time to be wasting on trying to get this chair right.

## Tuesday 29 August

I'm worn out. I had a bad day and I'm feeling pissed off with everything . . . but that is becoming pretty normal! I pushed this morning and started to feel all right for the first time in my new racing chair. The position was a little bit better and that was promising. But the afternoon session at Narrabeen was not so good. It was blowing hard and my neck and shoulders and the top of my back were really, really sore from pushing in the new chair. At the end of the session we changed my position again; tomorrow I will try it yet again.

The afternoon was also busy, and at night Karen came over to talk about some things and got kind of angry with me. After that I finally had dinner and a shower and now I have to ice my elbow.

I'm feeling a bit negative about things. It's almost eleven o'clock and I have to get up early tomorrow to train. I am just annoyed with everything at the moment. I want to be in bed earlier than this; I don't want to be having dinner at almost ten o'clock at night. I hope tomorrow will be better.

## Friday 1 September

It's the first day of spring, and I'm in a better mood than when I wrote the last entry! On Wednesday I pushed out at Homebush for the last time. Everything is being taken over there. I did a photo shoot with *New Idea*: three different shots with different clothes and stuff. It was OK.

Andrew called me during the shoot and was really excited. One of the top Swiss guys had announced he was going to quit, that he wasn't going to come to the Olympics or the Paralympics. If he pulls out of the Olympic demo race, Kurt Fearnley, who qualified ninth, will get a go. Everyone is waiting to see if that will happen.

It's exciting news. In the afternoon, I had a gym session, a *Rolling Stone* interview and then Karen came for tea.

Yesterday, after morning training at Centennial Park, I had a meeting with David Tucker from Nike. They have agreed to give me some clothing and gear for this year! My God, I was so excited – it's like Christmas has come early this year. David gave me a couple of catalogues and said, 'Go for it'.

I had physio yesterday – my elbow is giving me a lot of trouble. It is very sore, although at least my neck is now pretty good. Also my new racing chair is going OK now . . . for the last couple of days it has felt better. I have been in a good position and I haven't been *totally* sore any more at the top of my back and neck. That's promising, because I haven't got a lot of time left to break it in.

We trained at the track at Narrabeen again yesterday. I don't like Narrabeen. It is a slow track and it always seems to be so windy there. You can't seem to get any speeds up – and as Andrew has said, now is the time when I really want to be trying to get some speed into my pushing. Some of the other guys are training at ES Marks Field, Moore Park, which is annoying news; I understood there were no tracks open other than Narrabeen. The ES Marks track is old and hard and good for wheelchair athletes. I had my hair cut yesterday – for probably the last time until November.

Today I went back to Centennial Park again, using new gloves – and getting blisters, which is very annoying. I can't seem to get my knuckles healed up. But the really good news is that I am now not going to the Gold Coast to train I didn't want to be away, messing around with my chairs the way I am. I get to stay home.

As my diary has mentioned, the Olympic area was closed off early as Sydney went into lock-down mode – meaning that the tracks were just sitting there, unavailable, while people like me puzzled over how – and where – to get the proper facilities for the training we needed. The plan was firstly the Gold Coast, then Canberra, and finally Wollongong for the team camp prior to the Paralympics. It meant more travelling, closing my house down and boarding Penny out with friends. It meant packing up and leaving Sydney – and sleeping in a strange bed yet again. In the wash-up I didn't go to either the Gold Coast or Canberra and was very thankful for that.

\* \* \*

In early September, I contemplated my place in the scheme of things as the two huge carnivals of sport approached. In a reflective mood I told the Sydney *Sun-Herald*: 'I didn't initially go out there wanting to be a role model, but along the way I felt I could change people's attitudes about athletes with a disability or people with a disability – through being successful and getting known. I suppose that's what one of my goals has always been: to change people's attitudes and perceptions about people with disabilities. I enjoy opening people's minds to a little distant area they've probably never thought about before'.

The Sydney Paralympics represented a brilliant, once-in-a-lifetime opportunity for athletes with a disability, and I really wanted the people of Sydney – and of Australia generally – to come out and see what our sport was all about. That's why I was happy to get out and work so hard in promoting the Games. Sport for athletes with a disability generally doesn't get a lot of media coverage. This was the golden chance, and that's why I wanted it all to be so successful and to be a great representation of athleticism. I wanted everyone to come and share the experience.

I remembered Atlanta, and how nobody much came to the Paralympics. Finals were run at the highest possible level in our sport at the '96 Games – and there'd only be 100 or so people in the

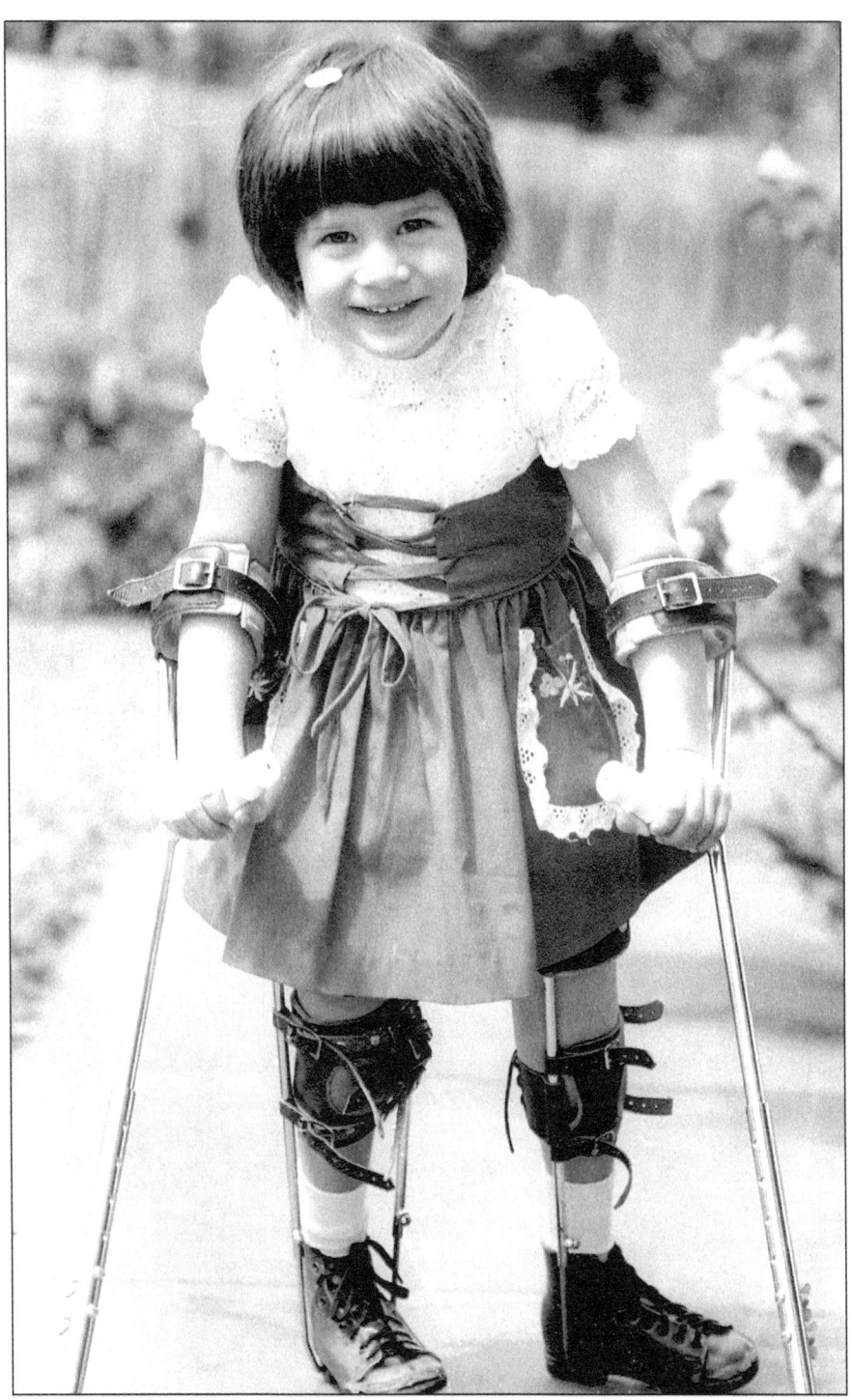

With callipers (leg irons) and a happy smile – me at three, and so proud to have been chosen as Channel Seven Perth's 1976 Telethon Child, to represent all disabled children in Western Australia. The photo, taken in the front yard at home, takes me back to one of my earliest memories in life.

Me at eight or nine months, in the back yard with my Raggedy Anne doll.

My christening photo at ten months, with Mum and Dad and a squinting sister Ann – out the front at the family home in Joondanna. Note the splints on my legs ... something I got rather used to.

The Sauvage sisters in 1974 – me with ball and, unusually, without plaster casts or splints.

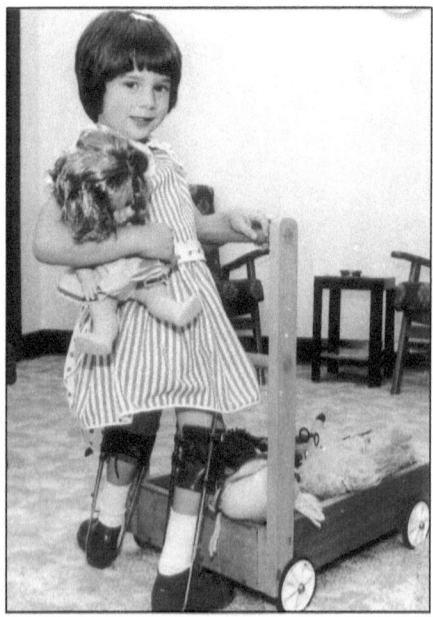

The Telethon Child of 1976, with a Womble and some other 'friends'.

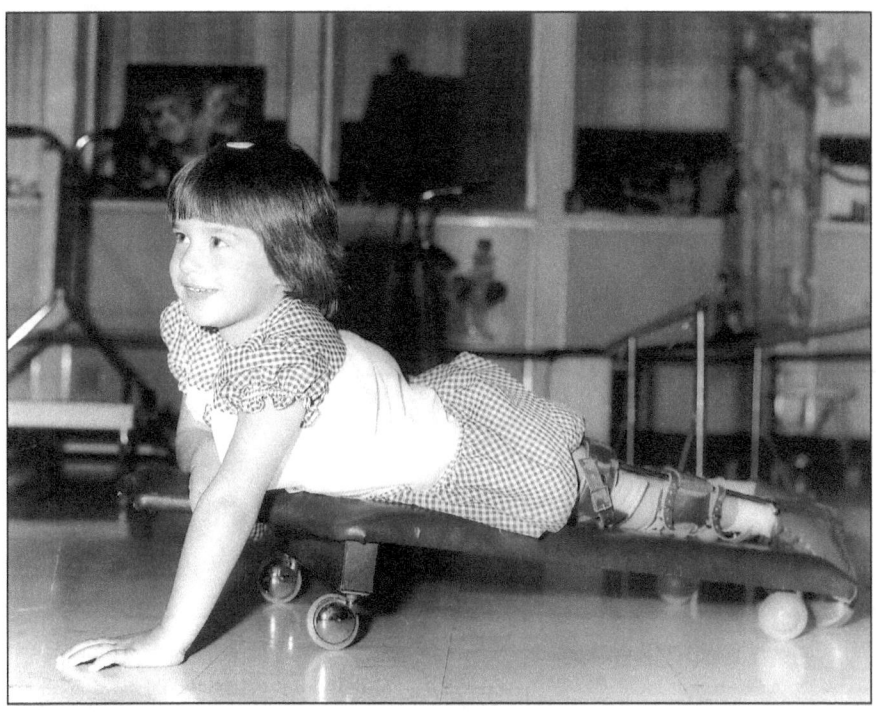

This was the hospital's skateboard – not the one that my dad was to make me later. It's 1976 – and I was to get pretty used to this method of 'transport'.

In the front yard at home – all dressed up and ready for a party.

I'm not wild about the look here, but it's a bit of history, I suppose – a photo from pre-primary days when I was four.

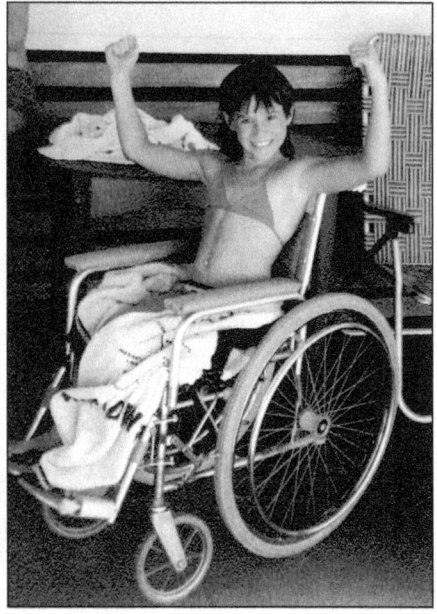

Ann and I in the Adventure Playground in King's Park, Perth. I'm six in this shot, Ann ten. In the background you can just about see the family dog of the time, Sparky.

How skinny was I here! And in a bikini! And how about the horrible old-fashioned hospital chair, bearing no comparison with today's sleeker versions! I was seven years old.

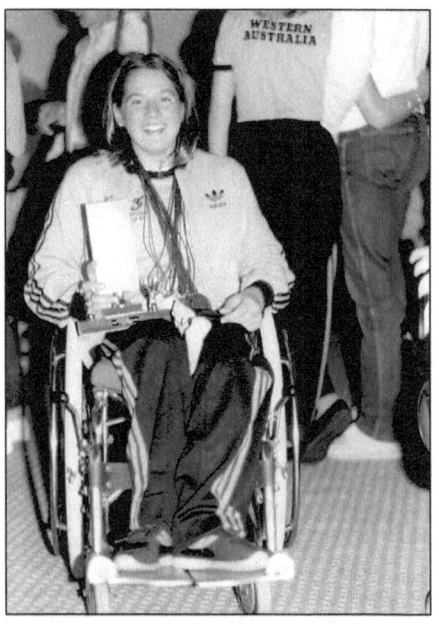

Proudly showing off my trophies from the Junior Nationals, Melbourne, in May 1985. The trophy on the right is for the best female performance in the swimming competition at the Nationals.

Perth Airport, May 1985, after flying home from the Junior Nationals in Melbourne – holding all my medals and trophies and feeling pretty proud about wearing the Western Australian team uniform.

This was the hospital's skateboard – not the one that my dad was to make me later. It's 1976 – and I was to get pretty used to this method of 'transport'.

In the front yard at home – all dressed up and ready for a party.

I'm not wild about the look here, but it's a bit of history, I suppose – a photo from pre-primary days when I was four.

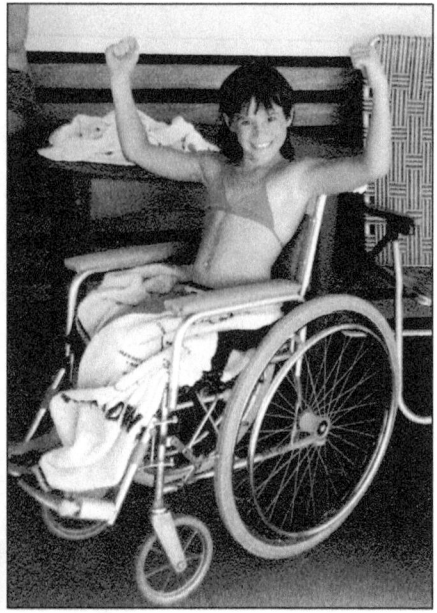

Ann and I in the Adventure Playground in King's Park, Perth. I'm six in this shot, Ann ten. In the background you can just about see the family dog of the time, Sparky.

How skinny was I here! And in a bikini! And how about the horrible old-fashioned hospital chair, bearing no comparison with today's sleeker versions! I was seven years old.

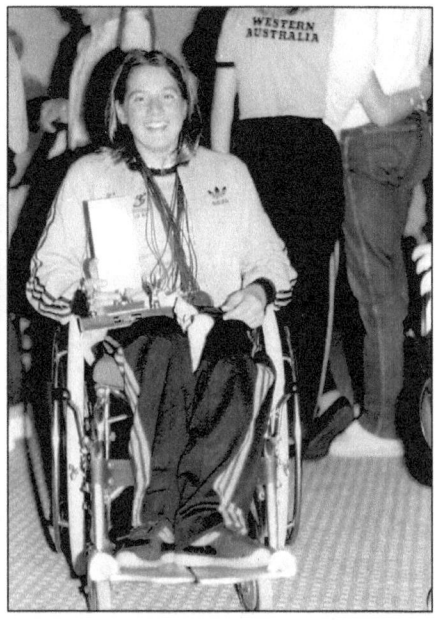

Proudly showing off my trophies from the Junior Nationals, Melbourne, in May 1985. The trophy on the right is for the best female performance in the swimming competition at the Nationals.

Perth Airport, May 1985, after flying home from the Junior Nationals in Melbourne – holding all my medals and trophies and feeling pretty proud about wearing the Western Australian team uniform.

'January was a whirl of competitive excitement for Joondanna lass Louise Sauvage', reported the *Community Guardian* of 7 February 1984. At ten, I had just come home from the National Senior Paraplegic and Quadraplegic Games in Sydney – where I had won two silver and three bronze medals.

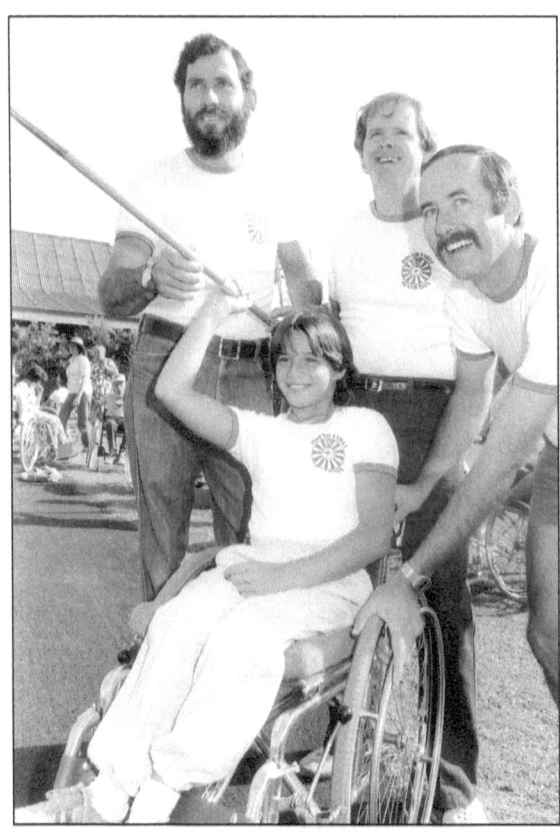

*left:* This photo represents a slice of history, recording the first time I was given some sponsorship support in my sporting career. I'm pictured with three members of the service organisation Perth Round Table, Neville Abrams, Steve Fletcher and Phil Capper. Round Table provided sponsorship support of $300 for me for the second National Junior Games for the Disabled, in 1983.

*below:* Joe Loval provides an anchor for my chair as I complete a discus throw (my best field event) during the Games. In the background looking serious is my first coach, Frank Ponta.

*right:* Ann and I attracted some newspaper attention in early 1983. I had been picked to compete in swimming, track and field events at the National Junior Games for the Disabled – and Ann, a few days before, had won the Under 14 Individual Championship at St Mary's College, Leederville.

*below:* The newspaper story that accompanied this photo tagged me 'The Joondanna Flash'. I'm at Perry Lakes Stadium in my first race chair, donated by Tuart Hill Swimming Club, before the National Disabled Games of 1984, to be held in Sydney. The photo shows so clearly how racing chairs changed once technology entered the equation. This old chair was pretty much just an adaptation of the day chairs of the time.

A photo taken by my sister Ann for a school project in 1985 – me with all the trophies and medals that I had won to that time.

A snap from the family's trip to east Africa when I was twelve.

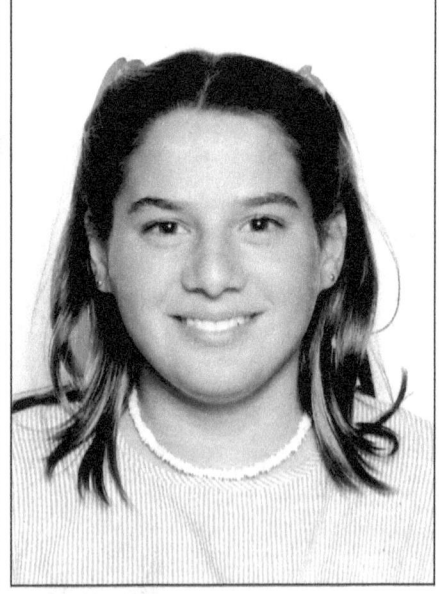

Wearing my favourite shell necklace, I'm in the summer uniform of Hollywood High – in my first year at the school.

My mum, such a great supporter over the years, was there to meet me when I flew home from the fifth Junior National Games, held in Queensland in 1989. I went as a member of the Junior Wheelchair Sports Club of Western Australia, and came back with a swag of records and medals. The big problem had been getting to Queensland at all during a national pilots' dispute. At one stage it looked like being a bus all the way – but in the end Qantas flew us to Sydney and a fifteen-hour bus trip got us the rest of the way to the Gold Coast.

Proudly showing off the first car I owned, a Nissan Pulsar Hatch, bought in 1990. In the background of this pic is Dad's yellow Kingswood. I was seventeen, and had just gained my licence. The arrival of my new car was a life-changing event – it meant freedom!

The back-yard pool at home provided hours of fun, day after day, year after year. This is a Sauvage family shot – and a pretty rare one of Dad in the pool ... he wasn't often there. In the background his grape vine is looking healthy. That's me in front – on the pool pony.

This is one of my favourite photos – of my cousin Jacquie and me at Mission Beach, Cairns, after we had safely negotiated a sky-diving adventure in 1998. It was a great Queensland holiday – with white-water rafting, snorkelling, sky diving and trips to the Barrier Reef.

A section of the Australian team training in Notwill, Switzerland, in 1998. At the back *(left to right)*: Andrew Dawes (coach) and Greg Ungerer (physio); and lined up in front *(left to right)*: John Lindsay, Geoff Trappet, me, Christie Skelton, Fabian Blattman, Paul Nunnari and Greg Smith.

On the track before one of my finals at the Barcelona Paralympics, 1992. I have just been introduced, and acknowledge the response of the crowd. This was my first international racing chair – and the last chair in which I raced with my legs down, rather than tucked underneath me.

This photo is recognised now as one of the most dramatic ever taken in our sport – the moment when I grabbed the 1998 Boston Marathon away from Jean Driscoll. Jean had already been hailed as the winner by the announcer and, as you can see, she has begun to raise her arms in anticipation of victory. I was in a state of shock after the race. It took quite a while for it to sink in that I had come from so far behind to win.

It's now well after the 1998 race and the medal presentation – and both Jean and I are little more settled as we pose for the cameras.

Shocked, but still gracious in defeat, Jean Driscoll offers her congratulations after the epic Boston race of '98. She couldn't believe what had happened – and neither could I. There has always been a lot of mutual respect between the pair of us.

In 1998 *Cosmopolitan* magazine picked their '30 Most Successful Women Under 30' of that year – and staged a dinner in celebration. I was honoured to be one of the thirty, as I was on two other occasions, and am pictured here at the highly enjoyable gathering which helped mark International Women's Week.

As my profile lifted in the sporting world, and corporate sponsorship became a fact of life, photo shoots became an occasional interlude in my life. This is one from the late 1990s.

Action from a Grand Prix event in the lead-up to Sydney's dual games of 2000 – and a perfect portrait of just how much racing chairs have changed in the years since I was presented with my first one, way back in 1983.

Here's me and my 'housemate' Penny, the Tenterfield Terrier who has shared my life these past couple of years. I love my 'Miss Penny' – notwithstanding the fact that she has dug up my rose bushes more than a few times! Thankfully she's more sensible these days.

This photograph marks a very special occasion: the Laureus International Sports Awards, held in Monaco in May 2000, a memorable night at which I was named World Sportsperson of the Year with a Disability. With me are Dawn Fraser, a member of the World Sports Academy which voted for the awards, and Marion Jones, who had just been named Female Athlete of the Year. It's a picture that means a lot to me.

It was Greg Norman *(left)* who passed the Olympic flame to me on the Sydney Harbour Bridge on the unforgettable day of the Opening Ceremony of the 2000 Olympics. Later Greg and I shared a car across to Channel Seven for interviews.

If you think it's relief that is the main emotion shining through from this photo of me winning the 800 metres event at the Sydney Olympics, then the vibes are coming through just right. I had struggled with health and fitness in the lead-up – and honestly felt pretty awful on the day. To win was just a mighty feeling.

The Sydney Olympic Games of September 2000 – and I have just won the 800 metres demonstration event. England's Tanni Grey-Thompson is urging me to take another lap of honour. But I decided not to – and I regret that now.

Thursday 28 September 2000 – after the presentation ceremony for the 800 metres wheelchair demonstration race, flanked by Ariadne Hernandez of Mexico (bronze) on the left and Wakako Tsuchida of Japan (silver) on the right, our medals firmly and proudly clasped in our hands.

The cauldron is lit – and I'm out there thinking, 'What a *massive* honour!'. It's the Opening Ceremony of the Sydney Paralympics, October 2000. In one way I was freaking out ... just at the immensity of it all ... and yet on the night I was much calmer than I had been in the practice sessions. On that great night, even with such a vast crowd watching, it felt ... just right.

'Team Sauvage', my own personal support team at the Paralympics – sporting the T-shirts my sister Ann had made up in my honour. The line-up is, seated behind *(left to right)*: my father Maurice (*not* wearing the shirt), sister Ann and mum Rita. In front *(left to right)*: Phil and Julie Crocker, my cousin Jacqueline Sauvage, Karen Long and Lee Hudson.

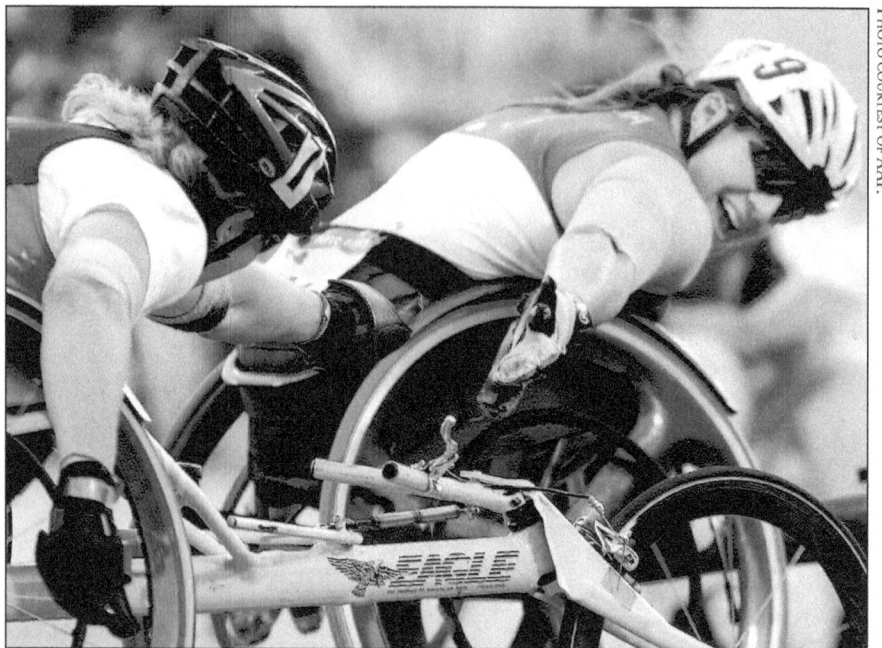

I have just won gold in the 1500 metres at the Sydney Paralympics – and my longtime rival Jean Driscoll is reaching over to pass on her congratulations.

The 2000 Sydney Paralympics 5000 metres final – and I'm away from the pack. But when no-one would come out with me, I eased back. My 'break' went for about a lap before I realised no-one was going to come and help.

*left:* On the dais at the Paralympics – a moment to acknowledge an always generous Sydney crowd, but also to think my own quiet thoughts of just how satisfying it was to win gold ... how all the hard work and sacrifice had paid off.

*right:* Monday 29 October 2001 was a pretty special day in my life – the morning when the 34-metre Supercat 3 Sydney Harbour ferry was named in my honour. I had problems getting the champagne bottle to break, but finally managed it – and so the *Louise Sauvage* was launched. I'm really chuffed to be in the company of some of the famous people who have had State Transit ferries named in their honour – the likes of Dawn Fraser, Evonne Goolagong Cawley and Susie O'Neill.

This is one of my all-time favourite photos – taken by my cousin Jacquie in Centennial Park, Sydney, one morning before the Boston Marathon of 1998. I'm with my coach Andrew Dawes, on a day on which the park was all but flooded. But the fact is that if you race in the rain – and sometimes you do – then you've got to be prepared to train in it. The photo to me sums up a basic truth of what successful sport is all about: if you're serious about what you do, about being the best you can be, then you'll be out there training in all weathers. You'll *never* miss a session. The photo also says a lot about the dedication of my coach Andrew. After all, he was out there in the rain with me!

stadium watching. So before Sydney I did my utmost to hammer out the message, whenever and wherever I got the chance. 'Come and support us ... come and see us race. You won't regret it and you won't forget it.' I must have repeated the message a thousand times. I stressed that the Paralympics were going to be bigger than the Commonwealth Games, bigger than the Winter Olympics ...

### Sunday 3 September

The Games are getting closer, and things are reasonable, although yesterday didn't start off too promisingly. I went training yesterday on the M2 with Christie Skelton – and my chair just wouldn't roll at all. It was horrible. Christie was drawing away from me – and I weigh maybe 15 kilograms more than her. This week I must find out what is wrong with the chair. I tried Kurt Fearnley's new wheels, because mine cracked – that was really nice of him.

Back home Penny had dug up both my rose pots and scattered potting mix everywhere. She had pulled out the brand new roses and chewed up all the leaves and spread mud all over my decking. I was so upset I started to cry. I spent the next hour cleaning it up. I was so mad with her I didn't want to even look at her. I didn't even tell her off. After lunch I went up to Parramatta and got some more potting mix and something to hopefully keep Ponny off the roses. We will see . . .

I caught up last night with Amy Winters, a fellow Paralympian with whom I had shared a house at one stage in Sydney. Amy stayed with me for three or four months soon after I moved into my new villa, while she was working to move into her own new place. We went to see *The Hollow Man*, which was a kind of gruesome movie – but good. When we came out of the movies they were giving away the next morning's *Sun-Herald* – and there I was on the front of the 'Tempo' liftout! I couldn't stop laughing – I looked so funny, just like a gypsy. My lips looked really red and I had big earrings on. The story was OK, although there were things in there that I wish I hadn't said.

Today, Father's Day, I slept in late – then rang my dad. He is at home by himself because my mum and sister are on holidays, and it was good to talk. Penny and I went around to Alison Quinn's house, and she has two big dogs so Penny was kept on her toes all day. (Alison is a fellow Paralympian – a sprinter – whom I have known for years.) This evening I watched a TV show, 'Winning Spirit', presented by Ray Martin, focusing on some Olympic athletes and their preparations for the Games. Something like that really motivates me, reminds me that I am not the only one out there doing the work. It is good seeing other people in the same situation as me. Then I watched '60 Minutes' – and that was special, because Sandy Blythe was on and I have been waiting forever to see his story. I have a lot of admiration for him; he is very genuine and a really nice guy. I read his book while I was on tour recently.

I usually don't get a lot of time to read; my days are full of training and preparation for the next thing ahead. But when I do read – which I do more of when I'm away from home – I like true stories, biographies . . . things that are real. In the search for balance in life, a couple of hours with a book is a great way of getting away from it all, losing yourself in a different world.

### Monday 4 September

For the first time today I felt really comfortable in my new racing chair. But the chair still won't roll, and that's bad, and worrying. I honestly think we are going to have to try another chair – or go back to the old one. Today I have hooked up the other new frame and we will give that a go tomorrow.

## Tuesday 5 September

I've had a terrible day and I am really, really tired. The morning session was OK. I tried the new racing frame, and it felt all right and rolled heaps better than the other one. But this afternoon at Hensley Field, Botany, it was so windy I could hardly push and I couldn't even stay in the draft; Andrew got really angry and frustrated and so did I. He said I should go back to my old chair, which I don't want to do. But it's looking more and more like I might have to. I ended up not doing a session and now I have to make it up on Saturday, which is a pain.

I spent an hour and a half at home trying to fix my old chair. I couldn't do it – and I'm going to have to go and see Jeff Wiseman, who is in Dee Why. (Jeff was one of the first wheelchair racers in Australia and runs a wheelchair repair services these days.) Tomorrow I'll use my new chair again. Nothing is proving easy.

## Wednesday 6 September

Tonight I'm in a better mood. Today was OK. I pushed in one of my two new racing chairs this morning and it was fine. But at home the dog has dug out my rose plants again. I could kill her.

Personally, I'm feeling quite good – my neck is *really* good and my elbow is OK. I'm still juggling chairs and went around to Jeff Wiseman's place and left him with one of the new chairs. He is going to try and fix it. It was way off track, toeing in, with the whole chair veering off to the left; hopefully that is the reason why it rolls so badly. Meanwhile my old chair is up and running once more. Jeff fixed the front end to stop the movement and we put in new bushes; I will push in it tomorrow, and hopefully everything will be fine.

Everyone else has gone up to the Gold Coast to train and compete this weekend. John MacLean and I were the only two who didn't go from New South Wales. But the place where they're staying up there sounds good. The track is great and there's a big meet on. Andrew rang to tell me about it. But I have no regrets . . . I've got so much on here in Sydney. Trying to get these chairs organised is the big task.

**Saturday 9 September**

On Thursday morning I pushed in my old chair and it was OK, but in the afternoon I went to the ES Marks track with Gary Foley – and pushed poorly again. No speed. I was doing 400s and I couldn't even get under a minute. For me a good training time in those sorts of circumstances is 56 or 57 seconds. I was feeling very bad.

On Friday I talked to Andrew and let him know that I'm not really happy with a lot of things. I don't know why exactly. And I don't know why I am pushing so badly either. Andrew and Gary don't seem to think it is that bad; I am more stressed than they are. With me, if I don't push well, I don't feel good.

In the evening I drove to the airport and picked up Lee Hudson from England, whom I have known for much of my life, through the family. Lee has been here before and has come back to work and travel. It's like a zoo out at the airport – with so many people it's unbelievable.

Today I trained two sessions – one to make up for the bad session on Tuesday. We pushed in the morning on the M2. Lee came on a bike that we borrowed and Gary came too – and we had a really good session. I rolled pretty well and felt strong, so I am quite happy about that.

Then it was off to Hardwarehouse to get some chook wire to keep Penny out of my roses – hopefully!

At ES Marks in the afternoon it blew a gale again. I don't think there has been a non-windy day in Sydney since I came back from overseas. But I pushed OK – I got up some speed for the first time in three weeks. I feel quite happy with today's sessions.

## Tuesday 12 September

I know I should be doing this diary every night – but I keep thinking Lee is going to hear me talking to myself and think I am a bloody idiot. My days have been full and a bit of a mixture as the opening of the Games approaches.

Yesterday I went back to training in Centennial Park, and did 1000s and felt pretty good. My Cateye speedometer has been playing up, so my 1000s were either just over or just under, which really annoyed me. I just couldn't get it to work. Then I went to the gym – and couldn't find my gym program. I think I'm going mad! Andrew tried to fax it from the Gold Coast, but the people in the office misplaced it, and now the only copy he has is on his computer back home. I did a gym session anyway and later went to the ABC studios at Gore Hill, where I did a prerecording for the show 'The Fat'. I was the only female on the panel, but it was OK. I wasn't too stressed. Tony Squires, who hosts the show, is a really nice guy.

Every day there seems to be something up. This morning when I went to Centennial Park for training the gates were closed. I ended up parking in the street. Like yesterday, my Cateye wouldn't work in training and I got angry again. I seem to lose my temper very quickly these days! It doesn't seem to take much to stir me up.

Afterwards I hooked up with Indra Reinpuu, one of the coaches of the Olympic women's volleyball team, and with some of the other volleyball people. It was so good to finally meet them all; Indra has been e-mailing me for a long time now and I felt like I knew them, although I had never met them until now. I enjoyed having breakfast with them – and thank you to the IOC for paying!

At ES Marks this afternoon I did 400s, and they were quite good considering that I have been struggling lately. I recorded a couple of good times. As we left the ground, there were a number of Olympic athletes coming in, which was exciting. The Opening Ceremony is in three days' time! Tonight Lee cooked me dinner, which was lovely. I am really tired, though.

**Thursday 14 September**

Today has been full-on: training in the morning and then out to the Uni of Western Sydney at Rydalmere for Olympic team processing – at which we received all our uniforms and tons and tons and tons of stuff, all sorts of clothing and other gear. We had our blazers presented to us and there was a singing group from the University, who were really good. After processing we went to accreditation, and finally home after a long, long day. I am so tired – and I know I have to be up just after three in the morning so I can get to the Town Hall to catch the bus and do my leg of the Torch Relay. I am carrying the torch over the Harbour Bridge and then going to the Opening Ceremony. It is going to be a very big day . . .

I had known for quite a time that I was going to get the chance to carry the torch. The Olympics Minister Michael Knight had rung me earlier in 2000 and asked me if I could like to take part. The answer, of course, was yes! He said he couldn't tell me exactly where or when I would be carrying the torch but that I would have a 'pretty prominent place'. It was such exciting news and I really had no-one to tell – except there were some workman out the back of my place, putting in the decking. So I shared the news with them. It was only later that I learned Greg Norman would be passing the torch on to me, and I would be carrying it across the Harbour Bridge . . .

CHAPTER 17

# LET THE GAMES BEGIN

The long wait was finally over. Living in Sydney, it seemed that the city had virtually held its breath for months . . . years, really . . . waiting for the arrival of the Olympics. I think that most people accepted that it would be a once-in-a-lifetime thing; they remembered Melbourne, so long ago now. The city was all geared up to make the most of the opportunity. Absolutely. And at last, on Saturday 16 September, in my diary I could write the words: 'The Olympic Games are on!'.

**Saturday 16 September**

The Olympic Games are on! Yesterday was just a massive day. I was up at 3.15 a.m. and headed into the city with Karen, my racing chair in tow. Greg Norman was there – and so too a few people still partying from the night before, who were a bit the worse for wear.

It was all pretty exciting. We got on the special buses and I was a bit stressed about my chair – and about the whole thing, I suppose. On the bus we met our guide runners and all the other torch bearers for that leg of the Relay, and learned how they got involved.

I got off the bus on the Bridge, leaving my day chair on board, and there were so many people gathered there it was just unbelievable. The crush was so great the organisers ended up closing the Bridge to traffic.

Eventually the torch came to me, via Greg Norman – and he gave me a kiss and a hug. Then, after a brief moment when I thought it wasn't going to light, off I went. They put the torch in a little holder attached to my chair so that I could push without having to hang on to it, but I got them to take it out of that and I ended up carrying it, then passing it on to my guide runner, Lucy, for a little while. At the end I handed it over to Nicole Kidman's dad – although I didn't know then who he was. On the bus we'd only used first names.

Everyone was screaming and yelling. The atmosphere was unbelievable. People seemed so proud and happy that the torch was there. And I was carrying it – and it was quite overwhelming.

Afterwards, Karen and I travelled with Greg Norman to Channel Seven, to do the 'Olympic Sunrise' show with Joanna Griggs and Andrew Daddo. Greg Norman is really nice and he signed an autograph for a friend of mine. I was home by eight – drained, but elated. I was just getting to sleep when my mum rang; they had just seen my leg of the torch relay via a delayed telecast in Perth. She was all excited and happy. Afterwards sleep wouldn't come – I just lay there thinking about it all.

The day had really only just begun. In the afternoon, Andrew, John MacLean and Kurt Fearnley (who is now competing in the men's 1500!) met at my house and we headed to the Olympic Village and got changed there to march in the Opening Ceremony. It was so great to see all the Aussie athletes, all the ones you don't see very often – in the flesh, anyway.

We assembled in the Superdome, just across from the Stadium, and for us it was a long wait. Being the host country, we were the last out . . . and had to wait for the other 196 countries to head off. Big screens gave us a look at the spectacular taking place next door. In the Superdome, among the many other athletes I talked to, I met Monica Seles. Well, I didn't really get to *meet* her – but at least I had my photo taken with her. That was amazing. I'm a big, big fan of Monica's. That was close to my highlight of the night!

At last we filed out. Everyone was yelling and screaming although we weren't even in the Stadium yet. Down the tunnel were all the performers who had been part of the opening so far – and they were just going wild! The noise in the tunnel was deafening. I was sitting next to Alison Inverarity and all of a sudden she started to cry. And I was telling her, 'Don't cry. This is really happy . . . come on'. But she just couldn't help it . . . and I understood. Then we were out in the arena . . .

I was three rows back. There was Cathy, Melinda and then me on the outside, closest to the crowd. And it was just amazing . . . the cameras flashing, the noise just unbelievable right throughout our slow march. We finally reached our spot at the head of all the nations – and stayed there to watch it all unfold. The torch went around from one great Australian female athlete to the next . . . and then finally to Cathy Freeman. It was wonderful. Amazing. I am so glad I was there. The funny thing was it all seemed over very quickly, as if time had sped up.

After it all ended, we hooked up with Julian Foxton, who lives up the road from me and had been in the audience, and they organised a couple of buggies to drive us back to the site and then home. It was 1.30 a.m. when I got home. A couple more hours and I would have been awake a full twenty-four. What a day! I was unbelievably tired.

I slept in this morning – no surprise there – then went training in Centennial Park late morning. It was back to some degree of reality. I was meant to head off to Canberra today – the whole New South Wales wheelchair squad was scheduled to go there for a week or more. But there are problems with our accommodation at the training venue; the hotel we wanted to stay in is booked out. After training we held a meeting – and decided that we wouldn't go to Canberra after all.

### Sunday 17 September

I was close to the Olympic Village today, in Carter Street at the Qantas Club they have set up. I went with Karen, and Dominique Maher from Qantas was there – and it was really good, with a big screen, nice food and a relaxing atmosphere. We just chilled out . . . no official duties or anything.

Tonight Karen rang me. 'It's your birthday tomorrow,' she said. 'We've really got to do something special.' I hadn't even thought about it, the fact being that I was supposed to be in Canberra. But the decision was that if the weather was good a barbecue at Karen's would be an ideal way to celebrate.

### Monday 18 September

I got some good prezzies for my birthday: a photo frame with 'Rrrough' on it for a pic of the dog, a wind chime, some lipsticks from Aunty Margaret and a bear that you put in the microwave and take to bed all nice and warm. I trained twice, and while I was there Paul Nunnari, a good friend and fellow racer, gave me a big bunch of flowers.

In the end we were a bit short on numbers at the barbecue because the notice was so short – but it was a good group, and a lot of fun, especially when some marijuana that someone had stashed under the communal barbecue of the apartment building finished up on the fire, smelling the whole place out! We had three kinds of ice-cream cake. I admit to *loving* ice cream. It was a good birthday, a nice interlude in between all the hard work . . . and with the Olympics going on all around us.

### Tuesday 19 September

Today was nothing mega – but my speed in training wasn't bad at all and I felt pretty good for one of the first times.

### Wednesday 20 September

Training, then physio – I am pretty happy with the way things are going. There was a phone link-up of the athletes who are on the Australian Paralympic Athletes' Committee (including me) to go through the nominations for the captains of the Australian Paralympic team – and the flag bearer. I was nominated for both, but I pulled out of the running for the captaincy. I didn't really want that responsibility. But I would love to carry the flag. That would be a huge honour . . .

### Thursday 21 September

My three 600 metres time trials this afternoon were good news. I was only scheduled to do two, actually – but the first was kind of slow, then the second faster and better. I decided I wanted to have a third shot at it and recorded a faster time again, although probably not as fast as I would have liked. But I was pretty happy with it.

Tonight Lee and I decided to go to the Qantas Club for dinner to watch the swimming on the big screen. At the club Steve Loader asked us if we'd like to go one better – and actually go down to the swimming. Would we! So we ended up at the Aquatic Centre, sitting in the Olympic family section – about four rows back and across from Chelsea Clinton. Lee and I were very excited. We caught up with Steve later and headed back to the Qantas Club.

## Friday 22 September

My race is getting close, and I'm tapering. I pushed in Centennial Park this morning, but I'm not really doing anything full-on. Today was a day for running around – getting odd jobs done. Kurt and Andrew came round and we all decided we would go to the Village, check out the transport and have dinner there. A couple of volunteers recognised us, but I'm sure most people were confused as to why we were there.

I had a phone call from my sister Ann today, which surprised me a little. She rang to wish me good luck for Thursday and was telling me to believe in myself – that I had the experience and that's what was going to matter. I don't really talk with my sister much about things like that – but I know my family want me to win more than anything. It was nice, really thoughtful of her to say those things.

## Saturday 23 September

Last night was pretty late, watching events at the Olympic Stadium with Kurt and Andrew. It's kind of scary to think I am going to be down there soon competing myself.

I went to Centennial Park today and did 1000s. I was supposed to do six 1000s, but did only three and they were totally different. Andrew is really toning down and tapering what we are doing. I felt pretty good – got some good speed up and was happy.

### Sunday 24 September

Today I dropped Penny off at her friend's house. Penny is very fond of Amy, a little white Bichon who belongs to my neighbours, the Foxtons. Then I headed out and picked up a sander to try and get the stains off my decking so we could paint it. But it didn't work too well – and I ended up painting Penny's dog house instead, a purpley-mauve colour. I am sure she won't be impressed. I am tired these days, and not sleeping well. Just three training sessions now until I race.

### Monday 25 September

Tonight I watched on TV as Cathy Freeman won a gold medal in the 400 metres. I can't really imagine how she feels. Very relieved, probably. There has been so much pressure on her – with the whole country expecting her to win. Tonight that dream came true and it was fantastic. I was so excited, I could hardly contain myself. It was just a great feeling.

Up until now I have just been *watching* the Olympics and I know it is going to freak me out a bit to actually be there on Thursday. I really must stay calm and focused. The scenarios go endlessly through my mind: win, lose or draw. But in my mind you come first or nothing. I want to win gold more than anything – but who knows? I think I really have to try and convince myself a bit more that I can win! Hopefully I will be prepared on the day . . . hopefully it will all come together then. I am getting lots of good wishes and cards, and people saying they believe in me and it doesn't matter what I do . . . they'll still admire me. That's so nice.

As the race neared I remember I grew more and more stressed. I couldn't sleep and I became increasingly tired as the days rolled on. I was starting to think over and over about all the things that could go wrong. Eventually my body broke down and I picked up a really bad head cold.

### Tuesday 26 September

Today it is raining and thundering, and last night I had a terrible night's sleep. I don't know . . . I just can't seem to sleep. I didn't have to get up early and train this morning and I thought that would help. But no, if I put pressure on myself to get some sleep . . . I can't.

This morning I took Lee to have a hit on the tennis courts at Wheelchair Sports in Ryde and then moved on to the physio, Kingsley Gibson from the State Sports Centre, who is really good. I trained in the wet at ES Marks this afternoon – not a fantastic session but a consistent one considering the conditions.

I feel a bit off-colour – as if I am getting a cold. I can't even *allow* myself to think of that, though – and hopefully it will be all right. Tonight, two days from the race, there were some phone calls from people ringing to wish me well, and I packed my things for moving into the Olympic Village tomorrow. It is raining. I don't want it to rain on Thursday.

### Wednesday 27 September

This morning, before I moved into the Village we went for a push in Parramatta Park. It was storming and raining and horrible – and we got *saturated*. Back home, I sorted out Penny; she is going to stay with the Foxtons. Finally settled in the Village, I am feeling less nervous today – certainly better than I did yesterday. I am not as worried. But I have more of a flu today; my nose is blocked and my head aches. I'm sure I've brought it on myself, not being able to sleep these last few nights.

When I think back on it now I can't believe how unfit I felt, on the eve of the biggest race of my life. My head was a jumble of worries and stresses – about the race, about not getting enough sleep. I suppose I wasn't the only athlete with those sort of problems. But the lack of sleep, the training that I was still doing in the lead-up, the stress – all of it added up to someone who was vulnerable. I pushed my day chair from where we were dropped off at the Village to our lodgings. By the time I got there, I was stuffed. I felt just awful. 'I can't believe this . . . I've got to race tomorrow night,' I thought to myself.

In the Village they'd put the wheelchair athletes into what in reality was a container – like a big box, with the beds up each end and the bathroom in the middle. The two male racers, John and Kurt, were up one end and I was sharing with Andrew down the other end. It was hot and pretty horrible. It was lucky we didn't have to be there long.

The night before our races the boys went to the track for a push. Because I wasn't well, Andrew and I decided that I wouldn't do any work that evening – but I went to the track to watch anyway, knowing that some of my competitors would be there. A fitful sleep that Wednesday night was punctuated in the early hours of the morning by rain drumming on the roof, just like the day before. 'Please don't let it rain tomorrow,' I said to myself again as I lay there. 'I don't want to race in the wet.'

But next morning I awoke to the sound of raindrops drumming on the roof. 'Just great,' I thought. 'I've got a cold . . . and it's raining!' Tuesday's rain had been the first in what had been a magical period during the Games, and on race day the clouds again hung low and heavy. I contemplated a wet racetrack, which would make things even harder. But by the afternoon of the 28th it had cleared to sticky hot.

The morning of the race dragged – a fairly late breakfast then back to the 'rooms' to change tyres on my racing chair, to tape numbers on, to cover sponsors' logos and to pack my bag ready to go to the track. I was still having breathing troubles, thanks to my cold. Fighting my illness, I dosed myself up as much as legally possible: I took some Panadol for my thumping head and had a nasal spray with me, but I didn't want to use it too early – I needed it to be effective for race time. I desperately wanted to feel a bit better for the race, but the truth was . . . I felt crap.

After lunch and a brief lie-down – a chance to get some mental focus, and to doze a bit – it was time.

The Australian team HQ informed us that there would be an accessible bus to take all the wheelchair racers across to the Stadium at 4.30 p.m. So the sixteen of us in the two races gathered at the transport mall for the bus – where it soon became apparent that no-one knew anything about it. So there we waited: sixteen athletes with day chairs and race chairs . . . and no bus. We Aussies wanted things to be right and squirmed when they weren't. The wait for an accessible bus, thirty-five minutes or so, was long enough for some of the athletes to give up and head off to push down to the Stadium, a fair haul.

Finally, at the Stadium, there was still time to fill in. I kept looking at my rivals. I hadn't seen them for a month or so, hadn't raced against them for quite a time. I wondered how they had been going. Amidst all the tension in that highly charged atmosphere everyone was getting into their race chairs early – something I definitely didn't want to do. So I just messed around, said g'day to everyone, and spent time talking to Dr Jeff Simons, Sports Physiologist with the Australian team. Jeff had been on hand, supporting me, when I had won the same race four years earlier, in Atlanta.

Marshalling for the women's race wasn't until 6.50, but most of my opponents were in their chairs by 6.00 – far too early, I thought. I knew I only needed twenty minutes for my warm-up, so I hung back. I didn't want to rush . . . I wanted to make sure I did everything according to my plan. Runner Tamsyn Lewis was down at the track practising her stars for the 4 × 400 metres relay and her coach Peter Fortune and I gave her a hand, marking out steps for her. It was the perfect distraction for me, and a lot of fun – Tamsyn and I still laugh about it today. The fact was that I had no idea how to start on blocks – and neither did she, being an 800 metres runner (blocks are only used for the shorter distances). But it really took my mind away from everything else. I couldn't believe how calm I was. It was so strange – I wasn't nervous at all.

My warm-up wasn't the best. I got very hot, very quickly – and when I finished I thought, 'Oh my God, my face is so red'. In warm-up I did a couple of pick-ups with Kurt Fearnley, to try and get my speed up. A pick-up is essentially working with someone fast as a pacer, so you can reach maximum speed. Usually, drafting behind Kurt, I can get up to 30 kilometres an hour. That evening I couldn't top 27 kilometres. I did a few starts with Andrew and then he said, 'That's it – just stop . . . there's nothing more you can do'. I was as red as a beetroot.

I was last into the call room and one of the officials I have known for a long time was checking the chairs for sponsorship logos, the Olympics being very strict in that area. I had taped mine up earlier, and as far as I was concerned all was fine. But on some of the chairs there were tiny little hub brand stickers – nothing to do with sponsorship, yet officials were adamant these too had to be covered, and there was some resultant hoo-ha which seemed unnecessary, and was certainly frustrating. This sort of thing had never happened before at World Championships or in Paralympic competition. In the end, for all the fuss, not everyone's stickers on hubs were taken off anyway – for either the Olympic or the Paralympic events.

Finally it was all done, and the waiting time in the call room passed quickly enough – and calmly enough. Despite the problems of the warm-up, I felt OK. I had used my nasal spray and my breathing was reasonably clear.

The eight of us wheeled onto the track, me at the front because I had drawn the inside lane – and even then the crowd was going nuts. People were screaming my name. 'Louise . . . turn around . . . we want a picture!' they shouted as the cameras clicked. I tried not to look. 'Shut up . . . I'm supposed to be concentrating on the race,' I whispered to myself.

At a time when I should have been deeply focused on what I had to do, all the noise and clamour shouldn't have distracted me. But it did. Australia's Jai Taurima was in the middle of his battle for the long-jump gold and the crowd was really full-on. Every time he jumped, the fans went ballistic. A further glimpse of green and gold as I entered the track revved them up still further.

It's funny how at times small things can shine out amidst the sort of turmoil that was the Olympic Stadium that night. Earlier that day I had spoken to a longtime friend, Kathy Lee, who had been involved in wheelchair sport for a long time and who was then with the Victorian Institute of Sport. She was to be in the commentary box that night, and I had given her some extra background on the girls I was to race against in the 800 metres. Finally, out in the middle of the great Stadium, we got to do a lap of the track before the start of the race. Everything around us was just a sea of colour and a great buzz of noise. It was impossible to focus on any individual thing. Nothing felt familiar, comfortable or right.

Then, through it all, I heard Kathy's voice over the public address, loud and clear. It was an enormous comfort – just the thought that a good friend was up there, keeping an eye on the race. She was the something familiar I was looking for. To me it was as if everything were OK as soon as I heard her voice come through in that blur of noise and colour. I knew *she* would get it right . . . and that it was up to *me* to do the same. From that moment I had the feeling that everything was going to be all right . . .

\* \* \*

I had drawn badly – Lane One – and neither Andrew nor I was at all happy about that. The situation of the race being a one-off, straight-out final meant there was a random draw for lane positions. And I drew the inside.

Lane One can be a draw fraught with danger because of the possibility that you can get boxed in and never see 'daylight'. And I had the thought that because I was the only Aussie, and the favourite, the others might get together and work against me in the race. But I had had a day to come to terms with it, to adjust my thinking and race plan.

The 800 is a fast race, with pressure on most of the way – and as in the longer races, tactics play their part. It's a race that requires snap decisions. The thing above all else is not to get boxed in, to make sure you are in a good position coming into the last 200 metres, where the moves are made. My plan was to get myself into the right spot – and to attack in the last 150 metres.

On the starting line I still wasn't nervous. Maybe it was all the good vibes the crowd was sending out. But to be honest, I was starting to worry about the fact that I *wasn't* worried. I knew it was going to be a tough race. Chantal Petitclerc, who had stolen my world record over the distance, was there, plus Cheri Becerra, world record holder over 400 metres, and Wakako Tsuchida, who had beaten me in the Oz Day race earlier in the year. It was a class field, although I was in the dark to an extent about my rivals because I hadn't seen them or raced against them for some weeks, thanks to my free ticket into this event. Focusing on my own sickness, and trying to feel as good as I possibly could, I hadn't had time to stress about the other competitors much at all.

It's on the starting line that I do my self-talk – and I did it in Sydney: 'I'm here now . . . there is nothing more I can do to get myself ready. I have done the work. I deserve to win this race. This is my race'. And I repeat those words over and over. I know all is right technically – the tyres are right, the wheels are right, the chair is right. It is down to me. Even at the start of a race at the Olympic Games, before 110,000 people, I can narrow the focus, ignore the crowd, and just come down to what I have to do . . . what I *will* do.

The race started fast ... then slowed down. Chantal and Cheri, who are both good at the start (unlike me!), got away quickly, and soon were way out in front. But if you watch a replay of the race you'll see that into the first 200 metres the two of them slowed down – and waited for me. I think if they had been smart, maybe they would have kept the pace on. Instead, for whatever reason, they hung back, enabling the rest of the field to catch them. At the end of 400 metres, I was in the lead.

The Olympic 800 was such a strange race, a tactical race and not overly fast – which was fine by me, as I wasn't feeling 100 per cent. For some reason no-one wanted to go to the front, no-one wanted to race fast. Chantal and Cheri have so much natural speed, and yet they hung back, reluctant to 'take it on'.

There was no way I was going to get myself boxed away in Lane One, so I pulled out to Two – and then to Three as we all headed around the bend into the straight of that first lap. I honestly would prefer pushing out in Lane Six, rather than taking the risk of being locked away on the inside. I kept looking back, but no-one was coming through – until Ariadne Hernandez from Mexico pushed through hard in Lane One. When she drifted out and Cheri Becerra tried to come around me I was in danger of being boxed in. So I picked it up a bit more – and pushed Cheri out almost into Lane Four. With about 150 metres to go, I decided I would try and make my move. 'I'm going to do it,' I said to myself – and took off.

And it was then as I headed for the line that the crowd picked me up. Everything got noisier and I just felt this rush of ... something underneath, pushing me along. It wasn't until later that I realised that the *something* had been the sheer power of the crowd as people rose to their feet, willing me to win, and the noise level lifted even higher.

It was so cool. I just pushed and pushed and pushed until I was across the line. Only then did I raise my arms. I had won in 1 minute 56.07 seconds by a chair-length from Wakako (a personal best of 1.56.49) and Ariadne (1.56.49).

It was as if a giant weight had immediately lifted from my shoulders. I was so relieved, so glad it was over. In a confusion of noise and colour, and with my thoughts racing, I wheeled around the track with the other girls.

When that was done English racer Tanni Grey-Thompson was saying, 'Go on, do another lap by yourself . . . go on!'. But I didn't. I still can't really explain why. And when I think back on it now, I'm sorry I didn't. After all, I'll probably never have the chance to experience that sort of atmosphere, that sort of home-town support again in my life. If I could turn the clock back . . . I'd be doing another victory lap.

Trying to relive it now, so much is a blur. There were familiar faces everywhere, people milling around – hugging and congratulating. Down from the stand came my neighbour Julian Foxton, yelling his congratulations across to me. 'My God, I can't believe you're here!' I shouted back. Others, though, I didn't see – such as Karen, Lee and my good friend Kellie Puxty, who were all in the milling crowd at the bottom of the stairs. It was all just a huge, happy confusion . . . The minutes just raced by. So much was going on – and it seemed hardly any time before I was being called for the medal presentation.

It was then that the International Olympic Committee reminded me that this, after all, was only a demonstration event. The gold commemorative medal that IOC President Juan Antonio Samaranch presented to me was half the size of the ones that the able-bodied Games winners were receiving. It was a reminder that, whatever I was, I was still not *really* an Olympian. I consoled myself with the thought that at least the reception the Sydney crowd had so generously given me was a full-sized one, and that they saw no difference between my victory for Australia and any other by our able-bodied athletes at the Games. This meant a lot to me.

Then came the best part: the playing of the national anthem, with 110,000 people singing along with me. It was amazing to be in the middle of that. It was something I will never forget, an experience so extraordinary that I find it hard to imagine now that it really happened.

It's hard to put into words what it was like sitting out there. Well, the simple thought occurred to me that it had all paid off – all those cold early mornings, all those times when I trained in the rain, all those sessions training alone. 'It has all been worth it to be sitting here in this place tonight,' I thought to myself.

Only much later did I turn my mobile phone on – and then I talked to various people, including my cousin Jacqueline, a tour guide in Perth, who had been in the process of changing a tyre on a tour bus at the time of the race! I rang Mum, who was very excited – and I could hear Ann yelling in the background. 'Oh, I wish it hadn't been so close,' said Mum. 'Don't make your races so close in future.' She had had a whisky to try and calm herself down!

I got home about 2.00 a.m. – my home, ten minutes away from the Stadium. Lee and I stayed up and watched the video replay of the race. We also watched Lee's own video coverage of the final – which was hilarious, with the camera bobbing up and down as the excitement grew and with Karen's screams of support coming through loud and clear.

When I finally got to bed, I lay there for a long time with my eyes wide open. I was desperately tired, but I couldn't sleep. So much was going on in my head – I was running over everything that had happened that night, the race and all that surrounded it. Even when I shut my eyes it was still there, buzzing around. One thing I knew for sure: to have won at the Olympic Games here in Sydney, my home, was one of the greatest thrills of my entire career.

\* \* \*

But like so many of my achievements, the gold medal provoked controversy. The *Sydney Morning Herald*'s Caroline Overington wrote a strong and provocative assessment, which appeared the next morning under the headline 'Memo IOC: Sauvage Raced, She Won and Deserves to Receive a Real Gold Medal':

*A tricky question, sports fans: what is the difference between a wheelchair and a bike? What, for that matter, is the difference between a wheelchair and a horse? A wheelchair and a canoe? A wheelchair and a sailing boat?*

*What, in other words, is the difference between the medal that Louise Sauvage won in the 800 metre track race yesterday and any other medal won by an Australian?*

*The difference is, the medal called gold, because it might as well be chocolate. When Australia adds up its medals at the end of the games, it will not count towards the total. For some reason (no reason really), the International Olympic Committee has made wheelchair racing a 'demonstration' sport.*

*In other words, it makes a distinction between going around a velodrome on two wheels, and going around the Olympic stadium on three. This is because the person going around in the wheelchair probably cannot walk. This, and only this, makes Sauvage, who won the 800 metres, different from, say, Michelle Ferris who won the bronze medal at the velodrome.*

*Sauvage won the race easily. She took the lead from the start, then spent two laps wondering why nobody tried to catch her. Afterwards, Sauvage agreed that it would be 'nice' if the IOC would give the wheelchair athletes real medals, instead of token ones. 'But it's not up to us,' she said. 'I just race.' Asked if she hoped she had inspired people with a disability, Sauvage said: 'Not just them. If I've inspired anyone, that's fantastic.' The crowd was the 'biggest and most biased' she had ever raced in front of, 'and with 150 metres to go, the noise was just deafening. I felt a rush of wind under me. It just lifted me.'*

*Ostensibly, the reason that wheelchair racing is not a full-medal sport is that the athletes have to use special equipment to compete. Like pole vaulters don't need a pole? Like fencers don't need a ... fence? No, sword. Fencing is a sport? Suspending yourself upside down in a pool with plugs up your nose is a sport? But hunching enormous shoulders over a wheelchair and belting around the stadium track at speeds approaching 40 kilometres per hour, every muscle straining, heart pumping, throat hurting, breath bated – this is not a sport?*

*The only reason Sauvage's medal does not count is because she has used a wheelchair since she was a young girl, having been born with a spinal complaint. In other words, she is being discriminated against on the basis of ability.*

*When you think about it, this is hysterical (or it would be, if it weren't so serious, and illegal). The idea that Sauvage isn't able-bodied is absurd. She is much more able than most. Likewise, the idea that she is 'physically challenged'.*

*For some, getting out of bed is a challenge. Sauvage competes in marathons, with cracked seats and bent wheels, until her hands are raw, her fingers blistered, her face beaten red by the sun.*

*It is offensive, having wheelchair racers compete, then refusing to recognise the performance. What is the difference between this and segregating disabled kids at school? All of Australia's wheelchair racers stayed in the Village, wore the team uniform and took part in the Opening Ceremony. In total, there were six [sic – three], although Australia's men fared less well than the women yesterday, with John MacLean spilling out of his chair and Kurt Fearnley finishing 4th in the 1500 metres event.*

> Sauvage's gold medal was presented by the IOC president, Juan Antonio Samaranch. She was probably too polite to ask why she couldn't have a real one.
>
> The shame of this is that there is more than an element of pity in Samaranch's thinking. There is also an obscure idea that wheelchair athletes at the Olympics represent the disabled. This is so much nonsense. Sauvage represents Australia. That's why they played the anthem.

I always knew that any medal I happened to win at the Olympics would not count on the Australian medal tally for the Games. For all that, I'll just say it would have been nice to have received the *same* medal as the able-bodied winners. When I won in Atlanta, the gold medal awarded was at least the same size as all the other medals given, although I am told it differs on one side from the other Games medals.

Able-bodied gold medal winners at the 2000 Sydney Olympics were also honoured by Australia Post with the release of a stamp bearing their images – plus a $20,000 grant. The stamps celebrating Cathy Freeman and Ian Thorpe and the Hockeyroos and all the rest soon became collectors' items. Heading into Sydney's Olympics, I signed exactly the same athletes' contract as everyone else, and I competed under exactly the same conditions as all the able-bodied Olympic athletes. Yet when my manager Karen McBrien went to the post office a day or two after my race and asked whether there would be a stamp marking my victory, they told her no – and she was very, very upset. I suppose a lot of my friends and family had assumed there would be. At least there came the belated but very welcome news that I would receive the $20,000 (Australia Post) grant plus the $15,000 gold medallists' bonus offered by the AOC to winners, which I had also received after the Atlanta Games of 1996.

The debate about these issues is an ongoing one, and looks like continuing for quite a time. The question of the size of the medals or whether they should count towards medal tallies, and the issue of other rewards for gold medallists are things that are completely out of my hands. The thing that mattered above everything else to me at the Sydney Olympics was the fact that the race was a chance to help demonstrate my sport. To showcase it at that level was just fantastic. My long-term goals in sport have always been related to raising awareness and helping educate people about sport for athletes with a disability.

\* \* \*

It is almost certain that Sydney was my last Olympics. On the grapevine the word initially was strong that the wheelchair demonstration events would not be run again at an Olympic Games – although later, very welcome indications pointed to a shift in thinking and the possibility that the events may not be dropped after all. But I have no idea where I will be in four years' time, anyway!

I don't believe that the IOC intention was ever that the two Olympic wheelchair races would become full-medal events. The newspapers have suggested that the reason for that is that the events could never be open to everyone. Well, as far as I'm concerned *everyone* can compete in my sport if they want to – with or without a disability. I'd open it up to all comers. And I think a lot of wheelchair racers would like it that way – at least for the major road races around the world, the Boston Marathon and all the others, although not perhaps at the Paralympics, which is a sporting event so specifically geared to athletes with a disability. The Paralympics' specific requirement that they are for athletes rated with a disability of 10 per cent or more separate them from road racing. The jury remains out on the wider question of 'open' wheelchair racing. It's an ongoing debate, argued strongly around the world from different points of view.

\* \* \*

With the Olympics over, and me the proud possessor of a gold medal, I now lifted my sights to the Paralympics three weeks away. This would be an event with a different kind of edge – something more familiar to me, yet just as challenging, and probably deep down even more important because of what I knew the event could do for my sport. September was over; I had already climbed one Everest, now I had to get ready for the next . . .

CHAPTER 18

# ONE DOWN...
# A LONG WAY TO GO

What a buzz the two weeks of the Sydney Olympics were! Once my competition was over I couldn't wait to check it all out... to go into the centre of town and be part of the experience. The city was absolutely packed and really humming with good feelings.

**Friday 29 September**

Relieved, happy and tired, I headed back to the Olympic Village with Andrew today and picked my gear up. Now it's onwards to the Paralympics. Tonight I was back at the Stadium with Karen, where we were guests in Michael Knight's box to watch the athletics. The Minister wasn't there, but we had some good food – and a really good night.

### Saturday 30 September

This morning I tried one of my new chairs again and it was still pretty bad, just not rolling very well – so I am not going to try it any more. I am going to stick with my old chair, as I did for the Olympics. Later, Lee and I caught the ferry from Meadowbank into the city. We went to Circular Quay, which was packed, and walked up to Darling Harbour; on the way I phoned Andrew to wish him a happy birthday. At Darling Harbour I kept getting stopped and asked for autographs and photos, which was kind of cool, although it took us ages to get anywhere!

### Sunday 1 October

I picked up my wheels from Stuart Andrews, a great guy and someone who can blind me with science when he talks about wheelchair design. He's a perfectionist. I had given them to him last week and he took them to Canberra and had them retensioned.

Steve Loader from Qantas managed to get tickets for us to go into the Stadium Australia Box for the Closing Ceremony tonight! But at the Stadium, around seven, I got a call from the security company to tell me my house alarm had gone off. I panicked after what happened in July. They sent a guy around and Karen went too and they checked it all out – and it seems thankfully there has been no break-in. I was worried about my medals, and also about Penny.

The Closing Ceremony was just about the *best* thing I have ever been to. Back at the big party afterwards at the Qantas Club I met Mick Doohan, our former world 500cc motorcycle champion. He was really nice, and it was a great night. I felt proud to be Australian.

That final night came far too quickly, and for most people it was an abrupt ending to the fortnight's festivities – an occasion that was both sad and joyful at the same time, leaving an empty feeling in so many lives. In one way it was like that for me, too. But it was also a beginning. My win in the 800 was now a few days behind me, but imprinted on my mind forever, and still rattling around in my head as that wonderful night went by, ending the first stage in surely one of the most wonderful times that Sydney will ever enjoy – our brief moment in the international spotlight. For me there was the acceptance that the clock had immediately started ticking towards Part Two of the great double challenge I had set myself. The Paralympics were just down the road . . .

The Stadium Australia Box had a fantastic view of the Ceremony. It was just the best night. Well, it had to get better than the evening's start, with the alarm at my house going off. 'Not another break-in!' I thought at the time. It stressed me badly, but the night that followed soon swept me up, and took me into a different world – as it did everyone who watched. Lee and I had a lovely dinner at the Stadium and then watched the whole thing from the comfort of our private box. It was just a wonderful night – a jumble of emotions and memories for everyone, I guess, and for me along with the rest. I looked down on the track and thought, 'I won a gold medal there'. That felt so good. I won't ever forget that night.

But too soon, it seemed, the last flash of the fireworks had faded and the last note of a night filled with music and colour had died. Reality check: the hard work was about to start all over again. For me and my fellow Paralympians, the final countdown had officially begun . . .

### Monday 2 October

My e-mail in-box is full of congratulations and good wishes. It's really nice. I sent a few messages off in response. Tonight I was asked to go to the Australian Olympic team party at the Capitol Theatre. I went, but really didn't want to be there. I'm not sure why exactly. It was just all too much, I suppose. Towards the end I went up on stage and accepted the Australian flag from basketball captain Andrew Gaze on behalf of all Paralympians. Andrew gave a great speech, talking about how the Paralympics were on in a couple of weeks and everyone should continue on with the spirit and get right behind the athletes. It was great to be recognised in that way. It was a big night – with Prime Minister Howard joining the athletes onstage at one point. But when it was over I was happy to get away, to my own thoughts and dreams.

It was sort of a weird time for me – that period between my 800 metres race at the Olympics and the Paralympics, placed an awkward month or so further on. For most of the Paralympic athletes it was business as usual – the maintaining of a powerful, single focus on the one event that had been in their minds for years. But for the likes of John MacLean, Kurt Fearnley and me it was different. We had already tapered for one big event, eased off our gym work and freshened up. Having done that, and raced, it would have been tempting – and easy! – to slip into the party mode that progressively swept through the Olympic site – and Sydney as a whole, it seemed. I was invited to so many parties and functions that I lost count – but in the main I said no. No way could I afford to be out late, to be drinking and partying. There was still hard business to be attended to.

### Tuesday 3 October

No training this morning – and this afternoon I was at the ES Marks Field, doing 200s mostly. It was OK, nothing fast. My neck is just so tight. I've got good movement, but the muscles down the right-hand side and across my shoulder are really tight. I went straight from the track to the physio.

For me, the clicking back into gear for the Paralympics really came at a track and field team training camp in Wollongong in the wake of the Olympics, followed by further days of training as a team back in Sydney. By then my focus had narrowed; I had again become the athlete, determined to succeed. That meant shutting myself away from media and public attention as much as possible.

### Wednesday 4 October

I'm in Wollongong – at the training camp. I drove down with Smithy (Greg Smith) – and it was really good talking to him. I did a couple of media interviews, then chilled out for the afternoon. It was really weird not to be doing anything. I just watched the telly. Later we had a team session talking about Paralympic Village life, headed by our Chef de Mission, Paul Bird.

### Thursday 5 October

We had a session today with Karen Hellwig, Media Liaison Officer to the Australian team, specific to athletics, and then we had an athletes' meeting. My neck is really, really sore. Our physio Greg Ungerer worked on it and made it hurt so much. But I am used to that now.

This afternoon we had a track meet down at Barton Park that was set up to give us some racing practice, and I did a 200 metres – which was really stupid. It hurt my neck; I did one start after it, then stopped. I won't be doing that again! This evening I did a 5000 metres – and that was much better. There was a pack of five of us, with two of the guys from Norway – and we did about 24 kilometres an hour the whole race. The guys from Norway have come out here early and have been looking for some competition – so they were allowed to compete with us at the track meet. The time was good, and I was happy. It was fast and a lot of fun . . . and in the end that is why I race.

### Friday 6 October

Tonight we had our last dinner together as an athletics team, because as soon as we go into the Village everyone will be mixed in with all the other sports. I was named as one of the team leaders. There's me, Smithy, Amy Winters, Hamish Macdonald and Russell Short. Tonight we also sang a song that one of the team members, Anthony Biddell, wrote last year. And I was invited to become a member of the Bat Club which is made up of a few of the guys. All club members have to get a tattoo of a bat . . . but I don't think I am going to do that. Today a lot of the guys had tattoos of the Paralympic logo done; they have been putting the hard word on me to get one too. I'm not so sure . . .

### Sunday 8 October

I had a broken night's sleep on Friday, worrying about getting up very early to go training on Saturday morning. I was awake much of the night, and was up at six. My nose is still blocked – the tail end (hopefully!) of the problem I dragged through the Olympics. I trained on the road with Andrew and it was busy and a bit scary at times. We went for uniform fitting and were given our travel gear for the Paralympics. It is almost the same Nike stuff as for the Olympics – just a bit less of it.

In the afternoon, I headed back home to Sydney. I spoke to Mum tonight. They are all coming over on Monday the 16th.

### Monday 9 October

A wet Sydney day. I trained in the park and it rained. The physio is working on my sore spots and I'm a lot better than last week, although my elbow is troubling me.

### Tuesday 10 October

A morning off training! – so I did a radio interview and some paperwork, then took Penny to the park down at the end of my street. In the afternoon, an OK session.

### Thursday 12 October

After training in Parramatta Park yesterday morning, where it was very windy, I did 'The John Laws Show' on radio. I couldn't believe it was two years since I was last there. The interview seemed to go on for a long time, and I did a couple of others that morning and was also on 'Club Veg'. Afterwards there was a photo shoot at home, and some photos with Penny down at the park for one of the papers.

Lee and I went to Grace Bros in North Ryde this afternoon and people were stopping us. One guy told us he was there on the night I won the 800 at the Olympics. I am really excited now – thinking about what lies ahead. At night I caught up with a friend of mine, Toby Roberts, who is in Sydney for a while; it was good to see him and we went and had some dinner.

Today I went to Karen's with Penny – and together we wrote an article that had been requested by the *Sun-Herald*. Later I took Karen to the Olympic Stadium, where she is working during the Paralympics, in the media liaison area. She looked pretty funny in her uniform! Over there today everyone was giving me a hard time about why I wasn't staying in the Village yet. It just drove me nuts. I ended up leaving. I hooked up with a good friend, Patrice Dockery, an Irish wheelchair racer out here for the Paralympics, and members of the Irish team, and a few of us had dinner. Tomorrow I have about fifty million interviews.

On Friday 13 October, with just about everyone else moving into or already staying in the Village, I made the trek across to the place that would be known as the suburb of Newington after the Games – to pick up my accreditation, and to have a look at what the Village had become, from the period of the Olympics to the Paralympics. In the back of my mind was the nagging memory of Atlanta. But the Paralympic Village, Sydney 2000, was just fine, although understandably it was a smaller general area than it had been for the Olympics. All was in place: dining hall, international zone, accessible buses in and out of the Village area. It was going to be OK. And they had even named one of the thoroughfares in the Village after me: the Louise Sauvage Pathway.

But I wasn't ready to move in just yet, despite all the questioners – and I must say that the visit of 'unlucky' Friday the 13th wasn't a great experience, and in fact slightly concerned me when I thought of what lay ahead. The volunteers at the Games (both Olympics and Paralympics) were just terrific, but for a time at the Paralympics – on that first day, and then when I moved back in permanently – I thought I was going to get swamped by them. I suppose mine was a very recognisable face and everywhere I went I was asked for autographs, or to pose for photos. It got very wearing, and not just for me, but for some of the other athletes too. Commonsense prevailed when the volunteers were quietly advised to please ease the pressure and give the athletes some space – at least until after they had competed.

### Friday 13 October

It's Friday the 13th – and I've had a bit of a bad day. Training in Centennial Park was OK, but it rained on us. I headed to Homebush to get my accreditation and then decided I would go to the Village and have a look at where I was staying. I got grilled by *everybody*. They all kept asking me why I wasn't moving in.

On my way to accreditation, Brendan Flynn, CEO of the Australian Paralympic Committee, rang me and told me confidentially that I was going to be one of the last six torch bearers inside the Stadium at the Opening Ceremony. That's sooooo exciting!

## Sunday 15 October

The weekend has been full-on. I trained early on Saturday – and by myself, because I had interviews to do there. They all went fine. At the park near my house I did an interview for 'Sports Women' – a TV show focusing on women in sport produced by We Media and the ABC – and then I came back and talked to a guy from Reuters.

I had to be at the Olympic Stadium at 6.20 p.m. There it was confirmed that I was going to be one of the last six torch bearers on Wednesday night. The other five are Katrina Webb (athletics), Lisa Llorens (athletics), Anthony Clark (judo), Michael Milton (a Winter Paralympian who competes as a skier) and Kevin Coombs (an ex-Paralympian in basketball). It was fantastic to be told that I was going to be one of the torch bearers for the last leg. Karen Richards, organiser of the Opening and Closing Ceremonies, was there too. Just before we were going off to rehearse Brendan Flynn said to Karen, 'Well, we need to say now who is lighting the cauldron'.

And they said I was.

I couldn't believe it. My dream was to carry the torch in the Stadium . . . but to be lighting the cauldron – unbelievable! The tears just welled up . . . and I cried. As I talk about it now, it still doesn't seem real.

After *that* news we went down to the Stadium and to wardrobe – and then we rehearsed three times with the music. I met Melissa Ippolito, who is going to sing at the Opening Ceremony. She is fifteen and has had open-heart surgery, to repair a hole in her heart. And I practised lighting the cauldron. It was a really freaky night. We were down there for four hours . . . and it was windy and

> freezing. I was shaking like a leaf – and it was nothing to do with the cold!
>
> Right now I don't know what to think. I came home and had dinner with Lee really late. I am sworn to secrecy – not allowed to tell anyone about it. Obviously the people who were there tonight know the news – but I can't tell Lee, or my mum and dad, or anybody else.
>
> Today I had to pack and get ready for the move into the Village tomorrow and I procrastinated. I just didn't want to get myself together. Sometimes I don't know why I don't make better use of my time. In bed this morning I couldn't stop thinking about the cauldron and lighting it and all of that. It has just about freaked me out – in the best possible way, of course.

Once I had been told that I was going to play the 'Cathy Freeman role' for the Paralympics, one of the toughest parts was keeping the secret. Down at our training camp at Wollongong they had been placing bets on me to light the Paralympic flame. But when I was told that it was me and I was sworn to secrecy I stuck to that. I didn't even tell Karen, and I think she was a bit annoyed with me. Since I hadn't told her she kept telling people that I wasn't doing it. I said to her later, 'Why did you do that when you didn't know for sure?'. 'Well, you didn't tell me,' she replied.

### Monday 16 October

> I moved into the Village today after training this morning in the park. It is good to be here – and I am sharing with fellow wheelchair racer Angie Ballard. I am carrying the torch tomorrow in George Street. Tonight my parents arrived in Sydney.

With my own house now full of members of the Sauvage family, I shifted into the Village and set about getting myself psyched and ready for all that lay ahead. In the Village Angie and I shared a quiet room at the back of a house. It was twice the size of the room we had in Atlanta – big enough to take two beds and two wheelchairs, side by side! Amazing.

Angie was the only one who had a clue about my lighting the cauldron – because she had a secret too: she was involved in the Ceremony, riding in the blimp, and she had to tell me because she was leaving early for the Stadium and wanted me to save a spot for her. I had to borrow a pair of blue team pants from her for my role (I had lent mine to Christie) – so I had to let on that I was involved in something too.

### Tuesday 17 October

I trained earlier than the others, because I am carrying the torch today to Sydney Town Hall. I did some very consistent 200s, and some starts – for the first time in about a week and a half. My neck is not too bad. Back home I caught up with my mum and dad and sister and Lee. They had had special shirts made up, which read 'Unofficial Support Team of Louise Sauvage'. That was so nice.

Then the car came to pick me up and take me off to my Torch Relay duties – and we went to the wrong bloody place, to Parliament House instead of Government House! Anyway, when we finally got there all was fine. I caught up with Dawn Fraser and Dawn Lorraine. Ann and Lee and Mum and Dad got into the VIP area. I am sure Mum talked them into it.

*Ann Sauvage: We [Rita, Maurice, Lee and Ann] managed to gate-crash the Town Hall event wearing our backpacks and sneakers. We were just hanging around and they found out who we were. 'Come to the cocktail party!' they said.*

I took the torch from Dawn – and that was a thrill on its own on such an exciting day. With the torch I headed up windy George Street . . . and it went out! A guy arrived carrying a little lantern with a flame in it. That went out too! Finally another guy ran up with another torch, and relit mine. I arrived at the Town Hall and headed up the ramp . . . and lit the cauldron. There were media people everywhere and I talked to them and signed autographs – I just don't know how many. It was full-on and I was glad to finally get inside to the reception.

Back at the Village I had lunch and dinner combined (I had missed lunch), got changed – and went straight to a big Australian team function. It was like a mini-concert, with occasional 'official' interruptions. They named the captains: Priya Cooper (swimming) and Sandy Blythe (basketball), with Amy Winters (athletics) and Hamish Macdonald (athletics) as vice captains. The flag bearer is Brendan Burkett, a swimmer. It was a big night, with performers like Wendy Matthews (whom I really like), Christine Anu and Geoff Harvey and his band. Kylie Minogue was there too and she came around and said hello. Tomorrow night it's the Opening Ceremony, which will be so exciting . . .

## Thursday 19 October

Today has been a very special day, one that I won't ever forget. It started with an early interview with Triple J and is ending now, more than eighteen hours later (1.00 a.m.) as I go to bed to try and get some sleep.

During the day I went training, went to the physio, then did a photo shoot and press conference at the Novotel in Homebush, followed by a few more interviews. Tonight we assembled in the Superdome and marched together into the Stadium. Amazingly, in the tunnel as I made my way through the thousands of kids waiting to take part in the ceremony, I saw my young neighbour Lucy Foxton, daughter of my friends Julian and Sue, and her friend Kara. It was so good. The atmosphere was really great – something I will always remember.

I headed off with the other torch bearers; we got changed very quickly and then I waited until I was told when to go out to my position. Out there in the middle I waited for Michael Milton to come around with the torch. I took the torch from him . . . and lit the cauldron.

The funny thing was that although I was trembling right through the practice session, and through the carrying of the torch up George Street the day before, on the really big night in front of the huge crowd I was fine. I wasn't nervous or anything – I just got up there and did it and was really cool and calm. The only problem was that the wind on Opening Night blew in a different direction from the way it had blown on practice night. I was on stage with Melissa Ippolito, the singer I met at the practice session, and we looked at each other with some apprehension as the flame got higher – and blew towards us. I could picture myself finishing up with a sunburnt forehead. If it had gone on for a few more seconds I would have had to put my hand up to my face. But luckily the flame died down as it was supposed to – and all was OK.

After the cauldron was lit, all the torch bearers had our photos taken together. Then I got changed and was able to relax and enjoy the rest of the Opening Ceremony, with performers including Kylie Minogue, Vanessa Amorosi and Christine Anu. There were so many people. And fireworks.

At the end we all pushed back to the Village. It was a great night and I'm glad it has all started. Now I can't wait to compete . . .

I still have to pinch myself when I think of the build-up to the Paralympics – and the wonderful, unbelievable experiences that I had in the process of it all beginning. I will never forget that in the space of two days I lit the cauldron at Sydney Town Hall and then lit the Paralympic flame at Stadium Australia before 100,000 people to begin the Games. I spent much of the two days shaking my head in disbelief!

The Sauvage family video tape of the night, which includes a running commentary, is a bit of a hoot. You see, my family still didn't know that I had been chosen to light the flame. So on the tape you can hear my mum saying, 'Oooh, there she is ... she didn't tell me anything, the little sod!'.

> *Rita Sauvage: Yes, she kept it a secret. My heart just burst when I saw it was her.*

That unforgettable night over, now it was down to business. The competition, featuring the best in the world, was about to start...

### Friday 20 October

Thursday dawned grey and miserable after the late night of the Opening Ceremony. There weren't too many at the morning press conference, which was good in one way, because we were all exhausted, but not so good in terms of coverage of the Paralympics. I trained in the morning, with the weather warming and improving, and organised my chair. Late in the day I had to rush to get to an interview with the ABC's Karen Tighe, which I had forgotten all about.

Now it's down to the serious competition. At early training I went through a careful checking process on my chair and changed tyres and decided what wheels to use; I am going to use the wheels that Stuart Andrews made me. They are kind of different. They spin well and I get really good top speeds with them, and good acceleration.

Today I also had X-rays done on my neck; the physio and the doctor decided that it would be good to see just what was going on. But the X-rays went 'missing' – and I had had to go back and do them again, at which point the originals turned up!

I got to see my friend Karen Long for the first time today, and that was great. She has come to Sydney to see me race! I watched Christie race the 100 metres and get through to the final, and Angie push a really good race for fourth in her 800. Cheri Becerra set a new world record in the 100 metres final, with Chantal Petitclerc second.

Tonight I got ready for tomorrow – my first heat, the qualifier for the 800 metres, at 10.45 tomorrow morning. I don't feel nervous at all and that's pretty weird. I am sure that will be different tomorrow.

### Saturday 21 October

I slept badly. It's funny how little things can upset you; I have this watch I use to check the time at night when I'm away from home – and I misplaced it. It was really stupid, and because of it I had a night of tossing and turning. At breakfast I tried to force down a piece of toast, which didn't really happen too well.

At the track my warm-up was OK, and the track felt OK too – although not super-fast. The nerves still didn't get me – in fact I haven't been nervous before a race for quite a while. In my 800 metres heat I drew Lane Eight in a random draw, and got the worst start. I missed the push rim on the left-hand side about three times. Cheri Becerra, who was in my heat, took off really fast – and it took me almost the whole race to catch her. On the last bend I finally passed her and won my semi. It was a really slow time – 1.57 something – but I still qualified second fastest overall. Chantal Petitclerc won the next heat; Christie was disqualified, but Holly made it through.

It was strange – back at the Village, I didn't really feel excited about the whole thing at all. I did an interview with Peter Harvey from Channel Nine outside the Village, and met Kim Beazley. I wanted to have a drive of one of the little cars in the Village, so he hopped in too – and the pair of us did a lap of the Village, with me steering and the Leader of the Opposition operating the foot pedals. That was fun. I had dinner at home – a roast that Mum had cooked.

Tomorrow night is my final of the 800 and I'm hoping I will have a better race than I did today. Maybe I will be a gold medallist tomorrow night . . .

### Sunday 22 October

It's Sunday night – and I am neither a gold nor a silver medallist, nor a bronze medallist, for that matter. The race will probably be talked about for quite a time . . .

No-one could possibly have predicted just how controversial the Sunday night 800 metres race would turn out to be. I had felt myself under pressure for many days beforehand. Everyone seemed to be constantly asking me, when was I racing? And it was a lot more than just 'Good luck and do your best'. Again and again the question of the 'first gold medal' was mentioned. And to tell you the truth, I didn't handle the pressure too well. I was quietly freaking out at all this building pressure, this growing anticipation. It seemed as though I was carrying the expectation of the whole team . . . the whole country. Unlike the Olympics 800, when I was sick and dosed up, I was well this time . . . sharp, and thoroughly aware of the weight of expectation I carried.

> *Rita Sauvage: We were on a media bus in the Olympic precinct and I heard a girl say that Chantal was going to*

> *go all out in this 800. I told Louise – but I don't think she took much notice!*

The race has its place in Paralympic history now. It was an event that was sensational in the true meaning of the word. After a characteristically slow start from my fairly average lane draw (Lane Three) I took time to get up behind the fast-breaking leaders, Chantal Petitclerc and Cheri Becerra.

My chase after Chantal, who had pretty much controlled the tempo of the race, has been shown a million times on TV now. When she moved wide on the turn into the final straight, I was forced wider still, two lanes wide. It was ground I just couldn't make up. I just couldn't muster the momentum I needed down the home straight. In that last 150 metres I slipped a couple of times on my wheels, and just didn't get the full drive with my pushes. The finishing line came up too fast – and Chantal had beaten me.

'Finally!' she kept saying. 'Finally!'. She was tremendously excited, continually turning around and looking at me as if she couldn't believe it. She was entitled to be happy. She had been trying to beat me for a long time. Now, she had raced aggressively – far, far better than she had at the Olympics a month before – and she had won. And I had lost my first race on the track in eight years . . .

It was only after the race was over that I learned something had gone horribly wrong further back in the field. What had happened, of course, was that there had been a three-way crash just before the 200-metre mark – sending Holly Ladmore (Australia), Wakako Tsuchida (Japan) and Lily Anggreny (Germany) tumbling onto the track. I discovered afterwards that my Irish friend Patrice Dockery had been deemed to have caused the trouble by coming out of her lane – and she was later disqualified. The incident created a storm that was to rage for days in the newspaper headlines.

Straight afterwards came the bombshell: the news of a protest on the result, entered by Japan and Germany – although there was no protest by Australia. This changed everything; we weren't even able to cool down, and I had to hang around and do a drug test. All of us just had to wait there for what seemed ages and see what was going to happen.

Eventually there came the news that the referee, Reg Brandis (Australia), had ordered that the race be rerun on the Thursday night. International Paralympic Committee technical delegate Chris Cohen stood by Brandis's judgment: 'There was a crash at 198 metres and the referee looked at the video evidence and felt the athletes involved in the crash were disadvantaged to a sufficient [extent] to be given another opportunity to race'.

> I guess you could say I have been given a second chance. I hope I don't stuff it up. I am going to change wheels tomorrow.
>
> I had a lot of media commitments tonight and it was all a bit overwhelming. Probably I had already become sick of people asking me to do photos and autographs and all that, even in the Village. It became even more difficult tonight. There is only so much you can handle, so much you can cope with. Tonight I was almost at the end of my tether. I did no media – and made a decision that I will do no more media and sign no more autographs in the Village.
>
> I called Mum at the Stadium on a mobile and she was an absolute mess. I told her I was fine and not to worry. Whatever would happen, would happen . . .

As it turned out I didn't get my second chance at gold on the Thursday. The Canadian team appealed against the referee's decision to the International Court of Arbitration for Sport. I was very disappointed with the attitude of the Canadians in the days that followed, and with the way they went about things. I was furious that they had named me in their press releases. Why name me? I had nothing to do with the protest. It wasn't Australia who had asked for the rerun – it was Germany and Japan. Yet the Canadians were inferring that the rerun decision had been made on my behalf. If the race was to be rerun it was on behalf of those who had protested – those who had lost their chance by the fall. And who knows? If there hadn't been a fall it might have been a different race. Who's to say that Wakako, for example – who raced so well to finish second in the Olympic 800 metres on the same track – wouldn't have been right up there at the finish?

The squabble continued until the Wednesday. After a longish hearing the International Court of Arbitration for Sport upheld the Canadians' appeal. Chantal had the gold, and I had the silver. And I will say right now that I am really happy with my silver medal. Chantal was the better athlete on the day, and I was always happy to accept the final verdict – whether it was to rerace, or not. Andrew Dawes spoke for himself and for me when he told the media: 'We both concede that Chantal won fair and square . . . '. However, there are still some points that I feel I must make:

- I have no doubt that the race should have been rerun for the benefit of those who protested. Of all the races that involved crashes at the Paralympics this was the only one that wasn't rerun. That was very disappointing for the athletes involved.

- If there is a crash within 200 metres of the start the rules are that they are supposed to recall the race. It is my belief that the starter should have recalled the 800 metres field. But I think the people in charge went into some sort of shock. They took quite a while to get the fallen people off the track. They should have stopped the race there and then, and either rerun it on the night or rescheduled it for another night, depending on the condition of the athletes who had crashed.

- Probably most disappointing of all was that the controversy stole attention away from just about everything else for three or four days. It was front-page news day after day when other Aussies were winning gold – and I was deeply embarrassed that it was still my face that appeared in the papers. Or Chantal's. At one stage she suggested she wouldn't take part in a rerun, if that were ordered.

I don't respect Chantal as much as I did before the Sydney Paralympics. I'd been racing her for years and it had always been friendly enough; we have had conversations about plenty of other things apart from our sport. But in Sydney, when I would say 'Hello' and 'How are you?' and stuff, she was very non-verbal. She seemed to find it hard to even say hello. Other athletes had the same experience; she didn't seem to speak to anyone. Chantal and I exchanged a few words at the 800 metres medal ceremony ... and that was about it.

I guess you could say the 800 was the low point of the Paralympics for me – in the controversy it sparked, and the attention it was to steal from other events and other people. As my diary reveals, my mum was a real mess that night when I finally got to see her and the rest of the family – she could hardly speak she was so worried about what had happened. I just kept reassuring them, 'I'm fine ... I'm really fine ... just go home'.

So they did. I didn't see too much of the family during the Paralympics, but now and then I managed to sneak across to my house to sample Mum's famous roast chicken dinner, or lasagna.

> *Rita Sauvage: My thought after the 800 was, 'Oh dear, the poor kid'. But I suppose I was pleased with the way the whole thing turned out, with no rerun. It saved a whole lot of trouble and controversy. It was very dramatic.*
>
> *Ann Sauvage: We all thought we'd jinxed her. Dad and I had really never seen her race, on the track anyway. When she started to race in Perth, I'd be down at the surf club, doing my thing. I think the only time Dad and I*

*had watched her was in the Perth City-to-Surf in 1999. I remember doing the Mexican wave as she went past. Just the two of us.*

But after the dramas of the 800 metres, including having to deal with a very upset family, the Sydney Paralympics became the event that I had dreamed they might be for me. For me it was a case of the Games having to go on . . .

### Monday 23 October

I didn't have a good night. I had a really bad tummy ache and got up at 3.30 and stayed awake for an hour. I felt tired this morning. But at least at the track I won my 1500 semifinal. Around the last corner Chantal tried to push me out – again. Then she stopped. It was a pretty slow time but I was the fastest qualifier. Kurt got a silver, which was so good, and Amy got a gold and there were some other great results for the Australian team. Smithy's race was after mine last night, and he also got gold in the 800 and that was excellent. I was so excited . . . I just wish I could get that excited about my own races!

### Tuesday 24 October

I had today off – no racing. Training was good; it was the best I have felt the whole time I have been here. I left the Village and picked Penny up from the shop at Seven Hills where I bought her – she's been staying with my friend Margaret Emerton throughout the Games. She was really excited to see me. I felt really happy today and I don't know the reason. I talked to a few of my friends and went home . . . and just felt normal, I suppose. Tomorrow night is the 1500 metres final and I am looking forward to that . . .

Really interesting things happened to me before the 1500 metres final, run three nights after the 800. The court decision not to rerun the race was announced that day, so I was under extra pressure there. By then I was also having elbow trouble again – maybe due to the lack of a proper cool-down after the 800. It became so sore that I had to tape it up, for the first time in eighteen months or so – something that really disappointed me.

On the night before the 1500 final all the stress and worry I was feeling seemed to reach a crescendo – and then all of a sudden something very positive happened. I guess I just let go. I suppose I just accepted that whatever happened would happen and that I should just get on with business. Suddenly the care was gone and it was as if a big weight had lifted from my shoulders. I thought to myself, 'I'll just keep racing, and do my best – do what I am here to do'.

On the night of the race I came out and beat Jean Driscoll and Ariadne Hernandez by a metre or so and won the 1500 metres gold. One journalist described the race as 'a tense psychological battle as much as a test of fitness'. I felt totally focused – even when Chantal came around me with a charge in the final lap. It had been a slow race (3 minutes 48 seconds), which I had dictated without working too hard. When she came around me there was a sort of gasp from the crowd – as if to say, 'Not again!'. But I was OK. I still had 400 metres to reel her in and I knew that I could do that because the race had been so slow. I had her measure at the top of the straight – then held off the challenges issued by Jean and Ariadne in the run home. Chantal finished fifth in the end. It was my eighth Paralympic gold medal.

> *Rita Sauvage: When she won the 1500 metres it was such a relief and such a thrill.*

Afterwards the media asked me about the 800 metres decision, which they were asked not to do. That was OK. The thing was that I had won my first gold medal at the

2000 Paralympics and that was excellent! Just as I went up to get my medal Jodie Willis Roberts threw a final shot in the shot put – and won gold. She did a victory lap while the anthem was playing . . . and it was just great.

Back in the Village I saw the doctor and the physio and was given some anti-inflammatories for my elbow. I'm just going to try and manage it as best I can and ice it a lot. After dinner in the Village I was struggling; I had ice on my elbow, a really bad headache and sore eyes. All the stress has caught up with me. And I have to train in the morning. Everyone seems to be in almost wind-down mode at these Paralympics already, which can be a bit frustrating for those of us who still have to compete. But that's just the way it is.

## Thursday 26 October

I had a sleep-in – and awoke to the happy realisation that my elbow was not too bad today. The anti-inflammatories must be working. I saw my friend Tracy Griffiths (now Harnett) today and Mum and Dad briefly, as well.

The medal ceremony for the 800 was on, so I headed back down to the track and received my medal. Silver. I talked to Chantal briefly and she seemed fine. I suppose I am still a little bit disappointed at how the Canadians handled what happened. I was at the track tonight when Smithy won gold again, with Aussie teammate Fabian Blattman second in a really close race. I watched from Michael Knight's box, which wasn't being used. The box next door sent us in some cake, which was a nice thing to do.

## Friday 27 October

Training today, and some time with friends and a quiet dinner with a couple of the guys in the Village. Tomorrow I have the 5000 metres final . . .

The 5000 was a straight final and a day or so beforehand I spoke to Jean Driscoll. 'Will you go with me in the 5000?' I asked her. She said yeah, she'd have a go. I wanted to make it a tough race, a hard, fast race.

> **Wednesday 1 November**
> It's been a while since I updated my diary. I have just been feeling tired and a bit sick, and battling a really sore throat – and I suppose it's not that unexpected considering what we have all just been through.
>
> I raced my 5000 metres last Saturday – and before it, waited to watch Kurt's 800. He pushed really well and finished second. I was really excited for him. Watching that race probably meant I didn't have quite enough time in the warm-up, but I was feeling pretty good all the same.

After a staggered start, in which I went out hard and set up a 10- or 20-metre lead, I soon realised that no-one was going to go with me – despite my conversation with Jean earlier. I then had one of those internal conversations that athletes continually conduct with themselves: 'They're going to let me do the work . . . no-one is going to go with me . . . why should I bust a gut? . . . I'm not going to be able to hold it for 5 kilometres on my own'. The debate over, I dropped back into the pack, and just did a share of the work from there. The two Japanese girls, Wakako Tsuchida and Kazu Hatanaka, did most of the work in front.

> On the last lap I got myself into a really good position and in the last 200 metres just put the power on and sprinted home for my second gold medal.

It was a very tactical race, featuring a lot of surging. My only worry throughout it was the fear of being trapped back on the inside. It didn't happen, though, and I felt totally in control the whole time. Just about all the way it felt like my race. I was disappointed that Wakako and Kazu didn't figure in the placings. They deserved to. Jean did barely anything up front, but finished third – with Ariadne Hernandez second.

> We raced before probably the largest crowd we've ever had at the Stadium and afterwards I did two victory laps. It was just awesome. And I realised it was probably the last time I was ever going to be in front of a home crowd that big. It was kind of a nice race to go out on.

The Paralympics finished for me that night with a second gold medal – and the acceptance of a painful reality.

My elbow was giving me a fair amount of trouble by then, and in the 5000 metres I raced with it tightly strapped. Throughout the week I had been consistently asked, would I race the marathon (to be run the day after the 5000 metres)? I hadn't really made a decision, but increasingly I thought the answer was probably no. My elbow was really bad and I knew the marathon journey would only make it worse, and considerably delay the healing process. So after the 5000, I conferred with Andrew – and we decided... well *he* decided, because I couldn't make up my mind... that I wouldn't contest the marathon. And so the Paralympics ended for me – with a second gold medal and the wonderful feelings that went with that.

> I did a press conference to explain my decision and spoke to many, many people. I headed up to the announcer's box to see Kathy Lee, to thank her for the excellent job she has done. Then it was back to the Village – and back over again to the Novotel, where I caught up with my family.
>
> On Sunday morning I watched the end of the marathon. Jean won as I thought she would, with Kazu second and Wakako third. It was a small field, a little disappointing really.

> Things were winding down. I loaded my car up with all my gear, drove it home – and just left it in the garage. The unpacking could come later, I decided. I came back to the Village and got ready for the closing. Having been nominated for the Whang Youn Dai Overcome Prize, I had to be back at the Village at six o'clock, before the Closing Ceremony. I was one of six finalists.

The Whang Youn Dai Overcome Prize is presented at every Paralympics to two athletes 'who best exemplify the spirit of excellence in sports and the Paralympic Games despite adversities'. Dr Whang is a medical doctor from South Korea who has polio and who has been an advocate of people with a disability for many years. In Sydney the prize was awarded to Martina Willing from Germany, silver medallist in the shot put. Martina is also a winter sports athlete and is visually impaired as well as being in a wheelchair. The second winner was Oumar Kone from the Ivory Coast, who competed in the 400 metres and 800 metres.

> After the award was announced I was able to rejoin the Aussie team in the stands and hear acts like Jimmy Barnes and The Whitlams. It was so much fun. The two Closing Ceremonies have been very different for me. I watched the Olympic ceremony from a box, and that was wonderful. But tonight was so special – I was part of it, out there with the rest of the team. It was so cool.
>
> We eventually made our way to the Australian team party, which was opposite the Aquatic Centre, down the road a bit from the Stadium. This was the biggest sprint I have ever had to make in my day chair. People were running after us, trying to stop us for photos and autographs. I just didn't stop. It was pretty mad – I was just going flat out.

I had never been scared of the general public before, but I admit I felt a bit of that around this time – as my diary indicates at various points. People were just relentless in wanting autographs and photos. It was full-on and I had never experienced anything like it before. People would spot me and some of the others ... and they'd just start running. During the Closing Ceremony I had already signed countless autographs and posed for I don't know how many photos – everyone was out in the middle of the Stadium that night, volunteers and plenty of others.

> The night subsequently was really good. There was an excellent cover band and a basic barbie, which was probably the best thing possible. It was such a good night, people just let go. Everyone got a bit trashed – there was plenty of free alcohol, although not enough for some people! I got home about 2.00 a.m.

\* \* \*

The immediate period that followed the Paralympics was not a particularly happy time for me, but I have gradually let go of that, allowing the bad memories to fade, letting them slide. In the big picture the positive overwhelmed the negative. But the post-Games schedule was heavy – with parades, travel and a range of appearances and commitments. There were long days and nights, and missing bags, and hotel rooms that weren't ready, and not enough sleep – and, for me, the onset of some virus thing that really knocked me around. I did the Sydney, Melbourne and Perth Parades, struggling much of the time – although I appreciated the enthusiasm of the public, realising how much the Paralympics had done to raise the profile of sport for athletes with disabilities in Australia.

> On Monday morning I went with six or seven others and did a prerecorded segment for that night's 'A Current

Affair'. Then we headed down to the Sydney Paralympic Parade, which was very good, but very tiring, and even a bit scary at times. There was an amazing response from the public – a wonderful display of support for the Paralympic movement. In fact there were so many people waiting for us to come out of the Town Hall that when I got to the bottom of the ramp I just couldn't get through. People were pushing and shoving and eventually Petrina Tierney, one of the masseuses, helped me through and came back with me to the Wentworth Hotel where we were staying – and I was so thankful to have her there. I was getting really upset. I think I cracked then more than any other time during the Games, and I was upset that had happened.

Back at the hotel with the others, we had to wait two hours to get our rooms. We were off to Melbourne the next day. The team night that followed at the Convention Centre, with the family there, was a pretty good one, though – well, most of it. Afterwards I got angry with some things that Mum said and we had a row. That was awful – I ended up breaking down and crying. I guess we were all so emotional and tired, and when you're like that the smallest of things can set you off. It just seemed that everything good ended up being not so good. I think emotions were running high, and I was tired ... everything just started to come out. However, it ended up OK, and I got to bed at one o'clock after a long day.

My family took a flight back to Perth the next day as I headed off to Melbourne. For me the Games had been all the more special because they had been there to share the experience with me. I think it taught them a bit more about my life to come and see a little bit of what I go through. One night during the Games Mum wanted me to go out with them for dinner and I just said, 'No, I can't; I'll just get hassled and approached and I don't want to have to deal with that right now'. I think when I told her that she couldn't understand – but as the Games rolled on, she realised how much I had to cope with.

> The next morning, Tuesday, our bags had to be outside the rooms at 5.00 and we had to be downstairs ready to go at 5.30. I was up at 4.00, but at 5.20 the bags were still outside the rooms. We ended up not leaving until after 6.00. We could have slept for another hour!
>
> In the Melbourne Parade, I was in the lead car with pentathlete Donnie Elgin – and for the first time didn't have to push. That was nice. We headed the Parade down to the Town Hall and went up on stage. There were loads of people there and they gave us another great reception, but I was so drained that I just didn't want to talk to anyone in the end and they let me go back early to the hotel where we were staying. Team staff member Jason Hellwig came back with me along with one of the Telstra guys, and we had a quiet lunch, which was nice. Then I just went to sleep until dinner.
>
> Today I have a day off to spend doing whatever I want around Melbourne.

### Saturday 4 November

> On Wednesday, my free day, I ended up having a good lunch with my friend Shona Casey and an enjoyable dinner at St Kilda with Greg Smith and his pal Richard Skender.
>
> I think it has all caught up with me. By last Thursday I was feeling quite sick, with a sore throat and flu symptoms. I had a rash on my chest and a temperature. At the airport I could hear the flights to Sydney being called, and I just wanted to get on one of those and go home.

> But it had to be Perth first . . . the last leg. I felt absolutely terrible. My ears were blocked the whole way over.
>
> At the airport, the guys from Telstra met me. (Telstra is organising the parades.) It had been a long flight for me; I was way below par and my mood was somewhere down there too. I was sick and tired. But I slept OK, in a big jumbo-sized bed, and went to the chemist the next day and got some paracetamol and stuff . . . and felt a little bit better.
>
> On Friday morning I went to a media reception at Government House, to which families of athletes were invited. I didn't know anything about that — the invitations must have gone to Sydney. So Mum and Dad weren't there. The parade that followed was great, though — down familiar streets in a familiar city. There were heaps and heaps of people there. The best reception ever, I think. They were loud and happy and it was really nice. But the best thing about the Perth Parade was that I saw all my family and heaps of friends. They all came out to see me and I had fun trying to spot them in the crowd.

I was doing it tough, but the Perth Parade turned out to be the best of the lot. It meant a great deal to me finally to be in my home town — and even more because so many of my friends and family were there to share the experience. They were all so proud of me. Yeah, I got a glow out of that for sure. This was the best parade, the best reception . . . the one that meant the most to me.

> It was a good day — although I started to feel sick in the afternoon and eventually headed back to the hotel. With Alison Quinn, and Greg Campbell (Assistant Chef de Mission, Communications, at the Paralympics), I caught the 3.20 flight home. That was all I wanted — to get home, see my doctor, see Penny . . . and try to get back to a normal life . . .

## Sunday 5 November

I went around to Karen's and had my hair cut for the first time since September – a fair bit off the bottom. But nobody seems to notice! Tonight we had McDonald's for tea. I haven't done that for a year and a half. I guess I can eat whatever I want now. I admit to having had some cheesecake the other day, too. But I must try not to get fat while I am not in training. I'm feeling better already; my cold has improved and my ears don't hurt as much.

Well, it's really over. At some time soon I have to decide what I want to do from here, and how I want to do it. One thing I *would* like to do is go to Boston next year (2001), and for that to happen I'll need to start training in December. Probably I'll do Oz Day, too.

It has been a good time. I suppose things didn't always turn out exactly the way I wanted them to – but in the end I was really happy. I have come away from these past two months with an Olympic gold and two Paralympic golds and one silver. You really couldn't ask for more than that. The two Games were just the best ever. So fantastic. The end of a year I suppose I won't ever forget.

\* \* \*

It's a year now since Sydney hosted the Olympics and Paralympics of September and October 2000. Rereading this diary for the first time I honestly can't believe just how much I seemed to see everything in a negative light. I am a little shocked. I was so focused on myself during that period, so self-absorbed – but then as an athlete I suppose you have to be, as you strive to perform at your best.

The diary couldn't be more honest. It is exactly the way I felt and reacted to things at that time of my life. It was a highly stressful – but successful – few months, and the diary indicates clearly that I had a one-track mind – centred on my competition, and what I had to do.

Everything in my mind revolved around being able to compete at my best. I just couldn't see anything else. I realise that now . . .

Because the fact was that there was a lot of fun along the way, things I didn't mention when I sat down each night to record the activities of my day. There were all the funny things that can happen in a team situation. I remember our amputee guys stealing the moose, the Canadians team mascot . . . fun nights in our house in the village with all the flatmates . . . the nights grouped together around the TV when we couldn't go down to the Stadium . . . and the friendship and shared enjoyment with my roommate Angie. Yeah, a lot of happy things did happen.

I realise only now that what I wrote was from the narrower viewpoint – of an athlete under pressure, who desperately wanted to do well. Perhaps any athlete tackling the double challenge of an Olympics then Paralympics would have had the same limited focus. As a primary document recording the way things were for a slice of my life, my diary is the truth. But a year on the memories are now wider and more balanced – expanding to take in the fun things and the happy times. They add up in total to good memories of a wonderful time in my life . . . memories that will be with me forever.

Something I will never forget is the public support we had during these Paralympics – undoubtedly the biggest and best ever staged. The people turned out in unprecedented numbers. A number of sports had sellout sessions. People were educated and entertained. I'm sure that in those couple of weeks in October many people were hooked on our sports. It was just terrific. The Paralympics and the people competing were the toast of Sydney for that magic time.

And young Australia came along in vast numbers through the innovative schools program. It was a masterstroke to virtually throw open the Paralympic gates to the school kids, to the next generation – and the schools got right behind it. It provided the kids with valuable lessons about sports for athletes with disablities – something that should be enormously beneficial to our sports in the future. Kids being kids, they made huge amounts of noise – and just went ballistic over any Australian competitor.

With an affordable $15 day pass, the Paralympics became 'The People's Games'. I don't know how many people came up to me and said they enjoyed the Paralympics more than the Olympics – because they could afford to actually be there. People just found the whole thing more accessible and more enjoyable – even the volunteers. We were constantly told that they were enjoying the Paralympics more than the Olympics.

This unprecedented response to the Paralympics proved one thing above all: that sport for athletes with a disability can at times be very big news indeed. This in its own way is a huge step forward for our sports, even if the media's coverage is at times controversial and troubling.

One negative aspect of the Games that the media unfortunately seized upon was the positive drug test results of a number of athletes competing in powerlifting and athletics. Other athletes with a disability have tested positive now and then on the international scene, but until the revelations of Sydney – which were no doubt a shock to the general public, if not to people within the sport – not many of these results had been brought to light.

As is the way of things these days, you hear talk in our sports of people who might be 'suss' when it comes to drugs. But in my experience, not too much of it. My sense of it is that not too many athletes with a disability go for drugs. There is not enough money, not enough reward in our sports to justify people taking the risks involved with using drugs. Obviously the million-dollar deals in able-bodied sport at the highest level are the spur for people to take the chances that they do with illegal substances. In sport for athletes with a disability, that sort of money doesn't exist.

But the fact is that there is some use of performance-enhancing drugs in sport for athletes with a disability – a revelation that emerged at the Paralympics. The total number of athletes testing positive, nine or ten, was a troubling one, and I think the statistics in Sydney confirmed that sport for athletes with a disability requires ongoing vigilance in the future – just as does able-bodied sport at *its* highest levels.

At a function held before the 2000 Olympics, in company with Ian Thorpe, I gave my public support to a passport devised by the Australian Sports Drug Agency, to be used by athletes to document their drug-testing history. Ian and I had been selected because we were the current Australian Male and Female Athletes of the Year. My support for the cause was heartfelt.

Drug tests are a fact of life for someone competing at my level in sport. And I'm happy to say that I have always tested negative, and always will. Drugs are not for me. Why do it? is my question. Life has so much to offer without them. What I have achieved I have managed through a combination of the talent I have and the hard work I have added to that. It is my belief that if you can't compete at the elite level in any sport without taking drugs, you shouldn't be there.

Leaving the drugs scandal aside, the huge and overwhelmingly positive coverage of the 2000 Paralympics lifted our sport, once such a quiet backwater in the big picture, to another level again. Over the decade in which I have competed internationally we have come a long way in the understanding and appreciation of sport for athletes with a disability.

But athletes with a disability still confront some brick walls. Inevitably it seems there will always be people who rate us as different and who want to treat us that way.

> *Tracy Harnett, friend: I remember a night out that Louise and I had in Perth in the year after the Barcelona Games. We were in the Aberdeen Hotel, and Louise was up on a bar stool – putting her up at the same height level as me. And this guy came up and said quietly to me, 'Isn't it great the way they can get away from the TV and get out of the house and come out and socialise?'. He was talking*

> about Louise. I thought it was hilarious – he was talking about someone who had been travelling all over the world that year, and who had spent only three or four weeks in Perth because of it. But his attitude was pretty common.
>
> One night in the early '90s Louise and I headed out – and I went in a wheelchair owned by one of her friends. We went to a restaurant. 'Oh, how sad ... won't you two ever walk again?' a girl there said to us. Afterwards we went to a nightclub and we were dancing – and people kept coming up to us and wanted to hug us and kiss us. It was a real pity-type thing ... a sympathy thing. On a later visit the same nightclub refused us entry. I think they only wanted to accept the 'beautiful people' – and what a joke that was when you consider all the glamorous fashion shoots and modelling shoots that Louise has done for magazines. There was some subsequent publicity about that – and the nightclub apologised, and invited us back.

In the Olympic Village in Sydney, as in Atlanta in 1996, many of the able-bodied athletes had no idea why we were there. It was understandable, I guess; we were there just for one race on one day – and a demonstration race at that. We just didn't feel terribly much part of the team. We had volunteers coming up to us and saying, 'You're here early, aren't you?' It was three weeks before the Paralympics!

Thankfully, though, the brick walls seem to be crumbling. The attention paid to the Olympic demonstration races, then the fabulous support and media coverage of the Paralympics, aided the cause enormously.

To be honest, I still prefer the Paralympic experience. John MacLean thought I was a bit weird when I told him that, but it's the truth. The Paralympics is an environment I know, with staff and teammates I know around me – although I also know that I'll never forget the thrill and honour of twice competing at the Olympics.

The wonderful response to the demonstration races, then the Paralympics, showed just how wide the acceptance of sport for athletes with a disability was in 2000. We have made progress, and will continue to make progress – at least if I have anything to do with it!

CHAPTER 19

# DOING IT MY WAY

Throughout my career I have found that with the rising status of Paralympic sport, curiosity about my life, and the things I do chasing the success I seek, has risen accordingly. I suppose you can say that I'm a public figure now; the recognition factor certainly seems high these days when I'm out doing what I do. And people often ask me questions about my training, the equipment I use, the sacrifices I make . . . the sort of life I lead. I accept that in a sporting country like Australia, such questions go with the territory for those who manage to achieve some success. So in this chapter I have attempted to address some of those most frequently asked questions, to share some corners of my life that people perhaps don't know about.

So, what is my life like these days? What is a typical day in the life of Louise Sauvage?

Well, my life today, focused on my career as a professional athlete, is pretty full, as I juggle all its various facets around the requirements of my training.

> *Karen McBrien: Nothing stops Lou getting up to train. No matter if all around her have been partying on. Even if she's not well, or is below par – she'll be up early and out there training.*

When I'm home in Sydney, my day runs roughly along the following lines. I'm up between 5.30 and 6.30, depending on where training happens to be. My furthest trek for training is to Penrith, about forty-five minutes away. Centennial Park in Sydney's eastern suburbs is about thirty minutes away. At Penrith a number of us use the International Regatta Centre, site of the Olympic rowing and canoeing events. An almost flat 5-kilometre road that loops around the site is really good for endurance and speed work. In Centennial Park we work in good spirits with the huge packs of cyclists who pelt around there early of a morning. They know us well, and take care. 'Wheelchairs ahead . . . coming through!' they'll yell before whizzing past.

Parramatta Park is an occasional training venue, and, more frequently, Sydney's M2 freeway – but only on weekends. The road is too busy during the week, too risky – but its cycle lane provides a good long run. If you see someone on a Saturday heading out along the M2 in a race chair, from Toongabbie back towards the city, it could be me. I'll push a hard 10 to 15 kilometres east, then turn around and push back to where I parked the car.

The mornings generally consist of ninety minutes or so of track or road training. Total mileage in an average week can be anything from 100 to 150 kilometres. Then in the afternoon there's another session, which can vary between track, road, gym (weights – free weights, mainly) and boxing. In the garage of coach Gary Foley there is a variety of equipment that I use as part of my training: a heavy bag, a speed ball, medicine balls, focus mittens and much more. The gym I most often use is the one at the State Sports Centre, Homebush – although the whole gymnasium had to relocate during the Games period, moving to Meadowbank, which luckily is close to my home.

Before big events like the Olympics–Paralympics double of 2000 my training changes. In the taper period before big events gym work disappears from my program. My training is focused just on working in the chair. Generally I don't do much training on the track, but in the build-up to the two Sydney Games I was doing at least two sessions a week on the track. I used to really hate training on the track, although not so much now. The more work you do on the track (and I did heaps in the build-up to the Olympics and Paralympics) the more you get used to it, and the more you see the benefits and appreciate them. Basically, though, I just feel better on the road... freer, more comfortable... and faster, because the surface is harder than the track. And it's more interesting than just going round and round, too!

Over the years my training routine has also changed; boxing, for example, is a fairly new addition, something I didn't do in the lead-up to either Barcelona or Atlanta. Swimming was part of what I did back then. It's not any more – mainly because of this elbow of mine, which needs to be treated with some care. But training is always changing, becoming more sophisticated. New techniques come in, new approaches. In another eight years it will be vastly different again. Whether I'll still be around competing then ... well, that's another matter completely.

\* \* \*

Because of Penny, I generally have a third 'training' session late in the day, taking her down for a half-hour run on the playing fields and parklands at the bottom of my street. Before the Olympics and Paralympics Lee or one of my neighbours would help out in walking Penny.

I also visit the physiotherapist frequently, generally for 'maintenance work' on the injuries that I live with – the problem elbow and the neck trouble. So any week is a mix: road, track, gym, deep tissue massages, boxing, physio. And, oh yeah, I forgot the travelling to and from – and that's a big part of it. When I tell people I train three or four hours a day, they'll say: 'Oh, that's not too bad'. But add on the travelling time to and from – and hurrying home to attend to other matters, then shower and get ready to do it all again that day – and you'll understand that it's a full program each day.

And in there somewhere is the rest of my life, my other various commitments – to the media, sponsors, public speaking bookings, the organisational needs of a busy life . . . myself. All of it is set out on a weekly basis in my diary . . . which is my life, my bible.

* * *

Apart from taking Penny to our local park, I have Sundays off. Then, on Mondays it starts all over again . . .

The day off is vital – a full day to consolidate, to attend to other things, to recover physically and mentally and to prepare for the next week. And I need that, because I'm the sort of person who will overtrain . . . get up and drag myself out and go training or compete even when I'm half dead. I have paid the price for that at times, pushing the limits too far and not letting myself recover from the cold or flu or whatever it might be.

> *Andrew Dawes: If she's exhausted or not up to it, I will advise her not to race . . . but even if she's half dead, I know she'll want to.*

Professional athletes walk a fine line. We unhesitatingly train in the rain because we know at times we'll have to *compete* in the rain. We know the chance is there that we might pick up a cold. But we train anyway. The real trick is to train hard, but not so hard that you lower your immune system and your resistance levels to the danger point, where you are more susceptible to viruses – and get sick. I've heard it said that many elite athletes are fit . . . but not healthy. I do my best to stay both.

Sometimes, though, it wears me down. One of the worst things about being an athlete is that you feel tired most of the time. Sometimes you really feel you are 'running on empty'. The lead-up to the Olympics and Paralympics in Sydney, for instance, was very full-on and very difficult, and for a time, as you've already seen, I wasn't handling things too well.

I'm a different person now from the one I was back in '92 when my first Paralympics were nearing. I am older (obviously) and more experienced, and have a lot more knowledge about my sport and about myself. It hasn't got any easier, though. I have been at the top of my sport for many years now, and I think the hardest thing of all is the challenge of staying there. There is a lot more pressure on me now – more stress, more decisions to make.

My perception of how much I have achieved is probably not as high as some other people's. I suppose for me achieving things in my life is as simple as getting day-to-day obligations done – and sometimes I really struggle even with that; I never seem to have enough time. Achievement is a funny thing. I think that we all tend to underplay the things we achieve to an extent, and that the achievements of people far away from the media and the spotlight can be just as significant as those of people who happen to be more recognisable.

\* \* \*

Of course, I owe some of my success to Mother Nature. I have pretty much the perfect body for what I do: not much in the way of legs, and really long arms, a considerable advantage. People like Kurt Fearnley and me have had our disabilities since birth. We had built a lot of upper body strength before we ever started racing – because we always relied on our upper body for everything. Some of the guys who have had accidents and become paraplegics or quads don't have that initial advantage when they take up the sport.

> *Andrew Dawes: Louise's success comes from a combination of things: firstly, she's very strong, has a*

*physical structure very suited to the sport, with long arms. She has relied on her upper body all her life and built up strength. Wheelchair athletes like her have relied on arm, shoulder and chest muscles virtually since they were born. At four years of age they would do four hours of upper body exercises a day . . . whereas an able-bodied child wouldn't experience that.*

*But in my view that might be less than half the reason [for why she's so successful]. There are a lot of people similar to Louise who haven't had anything like the same success. With her it's that inner strength – not her arms, or shoulder power . . . it's the strength that lies within. She is such a strong-willed person – hates to get beaten. I've heard athletes say that they have come up to her in a race and think they've got her beaten – then they see this glint in her eye that says, 'No, you're not going to get me this time'. She's so bloody competitive, even when the stakes aren't high – like in heat races where you've only got to qualify in the first three. She still won't take the easy option. No matter that you tell her to save herself . . . if it comes down to a race then she's just got to win it.*

\* \* \*

In my sport the equipment is, of course, vital – and I am very fortunate that seven years back, as I've already mentioned, I linked up with Top End in America, now Invacare, who custom-make my wheelchairs these days. But my first overseas-bought racing chair was the Swiss 'Kuschall' I had custom-made before Barcelona, one of the better chairs on the market at the time.

The three-wheel 'Eliminator' racing chair from Invacare that I use these days is worth about $6000 all-up, the price largely depending on what kind of wheels it has. There are carbon-fibre wheels, tri-spokes, quad-spokes and solids, and I use different tyres for different requirements, whether track or road. The chair is made of lightweight aluminium, is very aerodynamic and weighs between 7 and 8 kilograms.

My relationship with Invacare is an important cog in my story. I am a member of the Invacare Corporation's 'Team Invacare', a squad of wheelchair athletes and teams, taking in wheelchair basketball and rugby teams and individual tennis players and track and road racing athletes. Their support of me is both personal and professional – and greatly appreciated.

> *Michael Devlin, Director of Health Care Professional Marketing, Invacare: Louise's recognition today alongside able-bodied athletes demonstrates how far disabled athletes have come. We take great pleasure in providing them with specialised equipment, but it is clearly their own efforts and determination that give them the edge they need to gain such recognition.*

The most important thing of all is the set-up of the chair. In 1990, when I went to my first World Championships in Holland, I probably didn't have the best chair on the market. But I was set up right and had a good technique and so I did really well. For sure it wasn't all the chair. A good chair has to 'fit' you well – have the right-sized push rims for your arm length, and provide good body position.

Today's chairs are pretty advanced, and the changes coming into them now are only relatively minor. The sleek and sophisticated equipment I use these days is light years removed from my first racing chair, bought for me by the Tuart Hill Swimming Club when I was eight. That was a four-wheeler and didn't have any steering. But I loved it, and thought I was pretty hot at the time.

I do just about all the necessary work on my chair myself. I have got to know the workings very well over the years – I think it's important to know how your equipment works. And it's especially important if you happen to be overseas and something goes wrong. It's a message I always push strongly to the kids coming through.

But even though I do my best to look after my equipment, I have still managed to break various racing chairs over the years. It can even happen during competition – as in Boston in '99, when my steering unit snapped. In King's Park, Perth, one morning a few years back, I was doing hill repeats and the chair felt weird. Something was wrong. Then on an uphill push I noticed a long crack in the front fork. I tried heading back downhill, but it was no good – the fork broke, and eventually I had to get out of the chair and wait by the roadside. After a while someone stopped and gave me and my busted chair a lift. Then outside Newcastle on Boxing Day, 1997, I was training with Christie Skelton when the same thing happened – the fork broke clean through. I had to head back into town without a front end – with the front raised and me balancing on the back wheels!

\* \* \*

Generally I have to be very careful in watching what I eat. Basically I stick to a low-fat diet 99 per cent of the time. I have a nutritionist whom I see on a regular basis and who works out what, how much and when I should eat to gain the most energy from my food. There are endless books and dietary programs around for able-bodied people, covering their needs. But for people like me in wheelchairs, with different requirements and different energy usage, there is nothing to use as a guide. It's been trial and error to an extent – working out the optimum daily calory intake and that sort of thing.

My optimum weight for competition is around 60 kilograms, and by being disciplined I'm usually not far off it. I don't think my genes help me much in that area . . . I come from a fairly 'large' family and constantly have to battle to keep my weight at what it should be. That is one of the hardest things about what I do. Going to a place with a buffet is a particular temptation – particularly if they happen to have fifty million desserts. I went to a restaurant like that in Sydney not long before the 2000 Games and I remember gazing over the desserts and thinking, 'My God! Wait until November . . . I'm going to come back here and try every one of these!'. A newspaper asked me a while ago what I would want served at my last supper. 'Ice cream,' I said.

My training schedule has meant that I have constantly had to make sacrifices in my life, to let some things pass me by. I think all top athletes would say exactly the same thing. It can be no other way – the physical and mental demands of training and competition at the highest level dominate a life.

Something has had to give. With me it has not only been my diet, but also my social life. The fact is that when your commitment to sport is what mine has been for the last ten years or so, there has to be a price. I have paid that price, without complaint – although like every one of us I wonder now and then whether the path chosen could have been different.

Full-time professional sport hasn't left me too much time for a life outside. When you're training, travelling, competing, your sport *is* your life. I would say I definitely haven't had the life of a normal girl in her teenage years or in her twenties. Through my competition years I haven't been one to go out clubbing all that much and do all those kinds of things.

> *Karen McBrien: There's no doubt that because of the life in sport she has committed herself to, Louise has missed out on some of the 'ordinary' things that people take for granted. Before any big event, the partying, the socialising is just not part of her life.*

I've never been a great drinker. Occasionally I'll have a beer or champagne and maybe once or twice a year I'll have a night out with a few drinks. I don't have a favourite drink – it might be spirits . . . it might be something else; it depends what mood I'm in. But alcohol is not a big factor in my life, and probably never will be – to be honest, it doesn't appeal that much anyway, although I enjoy a party as much as anyone.

> *Ros Shaw: So many times we've been out, and Louise would be there having a good time – but not drinking. She loves to party, but she'd say, 'Nup, I can't drink'. Like everyone she likes to unwind now and then – but for Louie there's always another training session . . . always another race. I say to her that seeing she's missed out on a social life . . . I do it for her!*

I do go out, of course, but within reason, I suppose, because of what my days demand. And I do have big nights now and then. I've had some fun along the way, though.

> *Shona Casey: In 1995 we went on a* Fairstar *cruise of the South Pacific and after twelve nights partying, got off the boat, flew to Melbourne and jumped into my car for the three and half hours' drive to my home town, Birchip, to attend the B & S ball. By the Monday Louise was back in Melbourne, flying out to Japan to compete in a marathon [the Oita Marathon].*

Away from my sport, I still enjoy what everyone enjoys in life . . . I'm no different. Family, friendships, weddings, christenings, birthdays, a night at the movies, going to parties. A lot of it, though, is rushed. If I go out to lunch when I'm in full training, for instance, it's a pain in the bum – because most times I can't sit there and relax and enjoy the meal and the conversation. There's always another training session just ahead.

\* \* \*

Of course, what I do occasionally brings perks that most people never get to experience, many of which I have shared with you – glittering awards, dazzling functions attended by glamorous celebrities . . . But when it comes to people, the *really* important ones in my life and career do not have names that are widely known to most people. They are my 'network' – the family and good friends who over the years have helped me become what I am, helped me achieve what I have achieved – and who have stuck by me through thick and thin.

I haven't had a massive circle of friends like some people of my age. My life as a professional sportswoman locks me in, especially so since I moved to Sydney. When I arrived here I really didn't know anyone, except people associated with my sport – although I'm settled now after five years. I hasten to add that the friends I do have, here and overseas, are terribly important to me. With the sort of life I lead I don't get to see many of them too often – but it's so good to have them there. They understand me, understand if I can't keep in regular contact because of my commitments, would never expect anything of me. In the rather solitary occupation I pursue, I am not a prominent part of their lives but my friends mean a very great deal to me. They help me get through.

When I look back my career to date, and all the successes I have had along the way, I know for sure that I couldn't have done it without the help, guidance, loving support and wisdom of a whole lot of people. I think that any successful athletic career (or life, for that matter!) is essentially a 'team' effort, composed of many threads. Almost always there are quiet heroes and heroines in the background – people who have helped lay the foundation and who, sometimes, are left in the shadows, all but forgotten, while the athlete moves on to greater and greater things.

Most of them you have met already: there are my coaches over the years, Frank Ponta, Jenni Banks, Andrew Dawes and Gary Foley; and my manager up until the end of 2000, Karen McBrien. All these people have been key figures in the progress I have made on the sporting arena. But there have been so many others: my family of course (couldn't have done it without them!) and friends – Tanya Giglia in primary school, Karen Long in high school (and beyond), Shona Casey, my great friend since 1993, and Tracy Griffiths (now Tracy Harnett, married to Paul and with a little boy, Nikky), who has been a good and supportive friend since we first met when she was working for the Western Australian Disabled Sports Association – though we don't get to see each other much these days. And so many more.

Sometimes, too, I think about the people who used to come along to training in early days, just to help out. Maybe they read about me now and think, 'My God, I used to pick up discuses for her when she was eight years old!'. In whatever I have managed in the years since, all of them have played a part.

\* \* \*

I have never placed great emphasis on dating, or anything like that. The glossy magazines seem forever taken with the question of whether or not I happen to have a boyfriend at any particular time. In interviews before the Sydney Olympics and Paralympics, *Who* magazine asked me the question, and so did *Woman's Day*. My unspoken reaction was: 'Why is it that you guys keep asking that question?'. Eventually I simply accepted the reality that that's just the way magazines are. I told *Woman's Day*: 'I don't have a boyfriend, so Penny, my Tenterfield Terrier pup, makes the perfect companion. She's always pleased to see me when I come home and doesn't answer back when I tell her off!'. And as I told the last journalist to pose the question, Kate Cox of the *Sun-Herald*, back in September 2000, no, I didn't have a partner right then. I also told her that I did my best to steer questioners away from the subject of my personal life, and that in interviews I tried to keep things as 'professional' as possible, not wishing people to know everything about my life. I'm like everyone else – I need some private space.

In my dealings with the media I have learned what to say, and what not to say. I know that every time a camera is on me or a microphone is produced I go into a special 'zone'. I will never say anything that I don't want the media to print – because I know that any time I do step over the mark with an opinion, it will be there the next day in black and white.

\* \* \*

The media also want to know about my personal likes and dislikes, and I don't mind talking about those.

Music is a big part of my life; I spend a lot of time in my car and the radio, CDs or tapes are always on. I like a whole lot of different bands and singers.

At the movies, I'm a great fan of those Kathleen Turner and Michael Douglas films: *Romancing the Stone*, *The Jewel of the Nile* and *The War of the Roses*. And I loved *Romeo and Juliet*, and loved the music too. The CD is still one of my favourites.

'The X-Files' is my favourite TV show – by a fair way. I love Mulder and Scully ... I just wish that they would get it on! I doubt it'll ever happen, though; maybe right at the end. It's such a cool show – and I loved the movie as well. I like 'Friends' a lot too, and I watch things like 'ER' and the medical dramas. When I'm in America I usually watch a lot of TV. Between events I spend a fair bit of time in hotel rooms – and I reckon I can tell you when every major show is on over there. There is such a huge selection – a hundred channels or more.

At home TV is only an occasional escape for me at the end of the daily slog of training. And 'occasional' is the word – honestly, I don't get to see that much. My life is so full and at the end of the day I am forever trying to catch up on things that have to be done. For that reason I have never bothered about getting a pay-TV hookup for sport or for anything else. I know that I'd hardly ever have the chance of watching it. I was glued, of course, when the Olympic Games were on. But wasn't everybody?

* * *

So, there you have it, a snapshot of my life: a little bit of fun mixed in with a whole lot of hard work! Now all I have left to tell you about is what I've been up to since the end of the 2000 Paralympics ...

CHAPTER 20

# BACK TO THE FUTURE

At my final press conference of the Sydney Games, I told the media that while I had toyed with the thought of retirement, I had made my decision to keep racing. 'Now is the time to reassess what level of competition I want to compete at in the future,' I said.

And that was the way it was. I was heading on. For a couple of months I had laughed and cried and won and lost. Never had life been so stressful ... or so exciting. It had drained me physically, but it hadn't daunted my spirit. I was twenty-seven, and there were more races to be run ... and won ...

\* \* \*

It wasn't until two weeks before Christmas 2000 that I climbed back into my racing chair and faced up to the challenge of becoming an athlete all over again. By then, after a two-month break, I felt heavy and fat ... but a lot more normal too.

By the time I got back from the final parade in Perth I was way below par, my ears throbbing from a bug I had picked up. My injuries had flared up, and my general health was not what it should have been. I needed to get away from it all, right away . . .

And after a brief interlude in Victoria, that's exactly what I did, heading to New Zealand for ten days with my friend Kellie Puxty, and touring around the South Island.

The six weeks away from my sport were the break I had to have. In Melbourne I went to Derby Day on the Saturday and then Cup Day on the Tuesday – getting dolled up for the big day, as you should. There were a few of the guys from the Paralympics there on Melbourne Cup Day and we had a lot of fun, joining in the parties at the course and having a good night out afterwards. I even managed to back a couple of winners on Derby Day. Later in my relaxed summer I was back in Melbourne for the Australian Open Tennis final (Andre Agassi versus Arnaud Clement), and later still at the Grand Prix.

The time in New Zealand was wonderful – just what I needed. It was only November, but bloody cold – beautiful all the same. In Milford Sound it snowed. It was the first time in my life I had seen snow falling, and I was so excited. On a boat trip on the Sound we saw penguins and seals. Physically, I did nothing, absolutely nothing on that trip – no training, no physical exercise; I didn't even go for a swim. I ate what I wanted to, took it easy . . . and gradually started to feel human again, as the stress and tension lifted after one of the biggest challenges I would probably ever face in my life.

Six weeks into my break, though, I was starting to think, 'It's about time I got going again'. Once when I had a period away from racing I used to keep some sort of light training routine going. But not in recent years – and certainly not now, when I so needed to be away from it all.

But 2001 was going to be a big year for me. At the end of each year I sit down with my coaches Gary and Andrew and we spend time setting goals for the twelve months ahead, tracking the schedule that I have set out for the next twelve months. In 2001 the Boston Marathon and the IAAF World Championships in Edmonton, Canada, were the big targets. Still smarting from my controversial 800 metres defeat at the Paralympics, I knew that the Worlds would give me the chance to turn the tables on Chantal Petitclerc... and on her own turf.

So late in 2000, there came a day when I knew it was time to get serious once more. When it happened, and I climbed back into my chair to start all over again, it felt so strange. It was four weeks or so before I felt I was back in the groove, an athlete again.

What made it even tougher was the fact that if I was going to race the Oz Day race I had to return to training in the pre-Christmas period, when everyone is in party mood and eating and drinking are such a big part of life. It is not the ideal time to be losing weight. But by then I had my twelve-month program firmly in mind. Oz Day in January was part of it – and so it had to be that way. The last thing I wanted to do was to make a fool of myself at Oz Day!

The race meant a lot to me this year. I had won seven of them, but been beaten by Wakako Tsuchida at the start of 2000. I was keen to turn that around. And I managed it – even though I wasn't in perfect shape. It was a good race; Wakako and I were together for most of it, within a wheel's length of each other, and this time, unlike in 2000, I had the better finish, winning by a second, with Chantal Petitclerc third, almost two minutes further back.

It was the beginning of a competition year during which I hit form that was as good as, if not better than, anything I have done in my life. The slow start to the competition year, with me in relaxed holiday mode, culminated in a burst of form and record times that probably surprised even me.

It started in the February–March Grand Prix Series, when I raced in Newcastle, Sydney, Canberra and Melbourne. In Melbourne, racing against the men, I went 1 minute 48 seconds for the 800 metres – 2.62 seconds inside the world record that Chantal Petitclerc had established in August 1999! It couldn't be submitted as a world record, because the race wasn't sanctioned – but the time just blew me away. I couldn't really believe it. I guess I knew then that I was possibly on the verge of another new phase in my career as a wheelchair racer. And the competition year unfolded just as I had hoped, with success after success – despite increasing problems I was having with my left elbow.

In March I won the 8.8-kilometre Round-the-Bays race in Auckland and subsequently won the 800, 1500 and 5000 metres races at the Nationals in Canberra, racing well on the track considering I was building up for a marathon: Boston – again!

My elbow nagged at me the whole way through the build-up to Boston. Nothing I could do made it any better, so I just maintained it with daily icing and regular physio. There was talk of a cortisone injection before Boston, but I didn't want to take any time off training so that was put on hold. Despite the troubling elbow, I was pretty happy with my preparation; I hadn't done a lot of work in the gym, but I had done quite a bit of hill work, and felt comfortable.

This particular Boston, on 16 April, felt very strange indeed – for one very good reason. There was no Jean Driscoll. I had, of course, heard the reports of her retirement. But as I told the media before I left home: 'I won't believe it until I line up for the race, look along the line and see she's not there'.

Well, it was true. After eight victories in eleven years (punctuated by my three wins), the Queen of the Boston Marathon had finally called it a day and was now on the other side of the fence, as a commentator. I saw quite a bit of her this time and found her a chattier, friendlier person. It was not surprising; we were no longer rivals! On Easter Saturday, two days before the race, Jean kindly invited me to a pizza-pasta day at her coach's brother's home. There were a lot of people there I knew and it was really nice of Jean to think of me. So with Jean there, it was Boston as usual in one way . . . but so different at the same time.

Without Jean, I went into the race as favourite, with the Swiss girl Edith Hunkeler rated my main challenger. It was funny to go out to the start knowing that Jean wouldn't be there. It felt very different – but I was relaxed and fine.

If there is such a thing as a 'comfortable' marathon, this was it. Edith and I worked together, both of us taking turns out front and not pushing at an exceptional speed. I didn't go out of my way to do a fast time, or to take on a lot of the work. In the end I just set out to do whatever was necessary to win. Edith didn't try to break away at any stage and I knew deep down that I could outsprint her when it came to the crunch. Eventually it did down come to a sprint finish – and I ended up beating her by about 10 metres. The time was slowish: 1 hour 53 minutes 54 seconds. Probably there were people who didn't think it was very fair – Edith had done more of the work than I had, and no doubt deserved first place. But I went there to win . . . and I did it. I thanked Edith when she congratulated me at the end, and complimented her too on the way she had raced.

Then I told her, 'That was probably my last marathon ever'. 'No . . . no . . . don't say that!' she said. But I was deadly serious – I told the media the same thing at the press conference, and Jean too when she pulled me aside. 'Yeah, that's it,' I said . . . and told her about the seriousness of my elbow problem.

It was my fourth win, and my ninth and last Boston Marathon.

I guess I have been much in Jean's thoughts throughout the past few years, as she has been in mine. Her autobiography *Determined to Win* in fact starts this way: 'Louise's yellow jersey bobbed up and down in front of me as we cruised at more than thirty miles per hour, down the hill past the fifteen-mile mark'. She was telling the story of the 2000 race. I couldn't believe that – my name is the first word in her book!

In the copy Jean gave me in 2001 she wrote the following: 'To Louise – congratulations on winning your 4th Boston Marathon! You are a champion and are worthy of the accolades you receive! You have helped to redefine women's wheelchair racing. You have been a tough competitor and your résumé is impressive. Good on you! What else can I say? – Jean Driscoll'.

Months later, as I work on this book, I feel exactly the same: I have raced my final marathon after fifty or sixty in my career – although who's counting? But for all that, it was weird to leave Boston for the last time. Maybe I'll go back to the event as a spectator one day, just to enjoy all the things that go on around the big race. The place and the race have been such a big part of my sporting life.

\* \* \*

I came home happy that I had done what I set out to do, but with a seriously aching elbow. I knew the regular icing and anti-inflammatories could do no more than maintain it. I had made my decision to give up marathon racing with this thought in mind: 'I am going to have to push my day chair for the rest of my life ... and I don't want to be in pain for the rest of my life'. If I wanted to keep racing – and I did – something had to go. It was the marathon. I would reduce my training kilometres, still race, and hope that the elbow stood up for as long as I chose to keep competing.

So I headed back from Boston to some painful days. The elbow was sore in its own right – but sorer still when the doctor squirted in a cortisone injection and moved the needle around. That was disgusting, but it was only really painful for a day and then quickly settled down. Ever since – touch wood – it has been fine, quite manageable. I had two weeks off training after the treatment – and at the same time had all four of my wisdom teeth out, requiring a hospital visit. I came out looking like a chipmunk and was very swollen and sore for many days.

This set me back in a year in which my next big goal was the 800 metres demo race in Edmonton. But not too much. I raced and won a 10-kilometre road event in Darwin and had a few enjoyable days up there looking around. Then I travelled with some of the boys to Canada for the Championship trials, also held in Edmonton, then back into the US, to a training camp at a place called Cedartown, 100 kilometres out of Atlanta. I won a couple of road races there, but then had one of the worst training sessions of my life on the Sunday before the big Peachtree race in Atlanta in July. It was horrible. I just didn't want to race Peachtree because I felt terrible and I was so weak on the hills in my training. And towards the end of that race there are a lot of hills.

Well, I raced it in the end – and got beaten by a basketballer! I probably talked myself out of any chance of winning, and decided that one of the Americans, a strong girl named Christina Ripp, who had represented the US at basketball at the Paralympics, would probably win the race. There is a steep downhill at the start and she and I positively flew down it, and raced together, breaking away quickly from the rest of the pack. Well into the race I turned to her and said, 'When you get away ... just go ... because the race will be yours'. I was kind of encouraging her along the way, which is something I probably shouldn't have been doing – but I knew I wouldn't stay with her. After the injection and the teeth problems I just hadn't done the training I needed to do to be in top form.

So Christina won the race – and I just pipped Christie Skelton for second; Christie raced really well on a program of only four days a week training to fit in with her studies, picking me up on the hills a few times. I didn't really push too well – but I guess I had pretty much accepted that that was going to be the way of things before the race.

That was about the end of the bad news when it came to racing in 2001. Progressively I ran into a zone of really hot form. At the Metro Challenge in Toronto – the Canadian Wheelchair Nationals – I won the 800, 1500 and 5000 metres finals – although the times were nothing flash. But I knew the curve was heading upwards as the Worlds neared, and I was confident. By then I had done the necessary work, and my speed was good ...

\* \* \*

This was the first year since 1997 that demonstration races had been staged for wheelchair athletes at the IAAF World Championships.

After '97 they announced that our demonstration events would be replaced by events for blind athletes instead. In '98 the blind athletes were the only ones to demonstrate, but by 2001 there were six events for athletes with a disability: two for blind athletes, two for amputees and two for wheelchair athletes.

I had a comparatively long wait in Edmonton before my race; we arrived on the Sunday, and I didn't race until the Friday night. The time went slowly – but it was the first occasion on which I had had my coach Andrew Dawes all to myself at such an event and the build-up went really well. I trained well and we talked and planned extensively about the tactics and the race. We discussed all the different scenarios, the things that might happen, and mentally I was very, very prepared for all the possibilities.

With a big crowd roaring for Chantal, the 800 metres at the IAAF World Championships turned out to be quite a tactical race. I had again drawn Lane One – but happily I was able to control things basically from start to finish. Lane One wasn't great, but I reckoned there might only be a couple of my rivals that I couldn't catch in that first surge. Chantal was one of them; she had drawn Lane Six. It took her a while to get across, but by the 200-metre mark I was almost level with her, just behind. She tried to cross me, but I let her know where I was . . . and she stayed out. I raced then from the front; I knew what speed I wanted to do, and where I wanted to be in the run. The plan was always to get the lead from the start, and then to really suss out what I was going to do. The decision I made was to stay out there and set the pace – and I did it and managed to slow the field down.

Into the back straight on the final lap, Chantal came up alongside me . . . and the crowd went absolutely nuts. But I was comfortable with her challenging me . . . I wasn't worried. At the top of the straight I was feeling strong and in control. Chantal's challenge was fading – and in the end the challenge came down the inside, from Ariadne Hernandez, who sneaked through there when I left a gap. But the race was mine and I had half a chair to spare over Ariadne, with

Wakako Tsuchida third when we reached the line. Chantal really died towards the end, which surprised me. She finished fourth. I think she had pretty much run her race with the big charge she made in the back straight.

I was happy, but drained, and there was no big party afterwards. After the medal ceremony, drug testing and press conference I didn't get to leave the track until around 11.30 p.m. Back at the hotel with a few of the others, we caught the last dregs of dinner. My celebration was a bowl of ice cream with topping, although when I got back to my room, Trina, one of the hotel staff, had left me a baby bottle of champagne and some strawberries and chocolate. I was feeling like a zombie by then, but I had a glass of bubbly – and toasted my happy night alone.

It was the fourth time I had 'demo'd' at the World Championships, and the fourth time I had won. And this one was especially satisfying. The Championships proved to be a great success for the Australian team. Of the six events for athletes with a disability we won three, with Amy Winters and Neil Fuller also winning gold, and Megan Starr picking up a bronze.

* * *

In August, during the Swiss Nationals in Jona, something pretty amazing happened. Before the 5000 metres final a group of us agreed that we would 'go for it' on one of the quickest tracks on the international circuit. 'Let's work together ... let's make it a good race,' I said to the others before the start. And we did. I was up front throughout, along with the two Swiss girls, Edith Hunkeler and Sandra Graff.

Well, I won the keenly contested race on a hot afternoon – and glanced up at the clock as I went through the finish line. 'Hmmm, 13.14 ... not too bad,' I said to myself. It wasn't until I completed the cool-down lap that I realised I had in fact gone 12.14 – and smashed the old world record! The old record of 12 minutes 22 seconds belonged to Lily Anggreny of Germany.

They turned out to be great Nationals for me. Apart from the 5000 metres, I won the 800 and 1500 and ran second in the 400. Andrew got me to race the 400, which was no longer on my schedule, to help add the speed factor to my starts in the 800 metres. I once held the world record for both the 100 and the 200 metres, so I had to be OK at starts! But as time went on and I switched more to road racing and the chairs got longer, my technique changed. With the combination of all those changes, my starts deteriorated. I am continuing to work on that aspect of my racing.

\* \* \*

On 14 September 2001 I was booked to fly to the USA to compete in a couple of road races there – the Riverside Rumble in Wilkes-Barre, Pennsylvania, and a race in Boise, Idaho, that I hadn't tackled before. But three days beforehand, of course, the world changed, perhaps forever, with the terrorist attacks on New York and Washington D.C. Safely home in front of the TV in Sydney I watched the images of death and destruction in absolute horror . . . like everyone else. I don't fully understand why it happened, and just like most of us I probably never will. I guess about the only thing I knew as 11 September unfolded was that I wouldn't be going to America as planned – not just yet, anyway. The Boise race went ahead without me, and the Riverside Rumble was postponed, as people reassessed what had happened . . . and what might happen in the future. My inconvenience was minuscule and not worth mentioning, considering what had happened to so many others. I wondered if people would ever feel quite the same way again about international travel – and especially travel to the US. But I believe that no matter what happens life must go on. I am thoroughly aware that I could go out and get hit by a bus at training tomorrow!

So in October, with just a little trepidation, I flew to Pennsylvania and competed in the rescheduled 10-kilometre Riverside Rumble. It was a little scary, flying over by myself – but when I got to Philadelphia

I linked up with some of the other guys headed for the race and we travelled together, and things were fine. I found the attitude of the people over there was very similar to my own: that things have got to keep going, that life must continue as close to normal as possible.

The race was a tough one – but brought the result I had hoped for. I was not 100 per cent fit. I had been ready back in mid-September when the race was first scheduled, but since then had had a holiday in Queensland and a break from training. I went into the Riverside on only two weeks' training, which is not ideal. It proved just enough. I worked throughout the race with three American girls: Christina Ripp, the basketballer who had beaten me in the Peachtree race in Atlanta, Jessica Galli and Stephanie Wheeler. Over the bridge near the finishing line it was down to two of us – Christina and me. I knew she was strong and stayed behind her over the bridge before making my move. I got past her, but was dying a bit as the line neared and she came up on my left again. The finishing line arrived just in time. There was half a wheel in it.

\* \* \*

Back home I raced in the inaugural 10-kilometre Sydney Bridge Run, a promising event that unfortunately ended in frustration and disappointment for me. Not far from the finishing line at Fox Studios, Moore Park, they had changed the course from the one indicated in the program. A left turn indicated in fact meant a *hairpin* left. Like most of the other wheelchair racers I went left, but too gently – and kept going up the wrong street. I soon realised I was in trouble and I kept asking marshals and people at the drink stands: 'Am I going the right way for the 10k?'. 'Yeah, yeah,' they said, urging me on. But I wasn't – I was following the course for the full marathon, which was a separate event. Just about all the other wheelchair guys missed the turn – and got called back. They didn't call me back. I was set to finish second overall in the race, behind the men's winner, Grant Buckley. In fact I didn't finish at all, and eventually headed slowly back to where the finishing line was, rounded up my day chair, and went home. That afternoon the organisers rang me to apologise and they sent some flowers the next day, which was nice. They thanked me for taking the disappointment so well. 'Well,' I said, 'I wasn't too impressed . . . but these things happen'.

\* \* \*

On a glorious spring day the following week I found myself at the helm of New South Wales State Transit's 34-metre Supercat 3, surging east up the Parramatta River. Minutes before, after three unsuccessful attempts to crack the traditional bottle of champagne aboard the boat, I had finally launched the *Louise Sauvage* in a spray of champers at Homebush Bay Wharf, before a small crowd, with the railway band providing the musical accompaniment.

'My' boat proved fun to drive, with just a gentle touch required via the joystick. I know my mum's going to want to take a ride when she next comes to Sydney.

What a thrill, and what an honour! My name was chosen to go on the new vessel based on the results of a competition conducted by the *Daily Telegraph*. I was in illustrious company. The names adorning other Supercats, Harbourcats and Rivercats included Dawn Fraser, Shane Gould, Betty Cuthbert, Evonne Goolagong Cawley, Susie O'Neill and Mary MacKillop. On board the *Louise Sauvage* is an impressive pictorial feature, featuring photos of me, my record as a wheelchair racer and the message 'You'll never know what you can do or achieve until you try'. It is a motto that has underpinned my life. How true I believe it is!

Yes, 2001 proved quite a year.

\* \* \*

In terms of financial support things changed for me after the Olympics and Paralympics, as they did no doubt for a lot of athletes. I lost a couple of my sponsors and that was disappointing. But I suppose a lot of corporate plans were targeted just up to the September–October 2000 period, and then things were scaled down.

Later, though, I linked up with an excellent new sponsor, the German-owned telecommunications company Siemens. I also joined a new management team, Elite Sports Properties, headed by former Olympic swimmer Rob Woodhouse.

It was quite a wrench splitting with my friend and manager Karen McBrien, who had been such a part of my life since I moved to Sydney. But Karen decided after the Paralympics that she would take a different career path and would no longer manage athletes. I appreciated all she had done for me. She had been a great manager ... and best friend. And she still is. I knew I would miss the caring, personal touch that she provided, but life changes and it was a very amicable parting. I talked to a few possible new managers as I looked to my future on and off the road and track. Rob and ESP came very highly recommended and I was very happy to join their team, which includes the likes of Susie O'Neill, Michael Klim and Shane Gould.

Probably the question I was most asked along the way in the twelve months following the Olympics and Paralympics was: when was I going to retire? I still can't answer that question. I can only tell people the truth: that some time after the Sydney Paralympics I sat down with my coaches and mapped out a program for the next two years, 2001 and 2002. I committed myself fully and enthusiastically to that period. There were terrific stepping stones along the way – the Boston Marathon and IAAF Championships of 2001, and, in 2002, the IPC World Championships in Lille, France, and the Commonwealth Games in Manchester. After that ... well, I don't know.

The thought is at the back of my mind that to go to the Commonwealth Games – where there is a full-medal event on offer for the first time, an 800 metres – would be a wonderful way to cap my career. It is a huge breakthrough for athletes with a disability in general to have a full-medal event for the first time at an able-bodied meet. And the fact is that I have won gold medals at all the other major events – Olympics, Paralympics, IAAF and IPC World

Championships. To win one at the Commonwealth Games would be a very nice way to finish.

But I am making no statements or promises . . . because I simply don't know! I will be twenty-eight when the Commonwealth Games finish in the northern summer of 2002. I'll step back some time after that . . . and think about the next two years. There will be temptations to keep going, I know, with the Athens Olympics and Paralympics only two years away at that point. I'll just see how I am. Already I am being asked endless questions about Athens. 'It's only a few years away,' they'll say. 'And you're a long time retired.' And I think, 'Yep, and I've been a long time competing, too'.

The funny thing is that with a more relaxed and carefree approach to my racing in 2001, after the intense pressure of 2000 my form, as I said, has been as good as at any time in my career. And the enjoyment factor has increased considerably. Olympic year was so full-on that I made up my mind that in 2001 I would take it a bit easier. I wasn't as strict on diet – and if someone asked me out for drinks on a Saturday night, well, yeah, I'd probably go. In 2000 I wouldn't have contemplated it. I decided I wasn't going to get stressed about whether I was getting enough sleep or not. I don't sleep well at the best of times.

I decided I was going to enjoy life a bit more. And I did . . . and still am. And I reflected now and then on just how tough 2000 was, and how I hadn't coped very well at all – although the results were what I had hoped for in the end. Everything was a hassle, and if, as I said elsewhere, I appear whingeing and negative at times in telling the story of it in this book . . . well, that's just the way it was. I wouldn't want to be like that again . . . or go through that again.

Even the state of my backyard has improved. The roses have fences around them these days, and are growing very well. The yard is more or less 'Penny-proofed' – although she's become a lot better now that she's older . . . and wiser!

\* \* \*

My future beyond sport is perhaps already taking shape.

The focus of my life to this point has been my sport. It is what I do, and on a daily basis my life revolves around the things that I have to do to gain the success I achieve. It is a structured life much of the time ... because that is the way it has to be. You could probably say that I am *consumed* by it most of the time. But more recently one focus of interest away from sport has been my foundation, the Louise Sauvage Aspire to be a Champion Foundation (www.aspire.au.com), started in partnership with the Northern Eagles NRL Club in 2000.

That first year I didn't have a lot to do with it, because of my total commitment to getting ready for the two Sydney Games. In 2001 it was different, and I was really delighted to play an active role in developing the Foundation to the point where we distributed four individual financial grants and one team grant. I'm on the panel that makes the decisions. We also have fundraisers and look at doing promotions, such as one we did with Bonds around Mother's Day in 2001. Ten per cent of any Bonds products sold by Big W in a two-week period went to the Aspire Foundation.

The whole thing has now become a major part of my life. Yeah, it still involves my sport, but at a completely different level. It was set up to help any athlete with a disability, and I know how much I'm going to enjoy following the progress of the athletes who are recipients of support through the Foundation. I guess I know as much as anyone in our sport how hard it is to gain support or sponsorship. And sport can be a very expensive business.

It's great to be involved – a huge buzz, in fact, to be able to give away the money, knowing it's going to help a career ... and a buzz too to see the reactions of those chosen. For me the Foundation is a chance to give back something to my sport – a part of my life that has given me so much over the years. And that's why I started it. The athletes chosen are the future of our sport ... and I hope to see them all represent Australia. I think they will.

\* \* \*

In addition, my work as a guest speaker has been consistent since the Olympics and Paralympics. I do quite a lot of public speaking these days, and enjoy it. My talks are mainly about how I got started in sport and what the turning points were for me. I almost always talk about Boston and *those* races – because the tale of those battles with Jean Driscoll tends to be something of a motivator. Through everything I do, of course, I try to raise people's awareness about the Paralympics and about sport for people with disabilities.

Most of the work I do is with corporate groups, translating the messages of my life as a professional athlete to the business arena. The ideals of success in sport cross many boundaries – and certainly relate to the business world, as has long been recognised.

I talk about the need for people to set achievable goals, and about getting help and support along the way as they chase after those goals. It is so easy to relate sport back to business . . . and to life generally. I think one of the best examples of that lies in the approach of one of the sponsors that have backed me, the National Australia Bank – in the way they have changed in recent years, how they now work towards getting their staff more motivated and do productive through offering incentives and emphasising the value of teamwork. It has opened my eyes, observing how people at companies like the National work together. There is no doubt that the positive messages of sport have been snapped up and used by many businesses.

But in public speaking the thing I enjoy the most is the chance to talk to children. I probably like talking to kids more than adults because young people tend not to have preconceived ideas about anything. Sit in front of them for a few minutes and they have fully accepted you. They don't give a toot that you are in a chair. Adults in groups tend to tiptoe around things a bit; they don't ask questions and they tend to assume things. Kids just blurt it out: 'So, what's wrong with you?'. They just don't give a toss, which is really good. Whereas adults *assume*, kids *ask*. I like that.

I tend to keep it fairly short with children, because if you hang around too long, their attention wanders. I often start off by asking *them* questions to find out what they know. Then I tell them about me and my sport and what I was doing at their age – I try to relate my story to them and their lives. When I tell them I was eight years old when I had my first sports chair, that generally strikes a spark. Most of them can relate to what it's like being eight. I always bring some gear along: they get to sit in the chair, inspect the helmet, the gloves. And I always bring some of my medals. When we talk about the helmet I tell them they must wear one when they're on their bikes . . . something I feel very strongly about.

Talking to older kids, I can make it a bit more technical. They tend to ask the best and most intelligent questions of all. 'Don't hesitate to ask anything you want to know,' I tell the groups I talk to, 'because I have been asked just about everything in the past . . . and it doesn't bother me, whatever you ask'.

In late 2001 the Australian Paralympic Committee paid for me to do a course with the Rogen people, on presentations and public speaking . . . and it was terrific, although very confronting at times. The course takes you right out of your comfort zone and is one of the most challenging things I have ever undertaken. I know the lessons I learned will help me in my future working life, whatever shape it may take.

I am a more confident person now than ever in my life, and no doubt the Rogen course has helped with that. It has made me a better speaker and helped me get my messages across more strongly. That way I can influence people so that they hopefully go away with a different attitude, and really think about the things I have said.

Once, long ago, I was just an athlete. But for a long time now, media obligations and an increasing number of public speaking commitments have been a big part of my life. I think those things are like anything in life. When you practise them, work at them, you become more confident and better able to handle what has to be said and done. Because of these public speaking abilities I am a more confident person, both within my sport and outside it.

*   *   *

But in telling this story of my life so far I am still very much in competition and training mode and I haven't really looked past my retirement as an athlete. There is no set plan that I am going to do this or that. What I will do is what I have done right through my career: review, reassess, set goals and plan when the time comes. One thing I know is that I would like to be involved in my chosen sport in some way in the future, when I retire from competition. Whether that will be in coaching, or whatever . . . I don't yet know.

Goal-setting has always been an important part of my life. From the time I competed at my first Senior Nationals I guess I've always had progressive goals in my career – although always realistic ones. I have never been a person who looks ten years ahead. As an athlete, the focus is always much tighter than that. For me throughout my professional career it's been essentially one year at a time – with a monthly focus, and a weekly focus, and a daily focus . . . of getting my training right, of concentrating on technique and the necessary hard work within the framework of a balanced life. Obviously the between-Olympics periods are different, with the acceptance of the reality of the four-year time period, and the raising of my sights to that . . . but all of it is still based on a year-to-year plan. There are no secrets – it is just the method I have used to achieve things in my years in sport.

But there are more personal goals too . . . the sorts of dreams that we all have. When I think about the house I am going to live in one day it is going to be really, really big . . . with a double garage. We all think about things like that. As to where I eventually want to live, I don't really know – I like all three of the cities I have lived in, Perth, Melbourne and Sydney. I do know that I'd like to live in Melbourne again some day . . .

*   *   *

When I look back I find it hard to believe what I have achieved. It was certainly never a goal that I would be the one in Australia to establish some sort of landmark for athletes with a disability. When people describe me as a 'pioneer' in my sport, I always think to myself, 'Well, I never set out to be that'. I am, however, quite comfortable taking on that role, quite happy to be out there promoting what our sport is all about.

As I said in the final presentation of my Rogen course, in September 2001: back in 1983 when I first started in sport I had no idea I would one day be standing up telling the story of how I had competed at the Olympic Games and Paralympics and so many other events around the world. At that stage it never even occurred to me. I was living for the moment . . . for the day . . . for the fun. Nowadays I think it might be different, in a sporting world that has become more professional, more structured. You get kids of ten saying, 'I'm going to go to the Olympics, or Paralympics, one day!'.

I'm sure that when the time comes for me to call it a day in my career, I'll know with some certainty. It won't just be me thinking I've had enough, or that I have done enough. I'm sure it will be things like elbows and necks that will have the final word.

When I think back on the decade or so since 1990, the first year that it all started to get serious for me, I think above all else of three events. My first Paralympic gold medal at the Barcelona Games in 1992 was a special thrill. The Paralympics, after all, were the pinnacle of my sport . . . and I had won gold. And I think of the Boston Marathon of 1998, when I came from what seemed an impossible position, and snatched victory away from Jean Driscoll in the final centimetres. I had won it the year before, but '98 was more satisfying. In 1997 Jean had taken a tumble crossing the tramlines – but in '98 we were both fit and strong and hungry to win. That year I broke through mental barriers – something that provided a new springboard for the achievements of the few years that followed. Thirdly, I think of the Sydney 2000 Olympics – and winning the 800 metres there, with that tremendous surge of energy from the crowd lifting me to the line. I will never forget these things. This was so very special, competing in front of a home crowd, and even more so, in front of my family and friends.

I am so proud of the medals I have won. For any athlete such prizes are the symbols of success – and a representation of all the hard work and effort invested. And I enjoy sharing them – showing them to people – because I know that often they mean almost as much to other people as they do to me. Some athletes tuck them away, put them in cotton wool, fearful that they will be scratched or damaged. I've never been like that. My theory is, what's the point of having a medal, or medals, if you don't share the enjoyment? So I'm pretty keen on passing them around if people want to have a look. I mean, they're the ones who came out and supported me and cheered me on. And I don't care if they get a scratch on them or a mark . . . that just adds a bit of character.

The medals and the trophies represent the milestones of my career as a wheelchair racer – a journey that has changed me in many ways. And yet I'm not so very different from the girl I was when it all began in Perth. Back then, on the edge of the career in sport that my life became, I was sternly advised now and then, 'Louise, you can't do that'.

But I did it anyway.

APPENDIX 1

# AWARDS & RECOGNITION 1990 TO 2001

## 1990
'Queen of the Straight' (fastest woman over 100m), Stoke Mandeville World Wheelchair Games, UK

## 1991
'Queen of the Straight' (fastest woman over 100m), Stoke Mandeville World Wheelchair Games, UK
Sportsmen's Association of Australia National R. A. O'Neill Award – Winner
WA Disabled Sports Association Sports Star of the Year – Winner

## 1992
Order of Australia Medal
Young Achievers' Awards WA, Channel Ten – Finalist
WA Disabled Sports Association Sports Star of the Year – Winner
Caltex Sports Awards, WA – Finalist

Australian Confederation of Sport Female Athlete of the Year – Finalist
Official Sports/Tourism Ambassador for the Australian Tourist Commission
ABC Sports Star of the Year Awards – Finalist
WA Sports Foundation Sports Star of the Year – Finalist

## 1993
Young Achievers' Awards WA, Channel Ten – Finalist
Caltex Sports Awards, WA – Finalist
ABC National Junior Female Athlete of the Year – Winner
MLC Junior Sports Foundation – Achiever of the Year

## 1994
Australian Paralympian of the Year – Winner
Coca-Cola Sports Champion of the Year Awards, WA – Winner
Young Achievers' Awards WA, Channel Ten – Winner
WA Disabled Sports Association Sports Star of the Year – Winner
Women in Sport Foundation, WA – Finalist

## 1995
Australian Paralympian of the Year – Finalist

## 1996
Australian Paralympian of the Year – Winner
Telstra Sports Awards – Finalist
Coca-Cola Sports Champion of the Year Awards – Winner
WA Disabled Sports Association Sports Star of the Year – Winner
Women in Sport Foundation, WA – Finalist

## 1997
Australian Paralympian of the Year – Winner
IOC Trophy within Australia, 'Sport for All' – Winner
Telstra Sports Awards – Finalist
Australian Institute of Sport – Athlete of the Year
Coca-Cola Sports Champion of the Year Awards – Winner
*Cosmopolitan* Magazine 30 Most Successful Australian Women Under 30
WA Disabled Sports Association Sports Star of the Year – Winner

## 1998
Australian Paralympian of the Year – Winner
Australian Paralympic Committee Female Athlete of the Year – Winner

Australian Confederation of Sport Australian Female Athlete of the Year – Finalist
Young Australian of the Year Awards – Finalist
Young Australian of the Year Awards, ABIGROUP National Sports Category – Winner
Young Australian of the Year Awards, WA Sports Category – Winner
AVON Spirit of Achievement Awards, National Sports Category – Winner
MMI Daily Telegraph Sports Star of the Year Awards – Finalist
*Cosmopolitan* Magazine 30 Most Successful Australian Women Under 30
'This is Your Life' Program

## 1999
International Female Wheelchair Athlete of the Year – Winner
Australian Female Athlete of the Year – Winner
NSW Sport and Recreation Awards for Athletes with a Disability, Open Category – Winner
NSW Wheelchair Sports Association Athlete of the Year – Winner
Australian Paralympic Committee Female Athlete of the Year – Finalist
*CLEO* Magazine 1999 Young Women of the Year, National Sports Category – Winner
*Cosmopolitan* Magazine 30 Most Successful Australian Women Under 30
Louise Sauvage Pathway named in the Olympic/Paralympic Village

## 2000
International Female Wheelchair Athlete of the Year – Winner
Sport NSW Annual Awards Athlete with a Disability, Open Category – Joint Winner
NSW Wheelchair Sports Association, Athletics Athlete of the Year – Winner
NSW Wheelchair Sports Association, Athlete of the Year – Finalist
NSW Young Australian of the Year, Sports Category – Finalist
Australian Sports Medal
Inaugural Laureus Sports Awards World Sportsperson of the Year with a Disability – Winner

## 2001
Sport NSW Annual Awards, Athlete with a Disability, Open Category – Winner
NSW Wheelchair Sports Association, Athlete of the Year – Winner
NSW Wheelchair Sports Association, Athletics Athlete of the Year – Winner
Ryde Sports Star of the Year – Winner

APPENDIX 2

# PERFORMANCE RECORD 1990 TO 2001

## 1990 PERFORMANCE RECORD

### Track

| Date | Event | Distance | Placing | Time | Record |
|---|---|---|---|---|---|
| April | National Senior Games, Canberra | | | Time not available | |
| 14–25 July | IPC World Championships in Athletics, Assen, Holland | 100m | 1st | 18.31 | World |
| | Stoke Mandeville World Wheelchair Games, Aylesbury, UK | 100m | 1st | Time not available | World |

# 1991 PERFORMANCE RECORD

## Track

| Date | Event | Distance | Placing | Time | Record |
|---|---|---|---|---|---|
|  | Stoke Mandeville World Wheelchair Games, Aylesbury, UK | 100m<br>200m | 1st<br>3rd | Times not available | World |

## Road

| Date | Event | Distance | Placing | Time | Record |
|---|---|---|---|---|---|
| 26 January | Oz Day 10K, Sydney, Australia | 10km | 1st Junior Woman | Time not available | Aust |
|  | 10th International Bloemen Marathon, Holland | 8-day stage race | 3rd (Team) | Time not available |  |

Overall Series Winner, Woman's Division, National Wheelchair Road Racing Grand Prix Series.

# 1992 PERFORMANCE RECORD

## Track

| Date | Event | Distance | Placing | Time | Record |
|---|---|---|---|---|---|
| January | VicHealth International Track Meet, Melbourne | 400m (demo) | 1st | Time not available | |
| April | National Wheelchair Games, Adelaide | 100m | 1st | Times not available | Aust |
| | | 200m | 1st | | Aust |
| | | 400m | 1st | | Aust |
| | | 800m | 1st | | Aust |
| August | Swiss National Championships, Zug, Switzerland | 100m | 1st | 16.75 | World |
| | | 200m | 1st | Times not available | |
| | | 400m | 1st | | |
| | | 800m | 1st | | |
| 3–14 September | Paralympic Games, Barcelona, Spain | 100m | 1st | 17.37 | Paralympic |
| | | 200m | 1st | 29.03 | World |
| | | 400m | 1st | 56.71 | Aust |
| | | 800m | 2nd | 1:54.88 | Aust |

## Road

| Date | Event | Distance | Placing | Time | Record |
|---|---|---|---|---|---|
| 26 January | Oz Day 10K, Sydney, Australia | 10km | 1st Junior Woman | Time not available | Aust |
| April | Australian Marathon Championships, Adelaide, Australia | 42km | 1st Open Woman | Time not available | Aust |
| 3–14 September | Paralympic Marathon, Barcelona, Spain | 42km | 6th Open Woman | Time not available | Aust |

Overall Series Winner, Woman's Division, National Wheelchair Road Racing Grand Prix Series.

# 1993 PERFORMANCE RECORD

## Track

| Date | Event | Distance | Placing | Time | Record |
|---|---|---|---|---|---|
| 23 January | New South Wales Sugar Games, Sydney | 800m (demo) | 1st | 2:05.83 | Aust |
| 29 January | VicHealth International Track Meet, Melbourne | 200m | 1st | 307 | Aust |
| | | 1500m | 1st | 3:40.7 | Aust |
| 7 February | Athletics Australia Grand Prix Meet, Perth | 100m | 1st Woman | 17.20 | Aust |
| | | 1500m | 1st Woman | 3:38.75 | Aust |
| 3–4 April | Athletics Australia 1st National Disabled Track and Field Championships, Canberra | 100m | 1st | 17.23 | |
| | | 200m | 1st | 30.13 | Aust |
| | | 400m | 1st | 57.77 | Aust |
| | | 800m | 1st | 1:55.35 | Aust |
| | | 1500m | 1st | 3:40.52 | |
| | | 5000m | 1st | 12:55.99 | Aust |
| 25–26 June | Metro Toronto International Wheelchair Challenge, Toronto, Canada | 200m | 1st | 31.47 | |
| | | 400m | 1st | 57.16 | |
| | | 800m | 1st | 1:54.44 | Aust |
| | | 1500m | 1st | 3:52.96 | |
| | | 5000m | 1st | 13:20.79 | |
| 20 August | IAAF World Championships, Stuttgart, Germany | 800m (demo) | 1st | 1:54.39 | Aust |

## Road

| Date | Event | Distance | Placing | Time | Record |
|---|---|---|---|---|---|
| 26 January | Oz Day 10K, Sydney, Australia | 10km | 1st Open Woman | 25:22.00 | Aust |
| 27 February | Gasparilla 15K, Tampa, Florida, USA | 15km | 1st Open Woman | 39:46.00 | Aust |
| 7 March | Los Angeles Marathon, California, USA | 42km | 4th Open Woman | 1:52.30 | |
| 14 March | Mobil 10K, Torrance, California, USA | 10km | 1st Open Woman | Time not available | |
| 21 March | Round the Bays, Auckland, New Zealand | 8.8km | 1st Open Woman | 19:05.00 | Aust |
| 19 April | Boston Marathon, Massachusetts, USA | 42km | 3rd Open Woman | 1:39:33 | Aust |
| 25 April | Toyota of Orange 10K, Orange County, California, USA | 10km | 1st Open Woman | 23:48.00 | Aust* |

*Fastest Woman wheelchair 10km time in the world for 1993 and second fastest time ever (by 2 seconds).

| Date | Event | Distance | Placing | Time | Record |
|---|---|---|---|---|---|
| 2 May | Lilac Bloomsday 12K, Spokane, Washington, USA | 12km | 2nd Open Woman | 34:28.00 | Aust |
| 6 June | Melbourne Marathon, Melbourne, Australia | 42km | 1st Open Woman | 2:03:57 | |
| 4 July | Peachtree 10K, Atlanta, Georgia, USA | 10km | 1st Open Woman | 24:12.00 | |
| 10 July | Kaiser Roll 10K, Minneapolis, Minnesota, USA | 10km | 1st Open Woman | 24:45.50 | |
| 31 July – 7 August | Bloemen Marathon, Holland | 8-day stage race | 1st Woman Overall | Time not available | |
| 21 November | Olympic Dream 10K, Melbourne, Australia | 10km | 1st Open Woman | Time not available | |

Overall Series Winner, Woman's Division, National Wheelchair Road Racing Grand Prix Series 1991–1993.

# 1994 PERFORMANCE RECORD

## Track

| Date | Event | Distance | Placing | Time | Record |
|---|---|---|---|---|---|
| 27 January | VicHealth International Track Meet, Melbourne | 100m | 1st | 18.08 | |
| | | 800m | 1st | 1:53.21 | World |
| | | 5000m | 1st | 13:14.00 | |
| 13 February | Athletics Australia Grand Prix Meet, Perth | 400m | 1st Woman | 57.11 | Aust |
| | | 800m | 1st Woman | 1:54.81 | |
| | | 1500m | 1st Woman | 3:51.70 | |
| 19–20 February | Victorian State Track and Field Championships, Melbourne | 400m | 1st Woman | 54.75 | Unoff. World |
| | | 800m | 1st Woman | 1:52.05 | Unoff. World |
| | | 1500m | 1st Woman | 3:26.81 | Unoff. World |
| | | 5000m | 1st Woman | 12:11.08 | Unoff. World |
| 11–16 April | National Wheelchair Games, Melbourne | 800m | 1st | 1:56.24 | |
| | | 5000m | 1st | 13:55.06 | |
| | | 10,000m | 1st | 26:31.06 | Aust |
| 25–26 June | Metro Toronto International Wheelchair Challenge, Toronto, Canada | 400m | 1st | Times not available | |
| | | 800m | 1st | | |
| | | 1500m | 1st | | |
| | | 5000m | 1st | | |
| 22–31 July | IPC World Championships in Athletics, Berlin, Germany | 800m | 1st | 1:51.82 | World |
| | | 1500m | 1st | 3:40.01 | |
| | | 5000m | 1st | 13:05.61 | |
| 20 November | Olympic Dream Exhibition Race, Melbourne | 1500m | 1st Woman | Time not available | |

# Road

| Date | Event | Distance | Placing | Time | Record |
|---|---|---|---|---|---|
| 26 January | Oz Day 10K, Sydney, Australia | 10km | 1st Open Woman | 26:39.90 | |
| 26 February | Gasparilla 15K, Tampa, Florida, USA | 15km | 1st Open Woman | 36:45.00 | |
| 27 February | Top End Criterium, St Petersburg, Florida, USA | | 1st Open Woman | Time not available | |
| 6 March | Los Angeles Marathon, California, USA | 42km | 2nd Open Woman | 1:54:38 | |
| 13 March | Mobil 10K, Torrance, California, USA | 10km | 1st Open Woman | 24:01.00 | |
| 18 April | Boston Marathon, Massachusetts, USA | 42km | 2nd Open Woman | 1:34:45 | Aust |
| 1 May | Lilac Bloomsday 12K, Spokane, Washington, USA | 12km | 3rd Open Woman | 41:33.00 | |
| 4 June | Sempach Marathon, Schenkon, Switzerland | 42km | 1st Open Woman | 1:49:39 | |
| 4 July | Peachtree 10K, Atlanta, Georgia, USA | 10km | 2nd Open Woman | 24:21.00 | |
| 25 September | Berlin Marathon (World Championship), Berlin, Germany | 42km | 1st Open Woman | Time not available | |
| 20 November | Olympic Dream 10K, Melbourne, Australia | 10km | 1st Open Woman | Time not available | |

# 1995 PERFORMANCE RECORD

## Track

| Date | Event | Distance | Placing | Time | Record |
|---|---|---|---|---|---|
| 2 February | VicHealth International Track Meet, Melbourne | 100m<br>1500m<br>5000m | 1st<br>1st<br>1st | 17.19<br>3:39.15<br>13:03.28 | |
| 25–26 March | Athletics Australia National Disabled Track and Field Championships, Canberra | 800m<br>1500m<br>5000m | 1st<br>1st<br>1st | 2:06.48<br>4:12.20<br>15:32.76 | |
| 23–25 June | Metro Toronto International Wheelchair Challenge, Toronto, Canada | 800m<br>1500m<br>5000m | 1st<br>1st<br>1st | 1:55.49<br>3:42.25<br>12:50.23 | |
| | Trial for IAAF World Championships 800m Race | 800m | 1st | 1:54.98 | |
| 12 August | IAAF World Championships, Gothenburg, Sweden | 800m (demo) | 1st | 1:52.60 | |

## Road

| Date | Event | Distance | Placing | Time | Record |
|---|---|---|---|---|---|
| 26 January | Oz Day 10K, Sydney, Australia | 10km | 1st Open Woman | 25:58.00 | |
| 18 February | Gasparilla 15K, Tampa, Florida, USA | 15km | 1st Open Woman | 35:58.00 | |
| 19 February | Top End Criterium, St Petersburg, Florida, USA | | 1st Open Woman | Time not available | |
| 5 March | Los Angeles Marathon, California, USA | 42km | 2nd Open Woman | Time not available | |
| 17 April | Boston Marathon, Massachusetts, USA | 42km | 4th Open Woman | 1:52:01 | |
| 7 May | Lilac Bloomsday 12K, Spokane, Washington, USA | 12km | 2nd Open Woman | 33:13.00 | |
| 4 July | Peachtree 10K, Atlanta, Georgia, USA | 10km | 2nd Open Woman | 25:17.00 | |
| 16 July | Gold Coast Marathon, Queensland, Australia | 42km | 1st Open Woman | 1:55:20 | |
| 27 August | Sydney Marathon, Sydney, Australia | 42km | 1st Open Woman | Time not available | |
| 10 September | Melbourne Half Marathon, Melbourne, Australia | 21km | 1st Open Woman | 1:30:33 | |

| Date | Event | Distance | Placing | Time | Record |
|---|---|---|---|---|---|
| 17 September | City to Bay 10K, Adelaide, Australia | 10km | 1st Open Woman | 24:30.00 | |
| 29 October | Oita Marathon, Oita, Japan | 42km | 2nd Open Woman | 1:51:57 | |
| 19 November | Olympic Dream 10K, Melbourne, Australia | 10km | 1st Open Woman | Time not available | |

# 1996 PERFORMANCE RECORD

## Track

| Date | Event | Distance | Placing | Time | Record |
|---|---|---|---|---|---|
| 30 January | Summer Down Under Series, Canberra | 100m | 1st | 17.00 | |
| | | 400m | 1st | 56.40 | |
| | | 800m | 1st | 1:54.20 | |
| | | 5000m | 1st | 12:59.70 | |
| 1 February | Summer Down Under Series, Melbourne | 200m | 1st | 30.43 | |
| | | 1500m | 1st | 3:47.50 | |
| | | 5000m | 1st | 13:36.01 | |
| 23–24 March | Athletics Australia National Disabled Track and Field Championships, Canberra | 400m | 1st | 56.26 | |
| | | 800m | 1st | 1:54.80 | |
| | | 1500m | 1st | 3:37.30 | |
| | | 5000m | 1st | 13:51.90 | |
| 14–16 June | German National Track and Field Championships, Heidelberg, Germany | 400m | 1st | 58.28 | |
| | | 800m | 1st | 1:56.76 | |
| | | 1500m | 1st | 3:49.61 | |
| | | 5000m | 1st | 13:55.87 | |
| 26–28 June | Trial for Olympic 800m Demonstration Race, Paris, France | 400m (heat) | 1st | 55.04 | |
| | | 800m | 1st | 1:56.97 | |
| 1 August | Olympic Games, Atlanta, Georgia, USA | 800m (demo) | 1st | 1:54.90 | |
| 15–25 August | Paralympic Games, Atlanta, Georgia, USA | 400m | 1st | 54.96 | Paralympic |
| | | 800m | 1st | 1:52.80 | Paralympic |
| | | 1500m | 1st | 3:30.45 | World |
| | | 5000m | 1st | 12:40.71 | World |

## Road

| Date | Event | Distance | Placing | Time | Record |
|---|---|---|---|---|---|
| 26 January | Oz Day 10K, Sydney | 10km | 1st Open Woman | 26:37.00 | |
| 24 February | Gasparilla 15K, Tampa, Florida, USA | 15km | 1st Open Woman | 35:29.00 | |
| 25 February | Top End Criterium, St Petersburg, Florida, USA | | 1st Open Woman | Time not available | |
| 17 April | Boston Marathon, Massachusetts, USA | 42km | 2nd Open Woman | 1:54:39 | |
| 8 June | Sempach Marathon, Schenkon, Switzerland | 42km | 2nd Open Woman | 1:53:28 | |
| 25 August | Paralympic Marathon, Atlanta, Georgia, USA | 42km | 4th Open Woman | 2:05:45 | |

# 1997 PERFORMANCE RECORD

## Track

| Date | Event | Distance | Placing | Time | Record |
|---|---|---|---|---|---|
| 27–29 January | Summer Down Under Series, Sydney | 200m | 1st | 30.22 | |
| | | 400m | 1st | 59.88 | |
| | | 800m | 1st | 2:06.67 | |
| | | 1500m | 1st | 3:49.92 | |
| | | 5000m | 1st | 13:47.86 | |
| 21–23 February | Queensland Invitationals, Brisbane | 400m | 1st | 59.41 | |
| | | 800m | 1st | 2:02.06 | |
| | | 1500m | 1st | 3:52.45 | |
| | | 5000m | 1st | 13:36.40 | |
| 8–9 March | Athletics Australia National Disabled Track and Field Championships, Canberra | 400m | 1st | 54.61 | Aust |
| | | 800m | 1st | 1:58.18 | |
| 27–29 June | French National Championships, Paris, France | 400m | 1st | 57.96 | |
| | | 800m | 1st | 1:57.13 | |
| | | 1500m | 1st | 3:50.94 | |
| | | 5000m | 1st | 13:03.74 | |
| | Trial for IAAF World Championships 800m Race | 800m | 1st | 2:00.28 | |
| 2 July | Midnight Mile Track Meet, Atlanta, Georgia, USA | 200m | 1st | 29.60 | |
| | | 400m | 1st | 57.97 | |
| | | 1 mile | 1st | 4:04.56 | |
| | | 5000m | 1st | 13:34.34 | |
| 11–13 July | Metro Toronto International Wheelchair Challenge, Toronto, Canada | 400m | 1st | 56.12 | |
| | | 800m | 1st | 1:52.86 | |
| | | 1500m | 1st | 3:52.64 | |
| | | 5000m | 1st | 13:17.22 | |
| 8 August | IAAF World Championships, Athens, Greece | 800m (demo) | 1st | 1:52.11 | |
| 9 November | NSW Sports Council for the Disabled State Championships, Sydney | 400m | 1st | 59.00 | |
| | | 800m | 1st | 1:59.20 | |
| | | 1500m | 1st | 3:53.80 | |
| | | 5000m | 1st | 12:46.60 | |
| | | 4 x 100m relay | 1st | 1:09.00 | Aust |

# Road

| Date | Event | Distance | Placing | Time | Record |
|---|---|---|---|---|---|
| 24 January | Manly Criterium, Sydney, Australia | 5km | 1st Open Woman | 14:35.00 | |
| 26 January | Oz Day 10K, Sydney, Australia | 10km | 1st Open Woman | 27:08.30 | |
| 1 February | Newcastle 15K, Newcastle, Australia | 15km | 1st Open Woman | 38:55.00 | |
| 6 February | Waitangi Day 10K, Mount Maunganui, New Zealand | 10km | 1st Open Woman | 26:43.00 | |
| 2 March | Los Angeles Marathon, California, USA | 42km | 1st Open Woman | 1:49:25 | |
| 21 April | Boston Marathon, Massachusetts, USA | 42km | 1st Open Woman | 1:54:28 | |
| 1 June | Atrium Classic, Darwin, Australia | 10km | 1st Open Woman | 27:47.00 | |
| 4 July | Peachtree 10K, Atlanta, Georgia, USA | 10km | 1st Open Woman | 25:04.00 | |
| 6 July | Piedmont Criterium, Atlanta, Georgia, USA | 10 miles | 1st Open Woman | 40:40.00 | |
| 13 September | Heidelberg Marathon, Heidelberg, Germany | 42km | 3rd Open Woman | 2:04:49 | |
| 21 September | Riverside Rumble (World Championship 10K), Wilkes-Barre, Pennsylvania, USA | 10km | 1st Open Woman | 25:46.30 | |
| 28 September | Berlin Marathon, Berlin, Germany | 42km | 1st Open Woman | 1:49:58 | |
| 2 November | Oita Marathon, Oita, Japan | 42km | 3rd Open Woman | 1:46:58 | |
| 16 November | Olympic Dream 10K, Melbourne, Australia | 10km | 1st Open Woman | 26:11.00 | |
| 14 December | Honolulu Marathon, Hawaii, USA | 42km | 1st Open Woman | 1:56:08 | |

# 1998 PERFORMANCE RECORD

## Track

| Date | Event | Distance | Placing | Time | Record |
|---|---|---|---|---|---|
| 28 January | Summer Down Under Series, Sydney | 100m | 1st | 17.98 | |
| | | 400m | 1st | 58.82 | |
| | | 1500m | 1st | 3:49.54 | |
| | | 5000m | 1st | 13:46.73 | |
| 4–5 April | Athletics Australia National Disabled Track and Field Championships, Canberra | 400m | 1st | 56.68 | |
| | | 800m | 1st | 2:04.53 | |
| | | 800m (invitation race with men) | 1st Woman | 1:46.93 | |
| | | 1500m | 1st | 3:45.85 | |
| | | 5000m | 1st | 13:36.25 | |
| | | 4 x 100m relay | 1st | 1:06.50 | Aust |
| | | 4 x 400m relay | 1st | 4:22.00 | Unoff. World |
| 25–26 July | Swiss National Championships, Jona, Switzerland | 400m | 1st | 55.71 | |
| | | 800m | 1st | 1:52.38 | |
| | | 1500m | 1st | 3:33.07 | |
| | | 5000m | 1st | 12:32.39 | World |
| 9–16 August | IPC World Championships in Athletics, Birmingham, UK | 800m | 1st | 2:01.81 | |
| | | 1500m | 1st | 3:46.43 | |
| | | 5000m | 1st | 13:41.83 | |
| | | 4 x 100m relay | 1st | 1:08.22 | |
| | | 4 x 400m relay | 1st | 4:26.28 | World |

## Road

| Date | Event | Distance | Placing | Time | Record |
|---|---|---|---|---|---|
| 24 January | Oz Day Match Race, Sydney, Australia | 1km | 1st Open Woman | 2:29.00 | |
| 26 January | Oz Day 10K, Sydney, Australia | 10km | 1st Open Woman | 27:32.10 | |
| 3 February | Newcastle 15K, Newcastle, Australia | 15km | 1st Open Woman | 40:39.00 | |
| 6 February | Waitangi Day 10K, Mount Maunganui, New Zealand | 10km | 1st Open Woman | 29:30.00 | |
| 15 February | Gasparilla 15K, Tampa, Florida, USA | 15km | 1st Open Woman | 40:53.00 | |
| 29 March | Los Angeles Marathon, California, USA | 42km | 2nd Open Woman | 2:00:55 | |
| 20 April | Boston Marathon, Massachusetts, USA | 42km | 1st Open Woman | 1:41:19 | |
| 23 May | Sempach Marathon, Schenkon, Switzerland | 42km | 1st Open Woman | 1:48:51 | |
| 31 May | Atrium Classic, Darwin, Australia | 10.4km | 1st Open Woman | 26:19.00 | |
| 12 July | Gold Coast Marathon, Queensland, Australia | 42km | 1st Open Woman | 1:51:19 | |
| 16 August | IPC World Championships Marathon, Birmingham, UK | 42km | 1st Open Woman | 1:59:14 | |
| 20 September | Riverside Rumble (World Championship 10K), Wilkes-Barre, Pennsylvania, USA | 10km | 1st Open Woman | 25:24.70 | |
| 13 December | Honolulu Marathon, Hawaii, USA | 42km | 1st Open Woman | 2:15:00 | |

# 1999 PERFORMANCE RECORD

## Track

| Date | Event | Distance | Placing | Time | Record |
|---|---|---|---|---|---|
| 28–29 January | Summer Down Under Series, Sydney | 400m | 1st | 56.09 | |
| | | 800m | 1st | 1:56.84 | |
| | | 800m (Invitational race with men) | 1st Woman, 4th Overall | 1:51.14 Time not available | |
| | | 1500m | 1st | 3:49.58 | |
| | | 5000m | 1st | 13:03.26 | |
| | | 4 x 100m relay | 1st | 1:03.87 | World |
| 6 February | Optus Grand Prix, Canberra | 400m | 1st | 55.90 | |
| | | 800m | 1st | 1:.55.01 | |
| 20 February | Optus Grand Prix, Sydney | 800m (Combined Open Men and Women) | 1st Woman | 1:50.23 | |
| 25 February | Optus Grand Prix, Melbourne | 1500m | 1st | Time not available | |
| 23–28 May | Arafura Games, Darwin | 400m | 1st | 58.70 | |
| | | 800m | 1st | 2:04.97 | |
| | | 800m (Combined Open Men and Women) | 1st Woman, 3rd Overall | 1:53.93 | |
| | | 1500m (Combined Open Race with Men) | 1st Woman, 4th Overall | 3:48.70 | |
| | | 5000m | 1st | 13:38.23 | |
| 5 July | Nightrider Mile, AmericaSeries, Atlanta, Georgia, USA | 1 mile | 1st | 3:51.56 | |
| 6–7 July | US National Championships, Atlanta, Georgia, USA | 800m | 1st in heat (no final) | 1:53.16 | |
| | | 1500m | 1st | 3:39.57 | |
| | | 5000m | 1st | 12:45.89 | |
| 10–11 July | Metro Toronto International Wheelchair Challenge, Toronto, Canada | 800m | 1st | 2:06.73 | |
| | | 5000m | 1st | 12:56.79 | |

| Date | Event | Distance | Placing | Time | Record |
|---|---|---|---|---|---|
| 29–31 October | Southern Cross Championships, Sydney | 400m | 1st | 58.53 | |
| | | 800m | 1st | 1:56.82 | |
| | | 1500m | 1st | 4:02.96 | |
| | | 5000m | 1st | 13:09.00 | |

## Road

| Date | Event | Distance | Placing | Time | Record |
|---|---|---|---|---|---|
| 24 January | Oz Day Prologue, Sydney, Australia | 1km | 1st Open Woman | 2:11.00 | |
| 26 January | Oz Day 10K, Sydney, Australia | 10km | 1st Open Woman | 27:07.90 | |
| 31 January | Centennial Park 15K, Sydney, Australia (Category 'handicap' race) | 15km | 1st Open Woman, 4th Overall | 39:27.60 | |
| 28 March | Carlsbad 5000, California, USA | 5km | 1st Open Woman | 12:56.00 | |
| 19 April | Boston Marathon, Massachusetts, USA | 42km | 1st Open Woman | 1:42:22 | |
| 26 May | Arafura Mile, Darwin, Australia | 1 mile | 1st Open Woman | 3:40.34 | |
| 30 May | Atrium Classic, Darwin, Australia | 10.4km | 1st Overall | 27:16.00 | |
| 26 June | North American Championship 10K, Long Island, New York, USA | 10km | 2nd Open Woman | 26:20.29 | |
| 4 July | Peachtree 10K, Atlanta, Georgia, USA | 10km | 4th Open Woman | 25:24.00 | |
| 29 August | Perth City-to-Surf, Perth, Australia | 11km | 1st Open Woman | 29:58.65 | |
| 19 September | Riverside Rumble (World Championship 10K), Wilkes-Barre, Pennsylvania, USA | 10km | 1st Open Woman | 25:41.03 | |
| 22 November | Olympic Dream 10K, Melbourne, Australia | 10km | 1st Open Woman, 4th Overall | 28:58.70 | |
| 12 December | Honolulu Marathon, Hawaii, USA | 42km | 1st Open Woman | 2:09:07 | |

# 2000 PERFORMANCE RECORD

## Track

| Date | Event | Distance | Placing | Time | Record |
|---|---|---|---|---|---|
| 15 January | Optus Grand Prix, Canberra | 200m | 1st Woman | 30.00 | |
| | | 5000m | 1st Woman | 13:21.53 | |
| 22 January | Interclub, Homebush, Sydney | 800m | 1st Woman | 1:51.67 | |
| 27–28 January | Summer Down Under Series, Sydney | 400m | 1st | 55.17 | |
| | | 800m | 1st | 1:51.98 | |
| | | 1500m | 1st | 3:45.68 | |
| | | 5000m | 1st | 13:07.17 | |
| 13 February | Optus Grand Prix, Homebush, Sydney | 1500m | 1st | 3:32.53 | |
| 27 February | Athletics Australia National Track and Field Championships, Sydney | 1500m (demo) | 1st | Time not available | |
| 2 March | Optus Grand Prix, Melbourne | 800m | 1st Woman | 1:50.61 | Unoff. World |
| 31 March –2 April | Warm Springs State Wheelchair Games, Georgia, USA | 800m (semi) | 1st | 1:48.51 | |
| | | 800m (final) | 1st | 1:55.27 | |
| | | 1500m (semi) | 1st | 3:36.91 | |
| | | 1500m (final) | 1st | 3:30.79 | |
| | | 5000m (final) | 1st | 12:36.75 | |
| 29 May | Columbier Track Meet, Switzerland | 800m | 1st | 2:02.70 | |
| | | 1500m | 1st | 3:56.92 | |
| 31 May | Daniela Jutzeler Track Meet, Switzerland | 800m | 1st | 1:59.50 | |
| | | 1500m | 1st | 3:47.15 | |
| 12–13 August | Swede Elite Games, Gothenburg, Sweden | 400m (semi) | 1st | 57.41 | |
| | | 400m (final) | 1st | 59.00 | |
| | | 800m (semi) | 1st | 1:51.98 | |
| | | 800m (final) | 1st | 1:54.10 | |
| | | 1500m | 1st | 3:37.48 | |
| | | 5000m | 1st | 12:52.60 | |

| Date | Event | Distance | Placing | Time | Record |
|---|---|---|---|---|---|
| 19–20 August | Swiss National Championships, Delemont, Switzerland | 800m<br>1500m<br>5000m | 1st<br>1st<br>1st | 1:53.25<br>3:45.91<br>12:52.35 | |
| 28 September | Olympic Games, Sydney | 800m (demo) | 1st | 1:56.07 | |
| 18–29 October | Paralympic Games, Sydney | 800m<br>1500m<br>5000m | 2nd<br>1st<br>1st | 1:54.61<br>3:48.52<br>12:46.65 | |

## Road

| Date | Event | Distance | Placing | Time | Record |
|---|---|---|---|---|---|
| 24 January | Oz Day Prologue, Sydney, Australia | 1km | 2nd Open Woman | 2:16.90 | |
| 26 January | Oz Day 10K, Sydney, Australia | 10km | 2nd Open Woman | 25:59.60 | |
| 30 January | Paramatta City 14K, Sydney, Australia | 14km | 1st Open Woman | 37:10.00 | |
| 19 April | Boston Marathon, Massachusetts, USA | 42km | 2nd Open Woman | 2:01:16 | |
| 30 April | Sydney Marathon, Sydney, Australia | 42km | 1st Open Woman | 2:07:44 | |
| 4 June | Sempach Marathon, Schenkon, Switzerland | 42km | 1st Open Woman | 1:47:16 | |
| 2 July | Atrium Classic, Darwin, Australia | 10.4km | 1st Open Woman, 3rd Overall | 27:58.11 | |

# 2001 PERFORMANCE RECORD

## Track

| Date | Event | Distance | Placing | Time | Record |
|---|---|---|---|---|---|
| 3 February | Telstra Grand Prix, Newcastle | 1500m | 1st Woman, 1st Overall | 3:52.18 | |
| 16 February | Telstra Grand Prix, Sydney | 800m | 1st Woman, 1st Overall | 1:42.17 ('Handicap' start) | |
| 18 February | Telstra Grand Prix, Canberra | 1500m | 1st Woman, 1st Overall | 3:07.14 ('Handicap' start) | |
| 1 March | Telstra Grand Prix, Melbourne | 800m | 1st Woman | 1:48.89 | Unoff. World |
| 6–8 April | Athletics Australia National Disabled Track and Field Championships, Canberra | 800m 1500m 5000m | 1st 1st 1st | 1:53.51 3:41.12 13:26.45 | |
| 3 June | New South Wales Sports Council Track Meet, Sydney | 400m 800m 1500m | 1st 1st 1st | 58.30 1:54.90 3:46.10 | |
| 24 June | Trial for IAAF World Championships 800m Race, Edmonton, Canada | 800m | 1st | 2:02.01 | |
| 6–8 July | Metro Toronto International Wheelchair Challenge, Canada | 800m 1500m 5000m | 1st 1st 1st | 2:00.15 Time not available 13:20.86 | |
| 10 August | IAAF World Championships, Edmonton, Canada | 800m (demo) | 1st | 1:56.86 | |
| 25–26 August | Swiss National Championships, Jona, Switzerland | 400m (heat) 800m 1500m 5000m | 2nd 1st 1st 1st | 57.65 1:51.66 3:32.20 12:14.94 | World |

## Road

| Date | Event | Distance | Placing | Time | Record |
|---|---|---|---|---|---|
| 25 January | Oz Day Prologue, Sydney, Australia | 1km | 1st Open Woman | Time not available | |
| 26 January | Oz Day 10K, Sydney, Australia | 10km | 1st Open Woman | 26.58.90 | |
| 25 March | Round the Bays, New Zealand | 8.8km | 1st Open Woman | 20:34.84 | |
| 16 April | Boston Marathon, Massachusetts, USA | 42km | 1st Open Woman | 1:53:54 | |
| 20 May | Atrium Classic, Darwin, Australia | 10.5km | 1st Open Woman, 2nd Overall | 27:21.00 | |
| 28 June | 5K Road Race, Cedartown, Georgia, USA | 5km | 1st Open Woman | 12:59.00 | |
| 4 July | Peachtree 10K, Atlanta, Georgia, USA | 10km | 2nd Open Woman | 24:57.00 | |
| 17 September | City to Bay, Adelaide, Australia | 10km | 1st Open Woman | 22.44.00 | |
| 21 October | Riverside Rumble, Wilkes-Barre, Pennsylvania, USA | 10km | 1st Open Woman | 25:53.00 | |
| 25 November | Olympic Dream 10K, Melbourne, Australia | 10km | 1st Open Woman | 29:18.00 | |

# INDEX

**A**
ABC  53, 94, 117, 173, 205, 210
ABC Junior Female Athlete of the Year Award 1993  70, 133
Aberdeen Hotel, Perth  230
Academy Awards  145
Agassi, Andre  247
Albert, Prince of Monaco *see* Prince Albert of Monaco
Amorosi, Vanessa  209
Amy (dog)  182
ANA Hotel, Sydney  121
Andrews, Stuart  198, 210
Anggreny, Lily  160, 213, 254
Anu, Christine  208-209
AOC *see* Australian Olympic Committee
APC *see* Australian Paralympic Committee
Appleby, Lois  165
Aranmore School, Perth *see* St Mary's School, Perth
Armstrong, Duncan  165
Armstrong, Lance  144
Art Gallery of New South Wales  109
Aspire Foundation *see* Louise Sauvage Aspire to be a Champion Foundation
Assen IPC World Championships in Athletics 1990  40, 43-47, 239
Athens IAAF World Championships 1997  107-109
Athens Olympic Games 2004  109, 259

Athens Paralympic Games 2004  109, 259
Athletics Australia  107-109
Athletics Australia Grand Prix Series 1999  78
Athletics Australia National Disabled Track and Field Championships *see* National Disabled Track and Field Championships
Atlanta Olympic Games 1996  68, 77-92, 99, 101, 137, 194, 231, 235
Atlanta Paralympic Games 1996  44, 77-84, 89-99, 101, 104, 137, 168, 204, 207, 235
Australia Day wheelchair road race *see* Oz Day 10K
Australia Post  194
Australian Broadcasting Corporation *see* ABC
Australian Female Athlete of the Year Award 1999  132-133
Australian Institute of Sport  47, 81, 118
Australian Institute of Sport Athlete of the Year Award 1997  118
Australian Olympic Athletes Program  118
Australian Olympic Committee (AOC)  194, 204, 262
Australian Open Tennis Final 2001  247
Australian Paralympian of the Year Award 1994  73

Australian Paralympian of the Year
 Award 1997  109
Australian Paralympian of the Year
 Award 1998  123
Australian Paralympic Athletes'
 Committee  180
Australian Paralympic Committee (APC)
 119, 144
Australian Sports Commission  118-119
Australian Sports Drug Agency  230

**B**
Ballard, Angie  117, 122, 206-207, 211, 228
Banks, Jenni  48-49, 79, 84-85, 100-101, 121, 243
Barcelona Olympic Games 1992  50-51, 89
Barcelona Paralympic Games 1992  50-60, 81, 83, 85, 89-90, 94, 96, 230, 235, 237-238, 264
Barnes, Jane  126
Barnes, Jimmy  126, 222
Barton Park, Wollongong  201
Bat Club, the  202
Bateman Park, Perth  22
Beazley, Kim  17, 143, 212
Becerra, Cheri  85, 131, 159, 188-189, 211, 213
Berlin IPC World Championships in Athletics 1994  54, 75, 130
Berlin Marathon, Germany  76, 106
Biddell, Anthony  202
Big W discount store  260
Birchip B & S ball  242
Bird, Paul  201
Birmingham IPC World Championships in Athletics 1998  116-121, 125, 137
Blattman, Fabian  219
Bloemen Marathon, Holland  45
Blythe, Sandy  94, 150-151, 170, 208
Boise road race, USA  255
Bon Jovi, Jon  146
Bonds clothing company  260
*Boston Herald*, the  129
Boston Marathon, USA  63, 65-68, 74, 77, 80-81, 97-98, 102-106, 110-116, 124, 127-130, 136, 138-141, 195, 227, 248-251, 258, 264

Botham, Ian  144
Boy George  74, 146
Boyle, Raelene  73
Brandis, Reg  214
Broncos NRL team  164-165
Buckley, Grant  256
'Burke's Backyard'  143
Burkett, Brendan  208
Busteed, Joshua  126
Byron to Bondi Challenge 1998  122-123

**C**
Campbell, Greg  226
Campbell, Naomi  146
Canadian Wheelchair National Championships *see* Toronto Metro International Wheelchair Challenge
Capitol Theatre, Sydney  199
Carlton, Mike  118, 120
Carney, Emma  121, 125
Cartier jewellers  144
Casey, Shona  69-70, 76, 111, 134, 225, 242-243
Centennial Park, Sydney  99, 164, 167, 179, 181, 204, 234, 173
Channel Nine Sydney  212
Channel Seven Sydney  117, 177
Channel Seven Perth  11, 73, 86
Channel Ten Sydney  133
Charles, Prince of Wales *see* Prince Charles
City-to-Surf, Perth  25, 217
Clark, Anthony  205
Clement, Arnaud  247
Clinton, Chelsea  181
'Club Veg'  203
Cohen, Chris  109, 214
Commonwealth Games  169 *see also* Manchester; Victoria
Coombs, Kevin  205
Cooper, Priya  54, 208
Corbett, Reen  125
Cosgrove, Peter  143
*Cosmopolitan*  109
Costello, Peter  119
Cowley, Michael  57
Cox, Kate  142, 244
Cracknell, Ruth  143
'Current Affair, A'  223

Curtin University gym  50, 79
Cuthbert, Betty  257

**D**
Daddo, Andrew  177
*Daily Telegraph*, the  117, 132, 147, 149, 151, 257
Daley, Laurie  165
Darwin Atrium Classic  251
Dawes, Andrew  101, 110-111, 114-115, 127, 129-131, 166, 171-173, 177, 181, 184, 186-187, 197-198, 202, 215, 221, 236-238, 247, 253, 255
de Vito, Danny  146
Deane, Lady  143
Deane, Sir William  143
*Determined to Win*  250
Devine, Miranda  147, 149-150
Devlin, Michael  239
Disneyland, USA  94
Dockery, Patrice  203, 213
'Doggie' (toy)  9, 121
Domain, Sydney  109
Doohan, Mick  198
Doyle's Restaurant, Watson's Bay, Sydney  133
Driscoll, Jean  64, 67-68, 74, 81, 85, 92, 101-106, 113-114, 128-130, 139-140, 157, 159, 218, 220-221, 249-250, 261, 264
Durack, Fanny  80

**E**
Eales, John  125, 146
Eastern Creek, Sydney  165
Edmonton IAAF World Championships 2001  248, 252-254, 258
Edmonton IAAF World Championships trials 2001  251
Elgin, Donnie  225
Eliminator race chair  238
Elite Sports Properties (ESP)  258
Elizabeth II *see* Queen Elizabeth
Emerton, Margaret  143, 217
'ER'  245
ES Marks Field, Sydney  167, 172, 174, 183, 200
ESP *see* Elite Sports Properties (ESP)
Ettingshausen, Andrew  165

**F**
*Fairstar*, the  55, 242
'Fat, The'  173
Fearnley, Kurt  158, 160, 166, 169, 177, 181, 184, 186, 193, 200, 217, 220, 237
Ferris, Michelle  192
Fitzsimons, Peter  85
Flack, Edwin  80
Flemming, Jane  86
Flynn, Brendan  204-205
Foley, Gary  126-127, 137, 164, 172, 234, 243, 247
Forsyth, Tim  83
Fortress wheelchairs  63-64
Fortune, Peter  186
Fox Studios, Sydney  256
Foxton family  182, 185
Foxton, Julian  179, 189, 209
Foxton, Lucy  209
Foxton, Sue  209
Franz, Dennis  146
Fraser, Dawn  144, 146, 207-208, 257
Fraser, Dawn Lorraine  146, 207
Frasure, Brian  146
Freeman, Cathy  94, 125, 132, 134, 178, 182, 194, 206
Frei, Heinz  124
Fremantle Hospital  36
'Friends'  245
Fuller, Neil  254

**G**
Gainsford-Taylor, Melinda  78, 121, 125, 178
Galli, Jessica  256
Garcia, Sergio  144
Gasparilla 15K, USA  63-64, 77
Gaze, Andrew  200
Gibson, Kingsley  183
Giglia, Tanya  14, 243
Goldie, David  117
Goolagong Cawley, Evonne  257
Goosey, Vicki  108
Gothenburg IAAF World Championships 1995  77-78
Gould, Shane  257-258
Government House, Perth  74, 226

Government House, Sydney 207
Graff, Sandra 254
Gregan, George 125
Grey-Thompson, Tanni 108-109, 189
Griffiths, Tracy *see* Harnett, Tracy
Griggs, Joanna 177
Grigorieva, Tatiana 150
*Groundhog Day* (movie) 140
Guttman, Dr Ludwig 52

**H**
Hall, David 149, 165
Hansen, Connie 45, 54, 58, 64, 75, 124-125
Harman, Nan 65
Harnett, Nikky 243
Harnett, Paul 243
Harnett, Tracy 61, 139, 219, 230-231, 243-244
Harvey, Geoff 208
Harvey, Peter 212
Hatanaka, Kazu 220-221
Hellwig, Jason 225
Hellwig, Karen 201
Hensley Field, Sydney 171
*Herald-Sun*, the 77
Hernandez, Ariadne 189, 218, 221, 253
Hinds, Richard 132
Hockeyroos, the 108, 194
*Hollow Man, The* 169
Hollywood Senior High School, Perth 14, 16-17, 32, 47
Homebush Bay Wharf, Sydney 257
Homebush State Sports Centre 166, 183, 235
Honolulu Marathon 106
Hootie and the Blowfish 88
Host City Marathon, Sydney 2000 141
Howard, John 200
Hudson, Lee 172-174, 181, 183, 189, 191, 198-199, 203, 206-207, 235
Hudson, Margaret (Aunty Margaret) 76, 117, 179
Huegel, Geoff 126
Hugg, Peter 49
Hunkeler, Edith 128, 249-250, 254

**I**
IAAF World Championships 186, 258
    *see also* Athens; Edmonton; Gothenburg; Stuttgart
International Amateur Athletic Federation *see* IAAF
International Court of Arbitration for Sport 214
International Olympic Committee (IOC) 109, 174, 189, 191,194-195, 214
International Paralympic Committee World Championships *see* IPC World Championships
International Regatta Centre, Sydney 234
Invacare Corporation 81, 238-239
Inverarity, Alison 178
IOC *see* International Olympic Committee
IPC World Championships in Athletics 58, 186, 258-259 *see also* Assen; Berlin; Birmingham; Lille
Ippolito, Melissa 205, 209

**J**
Jackson, Samuel 146
*Jewel of the Nile, The* 245
'John Laws Show, The' 203
Johnson, Deann 38
Jones, Marion 74, 144-146
Jordan, Michael 144
Judd, Ashley 146
Judy (dog) 13, 142
Jutzeler, Daniela 53-55

**K**
Kidman, Nicole 177
King Edward Memorial Hospital, Perth 6-7
King's Park, Perth 49, 239
Klim, Michael 143, 258
Klisc, Mrs 15
Knaub, Jim 67
Knight, Michael 120, 174, 197, 219
Kone, Oumar 222
Kowalski, Daniel 126
Kuschall race chair 51, 238

**L**
Ladies Professional Golf Association (LGPA) 132

Ladmore, Holly  117, 122, 137-138, 158, 212-213
Laureus World Sportsperson with a Disability Award 2000  144-147
Lee, Kathy  48, 70, 186, 221
Lee, Michael  36
Lewis, Tamsyn  185-186
Lilac Bloomsday Run  68, 77
Lille IPC World Championships in Athletics 2002  258
Lillee, Dennis  73
Llorens, Lisa  205
Loader, Steve  181, 198
Long, Ali  15-16
Long, Karen  14-16, 28-30, 121, 211, 243
Los Angeles Marathon, USA  64-65, 77, 103, 106
Los Angeles Olympic Games 1984  52
Louise Sauvage Aspire to be a Champion Foundation  260
Louise Sauvage Pathway, the  204
*Louise Sauvage* Supercat 3  257
Lucas, Ben  115
Lucky Dog Great Australian Dog of the Year Competition  143
Lucy, Judith  109

**M**
McBrien, Karen  98-99, 102, 105, 115, 120-121, 129, 135-136, 143, 147, 149-150, 163-164, 167, 176-177, 179, 189, 194, 197-198, 203, 206, 227, 234, 241, 243, 258
Macdonald, Hamish  202, 208
McDonald's  88, 106, 227
MacKillop, Mary  257
MacLean, Andrew  181
MacLean, John  158, 160-161, 172, 177, 184, 193, 200, 231
Madonna  126
Maher, Dominique  179
Malay Restaurant, Sydney  126
Manchester Commonwealth Games 2002  72-73, 258-259
Manchester United soccer team  144
Mandela, Nelson  74, 146
Martin, Ray  170
Matthews, Wendy  208

Melbourne Cup 2001  247
Melbourne Derby 2001  247
Melbourne Paralympic Parade  223, 225
Melbourne Town Hall  225
Milford Sound, New Zealand  247
Miller, Scott  109
Milton, Michael  205, 209
Minogue, Kylie  208-209
Monaco Grand Prix course  145
Monaco Royal Palace  145
Monaghetti, Steve  77
Moses, Edwin  144
M2 freeway  164, 169, 172, 234
Munro, Mike  120

**N**
Narrabeen track, Sydney  166-167
National Australia Bank  96, 261
National Disabled Track and Field Championships 2001  251
National Junior Paraplegic and Quadraplegic Games 1985  24, 36
National Junior Paraplegic and Quadraplegic Games 1989  37-38
National Rugby League *see* NRL
National Senior Paraplegic and Quadraplegic Games 1984  24, 263
National Senior Paraplegic and Quadraplegic Games 1990  39-40
National Wheelchair Games 1992  50, 54
Navratilova, Martina  144
'Neighbours'  76
*New Idea*  166
New Orleans Olympic trials 1992  53, 81
New South Wales Wheelchair Sports Association  101, 122, 126, 157, 183
Nicklaus, Jack  144
Nike sportswear  94, 167, 202
'No Second Prize'  126
Nordlund, Madelene  160
Norman, Greg  175-177
Northern Eagles NRL Club  260
Novotel, Sydney Olympic Park  208, 221
NRL Grand Final 2000  164-165
Nunnari, Paul  179

**O**
O'Connor, Jack  33, 36
O'Neill, Susie  94, 126, 132, 257-258

O'Sullivan, Sonia 77
Observation City Hotel, Perth 47
Oita Marathon, Japan 74, 106-107, 242
Olympic Airlines 108
Olympic Dream 10K, Melbourne 76, 69
Olympic Games 52, 95, 195, 258 *see also* Athens; Atlanta; Barcelona; Los Angeles; Rome; Sydney
'Olympic Sunrise' 177
'One Year to Go' Sydney Paralympic countdown launch 126
Order of Australia Medal 57
Overington, Caroline 191
Oz Day 10K, Sydney 58, 74, 77, 98, 103-104, 110, 124, 136-137, 188, 248

**P**
Paralympic Games 26, 50, 52, 59, 95, 186, 195, 258 *see also* Athens; Atlanta; Barcelona; Rome; Sydney
Paris Olympic trials 1996 81
Parliament House, Sydney 207
Parramatta City 14K 138
Parramatta Park, Sydney 183, 203, 234
Parthenon, Athens 109
Peachtree 10K, USA 68-69, 77, 106, 252, 256
Pele 144
Penny (dog) 142-143, 163-164, 169-171, 173, 179, 182-183, 198, 203, 217, 226, 235-236, 244, 259
Peris-Kneebone, Nova 108
Perkins, Kieren 57, 94, 126
Perry Lakes Stadium, Perth 49
Perth Paralympic Parade 223, 226
Petitclerc, Chantal 54, 85, 92, 109, 131, 157-158, 188-189, 211-213, 215-219, 248, 253-254
Philip, Prince see Prince Philip
Ploeg, Evert 117
Ponta, Frank 21-22, 25, 38-39, 243
Prince Albert of Monaco 146
Prince Charles 74
Prince Philip 143
Princess Margaret Hospital, Perth 6
Punch (dog) 12-13, 142
Puxty, Kellie 157, 161, 189, 247

**Q**
Qantas 96, 108, 179
Qantas Club 179, 181, 198
Queen Elizabeth 143
Quinn, Alison 170, 226

**R**
Rafter, Pat 125
Razer, Helen 109
Reed, Ron 77
Regent Hotel, Sydney 132
Reinpuu, Indra 173
Reuters 205
Richards, Karen 205
Richards, Viv 144
Riley, Sam 126
Ripp, Christina 252, 256
Riverside Rumble, USA 106-107, 255-256
Roberts, Toby 203
Rogen public speaking 262, 264
Rolex Golf Player of the Year Award 1999 132
*Rolling Stone* 167
*Romancing the Stone* 245
Rome Paralympic Games 1960 52
*Romeo and Juliet* 245
Roosters NRL team 164
Round-the-Bays Race, New Zealand 249
Royal Society for the Prevention of Cruelty to Animals see RSPCA
Royal family 74
RSPCA 142-143
Ryde-Eastwood Leagues Club, Sydney 165

**S**
Sailor, Wendell 165
St Mary's School, Perth 14
Samaranch, Juan Antonio 189, 194
Sauvage family 206, 210, 224-225
Sauvage, Ann 4-6, 8, 12, 14, 20, 24, 48, 53, 121-122, 146, 170, 181, 191, 207, 216-217
Sauvage, Jacqueline 43, 191
Sauvage, Louise 1-265
Sauvage, Mary (Aunty Mary) 10-11

Sauvage, Maurice  4-6, 8-10, 12-14, 20, 23, 40, 48, 53, 57, 86, 170, 206-207, 216-217, 219, 226
Sauvage, Nanna  5, 10-11
Sauvage, Rita  2-9, 12-14, 17, 19-24, 28, 32, 39-40, 48, 57, 67, 73-75, 79, 86, 115, 117, 122, 129, 132-133, 144-147, 170, 191, 202, 206-207, 210, 212-214, 216, 218, 219, 224-226
Scandinavian Airlines  154
Seles, Monica  178
Sempach Marathon, Switzerland  74, 141
Shaw, Chris  25, 79-80, 134
Shaw, Ros  25, 79-80, 95, 242
Short, Russell  202
Siemens telecommunications company  257
Simone, Nanny  9-10
Simons, Dr Jeff  85, 185
Simpson, Barney  24
Singleton, John  165
'60 Minutes'  170
Skelton, Christie  93, 117, 122, 154-155, 158, 169, 207, 211-212, 239, 252
Skender, Richard  225
Smith, Dick  143
Smith, Greg ('Smithy')  76, 155-156, 160, 201-202, 217, 219, 225
Soloti, Anne-Marie  22
Sparky (dog)  12, 142
Spastic Centre, Mt Lawley, Perth  19
Sporting Archibald Prize  117
'Sports Tonight'  133
'Sports Women'  205
Squires, Tony  173
Stallone, Sylvester  146
Starr, Megan  254
Steggall, Zali  132
Stoke Mandeville World Wheelchair Games  52, 45
Stuttgart IAAF World Championships 1993  69
Summer Down Under Series 2000  138
Sun-Herald, the  124, 142, 168-170, 203
Swan River, Perth  49, 99
Swede Elite Games 2000  152-153
Swiss National Championships 1998  116
Swiss National Championships 2000  142, 158-160
Swiss National Championships 2001  254-255
Sydney Bridge Run  256-257
Sydney Convention Centre  224
Sydney Harbour Bridge  174-175, 177
Sydney Morning Herald, the  55, 85, 118, 132, 191
Sydney Olympic Games 2000  1, 53, 89-90, 94-96, 98, 119, 124, 131, 136, 141-142, 147-148, 150-151, 155-156, 159-170, 173-204, 212, 215, 227-229, 231-232, 234-235, 237, 244-245, 257-260, 263-265
Sydney Paralympic Games 2000  2, 54, 89-90, 94-96, 98, 118-119, 122-123, 131, 136, 143, 146-153, 155, 162-166, 168-169, 196-197, 201-202, 204, 206-223, 226-232, 235, 237, 244-248, 252, 257-258, 260, 264
Sydney Paralympic Parade  223-224
Sydney Town Hall  207-208, 210, 224

T

Taurima, Jai  186
Taylor-Smith, Shelley  121, 125
Team Invacare  239
Telethon, Channel Seven Perth  11-12
Telstra  226
Telstra Grand Prix 2001  248-249
'30 Most Successful Australian Women Under 30'  109
'This is Your Life'  120-122, 125, 140
Thomas, Alan  138
Thomas, Sheila  138
Thomson, Andrew  119
Thorpe, Ian  126, 134, 194, 230
'Three Seconds from Glory'  117
Tierney, Petrina  224
Tighe, Karen  210
Tonelli, Mark  165
Top End Action  81, 238
Top End Criterium, USA  77
Torch Relay, Sydney Olympic Games 2000  174-177
Torch Relay, Sydney Paralympic Games 2000  207-208
Toronto Metro International Wheelchair Challenge, Canada  254
Tour de France  45

Triple J radio station 208
Tsuchida, Wakako 137-138, 157, 159, 188-189, 213, 215, 220-221, 248, 254
Tuart Hill Primary School, Perth 13
Tuart Hill Swimming Club, Perth 19, 23-24, 40, 47, 239
Tucker, David 167
Tunstall, Arthur 71-73
Turner, Kathleen 245
Twining, Mrs 121

U
Underwater World, Perth 42
Ungerer, Greg 201
United States National Championships 1999 130-132
University of Western Sydney 174

V
Victoria, Canada, Commonwealth Games 1994 71-73
Victorian Institute of Sport 186
Victorian Wheelchair Sports Association 69
Vizaniari, Lisa-Marie 78

W
Western Australian Disabled Sports Association 42, 47-48, 244
Western Australian Disabled Sports Association Sports Star of the Year Award 1990 48
Western Australian Junior Disabled Games 1984 24
Western Australian Wheelchair Sports Association 32
*War of the Roses, The* 245
Waugh, Steve 125
We Media 205
Webb, Dr F. B. (Don) 6, 18, 32-36
Webb, Karrie 132
Webb, Katrina 205
Webster, Tim 165
Wells, Jeff 117
Wentworth Hotel, Sydney 224
*West Australian,* the 50, 72
Wetterstrom, Monica 53
Whang Youn Dai Overcome Prize 222
Whang Youn Dai, Dr 222
Wheeler, Stephanie 256
Whitlams, The 222
*Who* 244
Wickham, Tracey 72
Wiggins, Paul 68, 86
Willing, Martina 222
Willis Roberts, Jodie 219
Wilson, Anna 132
'Winning Spirit' 170
Winter Olympic Games 169
Winters, Amy 149, 169, 202, 208, 217, 254
Wiseman, Jeff 171
Wit, Katarina 144
*Woman's Day* 244
Woodhouse, Rob 258
Woods, Tiger 144
World Championship Marathon *see* Berlin Marathon
World Championship 10km road race *see* Riverside Rumble
World Sports Academy 144
Worrall, Jodie 94

X
'X-Files, The' 245

Y
Yothu Yindi 126
Young Australian of the Year Award (National Sports Category) 1997 109
Yunupingu, Mandawuy 126

www.ingramcontent.com/pod-product-compliance
Lightning Source LLC
Chambersburg PA
CBHW022031290426
44109CB00014B/822